The Power of

Business Process Improvement

The Power of

Business Process Improvement

10 Simple Steps to Increase
Effectiveness, Efficiency, and Adaptability

Susan Page

AMACOM
American Management Association
New York • Atlanta • Brussels • Chicago • Mexico City
San Francisco • Shanghai • Tokyo • Toronto • Washington, D.C.

Bulk discounts available. For details visit:
www.amacombooks.org/go/specialsales
Or contact special sales:
Phone: 800-250-5308
Email: specialsls@amanet.org
View all the AMACOM titles at: www.amacombooks.org

This publication is designed to provide accurate and authoritative information in regard to the subject matter covered. It is sold with the understanding that the publisher is not engaged in rendering legal, accounting, or other professional service. If legal advice or other expert assistance is required, the services of a competent professional person should be sought.

The following are registered trademarks:
   Adobe Acrobat Reader®
   Adobe PDFAcrobat®
   Microsoft Office Access®
   Microsoft Office Excel®
   Microsoft Office Outlook®
   Microsoft Office PowerPoint®
   Microsoft Office Project®
   Microsoft Office SharePoint® or
   Microsoft Office Visio®
   Microsoft Office Word®
   Open Text Hummingbird Connectivity®

Library of Congress Cataloging-in-Publication Data

Page, Susan (Susan Ann)
   The power of business process improvement : 10 simple steps to increase effectiveness, efficiency, and adaptability / Susan Page.
      p. cm.
   Includes bibliographical references and index.
   ISBN-13: 978-0-8144-1478-1
   ISBN-10: 0-8144-1478-8
   1. Workflow—Management.   2. Organizational effectiveness.   3. Management.   I. Title.
HD62.17.P34   2010
658.5'1—dc22   2009023530

About AMA

American Management Association (www.amanet.org) is a world leader in talent development, advancing the skills of individuals to drive business success. Our mission is to support the goals of individuals and organizations through a complete range of products and services, including classroom and virtual seminars, webcasts, webinars, podcasts, conferences, corporate and government solutions, business books and research. AMA's approach to improving performance combines experiential learning—learning through doing—with opportunities for ongoing professional growth at every step of one's career journey.

Printing number

10 9 8 7 6 5

To Greg . . .
without his encouragement and ongoing support,
this book would never have happened

Contents

CHAPTER 10:
Step 10: Drive Continuous Improvement: Embracing the New Mindset

CHAPTER 11:
Create the Executive Summary: Getting the Recognition

The Power of

Business Process Improvement

The Roadmap

Learning How to Navigate

Have you ever had a problem that you know little or nothing about land on your desk at work? Does the problem make you feel overwhelmed and uncertain as to where to begin? Challenges like this usually occur when you already have a full workload, unrealistic deadlines, and limited resources. What can you do when you feel lost, like Hansel or Gretel trying to find your way out of the forest?

Learning to navigate through unfamiliar territory goes a long way toward easing the burden and can help you feel comfortable dealing with the unknown. *Business process improvement* (BPI) work, the systematic examination and improvement of administrative processes, can seem scary and overwhelming because no one teaches this navigation skill in school. But once you give it some thought, *everything is a process*, from making breakfast for yourself in the morning to building the space shuttle. In both cases, you follow a series of actions or steps to bring about a result. Making breakfast, no matter how informal, is still a process. You brew the coffee, cook the eggs, and toast the bread. If Vince Lombardi had run a business instead of a football team, we might remember him today for saying that process isn't everything, it's the only thing.

The techniques covered in this book help smooth the path to successful BPI by clearing away the unknowns and delivering the power of process improvement directly into your

1

hands. Whether you consider yourself an expert on the subject or do not see yourself as a process person, you will appreciate learning how to tackle process improvement work in a bottom-line, straightforward approach. For the inexperienced, *The Power of Business Process Improvement* guides you along a proven, step-by-step approach to a successful result; for the expert, it becomes a handy A-to-Z reference guide to help you engage an organization in a process improvement effort.

This guide cuts through the long, confusing, and difficult-to-comprehend explanations regarding BPI and takes you directly to the core of what you, the business professional, want to understand. It describes a pragmatic approach to business process improvement that I developed over the years and that anyone can use in real time to solve real problems. The ten simple steps to increasing the effectiveness, efficiency, and adaptability of your business processes start with the creation of a process inventory and end with how to keep a business process continually delivering value to the business.

If you want to evaluate how your company hires employees, secures sales, or manufactures a product, examining the underlying processes helps you better understand how the business works. Every day we experience challenges with inefficient or ineffective processes and, after you start thinking of business processes as the foundation to the business, you begin to see the power of having a process focus and wonder why you waited so long to change your perspective.

Bill Gates wrote in his book *Business @ the Speed of Thought: Succeeding in the Digital Economy* (Business Plus, 2000) that "A rule of thumb is that a lousy process will consume ten times as many hours as the work itself requires." We have all seen bureaucracy and red tape continually added to a business process. Bureaucracy happens not all at once, but incrementally over time. A business process can easily become bloated, leading to an ineffective, inefficient, and inflexible process.

Improving business processes enables you to stay competitive and to increase your responsiveness to your customers, the productivity of your employees doing the work, and your company's return on investment. The expertise to examine and understand how business processes work sets you apart from the rest because you have the power to demonstrate the value that the process delivers, its importance to your company, and the effect that a single change can produce.

People become interested in process improvement for any number of reasons. Do any of these scenarios sound familiar?

▶ Your customers, clients, or suppliers complain about the business process.

▶ You find that your department makes numerous errors and/ or makes the same one again and again.

▶ You want to understand how your department can improve its efficiency so that your employees can spend their limited time on more valuable work.

▶ You have accepted responsibility for a new business or department, and you want to understand the work.

▶ You discovered challenges with the handoffs between departments.

▶ You want to increase your department's productivity.

▶ You noticed duplication of data or tasks in multiple departments.

▶ You started a new job and want to understand how the department works.

If you encountered one or more of these experiences, then **BPI** can help. It improves your ability to meet your customer's needs, helps you eliminate errors, identifies opportunities to yield a more effective and efficient process, assists you in learning the end-to-end process for a new part of the business, makes clear the relationship between departments and the roles and responsibilities of each, improves your department's productivity, and eliminates redundancy.

Working on business processes helps demystify the process and makes a seemingly complex process less intimidating. Process improvement work also gives you the chance to engage a cross-functional team in the work so that everyone can learn the end-to-end business process, instead of simply focusing on his or her own piece of the process. You will find that, as you do the work, few employees understand the end-to-end process. Employees may understand their own piece, but not how the entire process works from beginning to end. When a team works together on improving business processes, the work itself provides a means for colleagues to talk about common topics, and the team effort promotes an understanding of the interconnectivity of their work.

When you focus on a business process, it appears less threatening to colleagues than focusing on the employees who do the work. The process of finding challenges and linking those challenges to the process instead of to a particular employee leads to easier, less threatening solutions. No one employee or group of employees has to worry about repercussions.

On the other hand, BPI does affect the entire business system, including the employees who do the work; the information technology systems that support the process; the measurements established to assess the effectiveness, efficiency, and adaptability of the process; and reward and recognition programs that exist in a company.

If you still find yourself wondering whether you should undertake a process improvement effort on one of your processes, ask yourself four questions. If you answer no to any of these questions, you should start examining your business processes:

1. Does your process include a high level of customer/client interaction?
2. Does every step in your process add value for the customer/client?
3. Have you established customer- or client-focused metrics for the business process?
4. Are your employees evaluated on their contribution to the business process?

Throughout this book, the term *customer* refers to someone external to a company who pays money for a product or service. The term *client* denotes an internal customer within a company.

If you work as an internal consultant in your company, then you probably work with clients. The client's business processes should support the company's business goals, which in turn should support the paying customer. Remember, in business process work, the customer is king, and you should always focus on the customer.

Can You Do It?

Many of the process improvement books on the market support the myth that business process improvement must be time-consuming and complex. *The Power of Business Process Improvement* shows that nothing is further from the truth. It presents you with numerous tools and examples that you can use to make the work simple and yet maintain high standards.

Perhaps you have shied away from process improvement because it looks like something that only an expert can do. In reality, you can do this work without having to learn the ins and outs of quality management or reengineering. This book shares my own unique approach to BPI, an approach influenced by both quality and reengineering, that works for me every time. I have successfully used the approach outlined with every employee level in different and complex situations. It works. It works even with people who start out as skeptics.

As you apply the ten simple steps introduced in this chapter and covered in depth in the chapters that follow, you will find yourself adopting several of the quality and reengineering philosophies because the focus on the customer is at their core, but you use them in a seamless way that makes the work palatable to the business.

I geared each step toward ease of use. This book answers basic questions and elaborates on how to perform each step by demonstrating its application. It explains topics that no one ever bothers to tell you about, either because book authors, consultants, or colleagues assume that you already know about them or because they do not want you to know the full story, believing that knowledge is power and wanting to hold onto that power.

The various BPI books on the market remind me of getting a favorite recipe from a restaurant, but with some key ingredient missing. This book tells you the whole story and gives you the power of knowledge.

You will feel comfortable with the formulas that I use throughout the book because they are the ones commonly used in business. You do not have to understand complicated statistical measurements of process capability or know how to use Six Sigma, Lean, Kaizen, or other quality methods. You have everything you need right now, so let us begin the journey.

The Journey

Anyone who has ever driven on vacation or taken a business trip knows how to read a roadmap to follow the best route to reach a destination. Roadmaps are easy to follow. To help you navigate through the ten simple steps to BPI, I developed the roadmap in Figure 1-1. Join me as I take you on a trip through

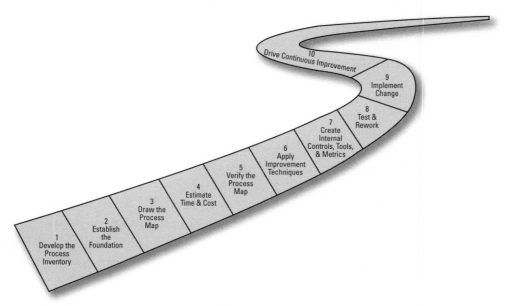

Figure 1-1 Roadmap to Business Process Improvement

process improvement, using the roadmap as a mental model of the ten steps.

The roadmap becomes a meaningful tool for you to use with your colleagues when engaging them in the work. Business professionals like to know what the voyage looks like and how long it will take; the roadmap describes the journey.

The objectives of BPI are:

► **Effectiveness:** Does the process produce the desired results and meet the customer's/client's needs?

► **Efficiency:** Does the process minimize the use of resources and eliminate bureaucracy?

► **Adaptability:** Is the process flexible in the face of changing needs?

These three terms appear frequently throughout this book:

► **Effectiveness** focuses on the customers/clients and whether the process delivers what they want.

► **Efficiency** focuses on the employees responsible for the overall process, the workers in a department or departments, and how easily they can use the business process.

► **Adaptability** evaluates how easily you can modify the business process on the basis of changing business requirements.

Chapters 2 through 10 focus on the ten steps in the roadmap, describing each step and explaining how it works. Each chapter includes tools that I created to help with the step, summarizes the key points in the chapter, and ends with a time estimate, so that you can see how long each step takes to finish. Chapter 11 then helps you to gain recognition for your work, and Chapter 12 discusses one of my process improvement projects from beginning to end. This last chapter also demonstrates how you can adapt the ten steps to changing circumstances because, just as you may encounter detours while driving a car, course changes also pop up during process work. As a result, you may find it necessary to alter your approach from time to time.

As you read this book, notice that the steps follow a specific order because the result of one step assists in defining the next step. In process terminology, you hear this progression described in terms of *inputs* and *outputs*. The output of step 1 in the roadmap leads to the input for step 2.

Now meet the people you will read about on our journey through BPI:

- ▶ The regional sales manager who did not feel that his sales team brought in a sufficient number of new customers
- ▶ The buyer who could not get her orders filled in a timely manner
- ▶ The marketing director who took too long to bring her product to market
- ▶ The training and development manager who wanted to reduce her team's course development time
- ▶ The human resource bank vice president who could not decide which business process to focus on first
- ▶ The human resource information system manager who needed to understand how system funding worked and how system costs hit his budget
- ▶ The compensation director who wanted to learn the head count requirements for his business processes
- ▶ The workforce analysis manager who wanted to understand why multiple groups in her company produced similar reports

The Ten Simple Steps to Business Process Improvement

Although each chapter focuses on a step in the roadmap, I will briefly explain each of them so that you have a snapshot of what is ahead.

Step 1: Develop the Process Inventory

Every department has numerous business processes to manage, but how do you decide which process to examine first?

Take the simple process involved in joining a health club: First you identify the available clubs in your neighborhood, and then you list your key selection criteria. Do you care more about the distance from your home, the age of the facility, the type of equipment, or the qualifications of the staff? You choose the health club to join based on what is most important to you.

Step 1 in the roadmap introduces the process inventory to help you decide where to start. The inventory lists the entire complement of business processes in a department or business area. The chapter describes how to:

- ► Identify the business processes.
- ► Create prioritization criteria.
- ► Apply the criteria to each business process in the inventory.
- ► Create a process prioritization table so that you can contrast a group of business processes to determine which business process you should address first.

At the end of this step, you have a list of the business processes and you understand the order of priority, so that you know where to start.

Step 2: Establish the Foundation

Once you create the process inventory in step 1 and select the business process to focus on first, step 2 introduces the *scope definition document*, your blueprint or foundation that guides you through the rest of your process improvement work.

Before starting a home improvement project, you should develop a plan so that you know the tools and materials you need. Whether building a deck on your house or simply painting a room, you always do prework to avoid those time-consuming trips back to the home center to pick up what you forgot. Likewise, in BPI you need to establish the boundaries associated with a process before you begin the in-depth process work, so that you avoid future time-consuming discussions about the beginning and end of the business process.

This is the role of the scope definition document, which includes the process boundaries, provides the baseline information about the business process you selected, and thus keeps you on track. The document works like a contract, but it does not seem as formal or as threatening to the business. It helps you avoid scope creep, whereby you veer away from the original purpose of the work without an increase in time, resources, or money.

At the end of this step, you have the basic information required to start the process improvement work, as well as specific boundaries to help you stay on track.

Step 3: Draw the Process Map

Drawing the process map enables everyone involved to understand how the business process works and where handoffs occur between departments.

The hardest part of many projects is getting started—taking that first step. You will find it no different when it comes to drawing the process map. Whether you work alone or with a project team, you may find yourself questioning where to start, how to handle conflicts that arise with a project team, and how to keep everyone interested and involved in work that can seem tedious at times. The scope definition document that you created in step 2 helps you get started with this step because it identifies where the process starts and ends.

In most cases, unless you own the process and work alone, you need other colleagues to help you build the process map. It helps to have a project team work with you throughout the ten steps or at least to have resources that you can go to with questions.

The process map you create in this step provides the information you require for step 6, when you apply the improvement techniques, and it assists in setting improvement targets. This step gives everyone involved in the work a better understanding of how the process works from beginning to end by educating the project team on the end-to-end process.

At the end of this step, you and the project team understand how the process works.

Step 4: Estimate Time and Cost

To measure an accomplishment, you need to know where you started. Whether you want to lose weight or run a marathon, you need to establish a baseline to know how much you have improved. How much do you weigh today, or how quickly do you run a marathon today? In process work, to establish an improvement target, you need to know how long a process takes and what it costs.

After drawing the process map in step 3, you understand the activities involved in a business process; step 4 aids in identifying what the process costs today. In the chapter on step 4, you learn about *process time* and *cycle time*. Process time helps you summarize the labor required to deliver a business process, and cycle time identifies how long the process takes from beginning to end, a key metric that customers/clients usually list as a top concern. Identifying the employee, overhead, and tool expenses associated with a business process brings a financial dimension to your work.

This step helps you define the process cost and cycle time, parameters you can use to set improvement targets.

Step 5: Verify the Process Map

Before adding a deck to your house, you would talk with your town's or county's code enforcement office and seek opinions from family members to ensure that you meet the town's setback requirements and keep family members happy. Similarly, you want to review the process map with the appropriate colleagues to validate that the map accurately reflects the existing process. Performing this review validates the baseline for your improvement targets and eliminates the possibility of any future challenges. It provides you with a solid foundation to start the next step, improving the business process.

By completing this step, you gain sponsor and stakeholder support, and you build a solid foundation on which to start the improvement work.

Step 6: Apply Improvement Techniques

If you weigh 200 pounds and want to lose 20 pounds in three months, you know that you need to make changes in your daily routine. You may change your eating habits and eliminate dessert, add an exercise like jogging, or partner with a friend for motivation. The same type of evaluation has to occur to improve a business process.

The *improvement technique wheel* provides an organized approach to improving a business process by introducing key methods to use, including:

► Eliminating bureaucracy.

► Evaluating value-added activities.

► Eliminating duplication and redundancy.

► Simplifying the process, reports, and forms.

► Reducing cycle time.

► Applying automation tools.

You learn how important it is to apply the techniques in a specific order and how applying the six improvement techniques, one at a time, aids in evaluating the business process in a planned and thoughtful approach.

By the end of this step, you have changed the business process so that it delivers business value.

Step 7: Create Internal Controls, Tools, and Metrics

Once you establish your plan to lose the extra pounds, how do you keep track of your progress so that you keep moving toward your goal? You probably weigh yourself at regular intervals and perhaps use an online tracking tool to view your progress. Without frequent measurement, you might easily gain the weight back. The same is true of a business process: Without regular measurement, it gets outdated, and without internal controls, human errors occur.

To bring the process to life—to move it beyond just creating a process map—you establish internal controls, you create tools to increase the effectiveness, efficiency, and adaptability of the business process, and you create metrics. Specifically:

- ▶ *Internal controls* identify points in the business process where mistakes can occur and explains how to prevent them.

- ▶ Creating *tools* to support the business process streamlines the process and assists in avoiding errors and training new employees on how to perform their jobs.

- ▶ Developing *metrics* shows you whether the process works as planned.

This book sticks to simple tools that anyone can use; it does not discuss large system implementations that you have no control over. In Chapter 7, I focus on getting the maximum out of everyday applications, using only the tools that you no doubt already have on your desktop computer.

This step helps you to minimize potential errors, create tools to automate the business process, and identify process metrics.

Step 8: Test and Rework

Before you purchase new software or join a health club for a year, you might want to accept a 30-day trial offer and test it out to make sure it meets your needs. Likewise, before introducing a new, improved process to an organization, you should test it and work out any bugs before implementing the change on a wide scale.

In this step you learn how to create a plan to test the new business process. The details included in the plan help to confirm that the new process and tools work as planned, and resolve any bugs before fully implementing the change. In creating a test plan, you answer questions like whom to involve in the testing, what items to test, what steps are involved, where you should conduct the testing, and when the best time is to conduct the test.

Testing the business process evaluates how well the business process performs, so that you satisfy such project goals as increased productivity or minimizing errors.

At the end of this step, you should feel comfortable that the business process, tools, and metrics work as planned.

Step 9: Implement the Change

When companies introduce a new product, they create a marketing plan that identifies the product price, customer base, distribution channels, and promotion strategies. Likewise, when you change a business process, you need to identify who has to know about the change, what they need to know, and how to communicate the right information to the right people.

Now that you have validated that the business process and tools work, this step explains how to introduce the change to the organization. Chapter 9 introduces a sample implementation plan that helps you successfully introduce the changes to the business process. The implementation plan includes phases like design, development, and implementation and further organizes each phase into tracks. For example, the implementation phase can have these four tracks:

1. *Change management track:* This track includes creating an impact analysis to ensure that you include the right colleagues in making the appropriate changes to the business process. In step 6, as you work with the project team to improve the business process, you identify changes that must occur in the organization to obtain the degree of improvement you expect. The impact analysis is a tool used to capture the changes that have to occur to ensure the success of the new business process.

2. *Testing track:* The steps in this track confirm that the process and tools work as expected.

3. *Communication track:* This track identifies whom to notify of the change, what they need to know, when they need to

know it, and the audience's preferred communication vehi-
cle(s).

4. *Training track:* This identifies who requires training on
what, when the training should occur, who delivers the
training, and the preferred training method.

At the end of this step, you have introduced the new
process.

Step 10: Drive Continuous Improvement

Now that you have lost weight, can you relax and allow
old habits to creep back into your life? Not if you intend to keep
the weight off for good. The maintenance phase of a weight loss
program should lead to lifestyle changes that become part of
your everyday life. Likewise, once you improve a business process, you cannot simply relax. Just as you need to keep weighing
yourself to maintain your weight loss, you have to continually
measure the business process to retain the strategic gains.

Continuous improvement means achieving a new mindset by which ongoing improvement is the natural course of business instead of an event. The *continuous improvement cycle
wheel* introduces four phases—evaluate, test, assess, and execute—to help you attain the new mindset. Each phase in the
wheel provides you with a degree of structure to help you think
through how to keep the business process up to date on an ongoing basis. Continuous improvement validates that the business
process continually delivers effectiveness, efficiency, and adaptability to the organization.

You now have a plan in place to evaluate the business
process on an ongoing basis, so that it stays relevant to your
customer's/client's needs.

After steps 1–10 are covered, there are two additional
chapters: the executive summary and a case study.

The Executive Summary

Chapter 11 assists you in gaining recognition for your
efforts. After all your work, this chapter shows you how to gain

the credit you deserve. An executive summary is a tool that allows you to present your work to senior management in the natural course of business. In this chapter, you learn how to write an executive summary and present statistical information in a thought-provoking manner. By the end of this chapter, you have a concise summary of your work, appropriate for senior management to read.

Case Study

Chapter 12 then presents a case study from beginning to end. You see the ten simple steps applied to a training and development case that I worked on for a financial institution. You can follow my journey, past the detours I had to take and all the way through to implementation.

When you reach the end of this chapter, you know how adaptable you can make the ten steps.

Chapter Summary

The journey to improving business processes should not appear threatening. I assure you that you can do the work. Just as Hansel and Gretel found their way out of the forest, you will quickly find that you are a business process person just by following the ten simple steps to business process improvement.

You can use the ten steps whether you work with a project team or on your own. If you work with a project team, the roadmap helps the team members understand what to expect, keeps them interested, and makes them feel part of the journey. If you work alone, the roadmap helps you keep track of your progress.

You can adjust the time spent on each step, spending as much or as little time as you see fit, depending on your goal. Always keep in mind the return on investment of your time. Expend as much effort as required to achieve your goal. That may mean delving deep into a business process or simply skimming the surface. Let your goal drive the amount of effort you invest.

Process	Business Process Owner
Human resource processes:	
■ Hiring	Ephron Levy
➤ Requisition process	
➤ Sourcing process	
➤ Job fair process	
➤ Orientation process	
■ Training	Fernando Ruiz
➤ Need identification process	
➤ Course development process	
➤ Evaluation process	
■ Compensation and benefits	Susan Gail
➤ Salary planning process	
➤ Budget process	
➤ Job-leveling process	
➤ New hire pay process	
Sales and marketing processes:	
■ Portfolio management	Bob Johns
■ Market planning/segmentation	Samantha Smith
■ Advertising	Steven Parker
■ Distribution	Hussein Riyad
■ Lead development	Abigail Adams
■ Account management	Lavali Chopras
■ Sales and marketing administration	John Smith
■ Revenue generation	Jennifer Harding
Finance processes:	
■ Budgeting and forecasting	Alejandro Izquierdo
■ Payroll	Darpak Gupta
■ Tax planning	Cybil Johnson
■ Risk management	Tim Seinfeld
■ Cash management	Susan Case
Information technology processes:	
■ Application development	Ajit Ganeshes
■ Change order	Isabel Munoz
■ Client relationship	Brigitte Dupree
■ Portfolio management	Bill Stein
■ Program management	Tom Williams
■ Incident management	Paul Reines

Figure 2-2 Sample Business Process Inventory

Since a single business process can have multiple subprocesses, you can further break down each main process into subprocesses. In this example, I broke the hiring process into four subprocesses: requisition, sourcing, job fair, and orientation.

As you build the process inventory, break major processes into subprocesses to make sure you do not overlook any business process and to identify the business process owner, that is, the person responsible for each process. Figure 2-2 shows the names of the process owners.

Another way to organize the process inventory is to group all business processes under general category names. If you work with an information technology department, you could group their business processes under fairly general categories that should work in most cases. For example:

1. *People/organizational processes:*
   - Performance management
   - Succession planning
   - Communication
   - Recognition
2. *Financial processes:*
   - Capital budgeting
   - Five-year plan
   - Annual operating plan
3. *Client-facing IT processes:*
   - Client relationship management
   - Change order
   - Issue resolution
4. *Internal-facing IT processes:*
   - Network administration
   - Security administration
   - Software development

The technique of grouping business processes under a few major headings works well when you have a long process list because grouping the processes helps manage the inventory and makes it easier to decide where to start. For example, you may decide to start with the collection of client-facing processes because they will improve the effectiveness of the department's business processes.

So, now that you know how to build the process inventory, let us move to step 2 and discuss how to develop the appropriate criteria so that you can prioritize the process inventory and pinpoint where to start.

Process Prioritization

Whether you have a list of specific business processes or just general categories, develop criteria and apply them to the items in the process inventory.

Remember Kendall Smith at the beginning of this chapter? He had to decide whether to focus on compensation's budgeting process, the job fair process, or their training process to better integrate new employees into the company. I had to find a way to help him prioritize his business processes so that he and his management team could easily decide where to start. The next section explains how to develop criteria to prioritize a process inventory.

Developing Criteria

The following four general categories help you determine the relative importance of one business process over another. Of course, you may have to vary these categories depending on the situation, and you should feel free to identify additional criteria if doing so helps to reach a better decision on where to start your improvement effort.

1. *Impact:* How much does the business process affect the business?
2. *Implementation:* How feasible is it to make the change?
3. *Current State:* How well is the process working today?
4. *Value:* What is the benefit, or return, of improving the process?

Figure 2-3 shows the continuation of the table framework with the four general categories of criteria added across the first row as column headers.

Process	Impact		Implementation			Current State			Value	
Process 1										
Process 2										
Process 3										

Figure 2-3 Process Prioritization Table Framework

The next step involves deciding how to measure each of the categories of criteria. For example, what does *impact* mean? What does *implementation* mean? To demonstrate how to accomplish this task, I will use the preceding four general categories and two typical business processes one might find in a compensation and benefit department: the annual salary planning process and the budgeting process.

Impact

Let us start with the *impact* category to define how we might measure the impact of a business process on the business. Two common criteria used for this category are *number affected* and *client level*. Figure 2-4 shows these two criteria added to the table framework in the second row (note the shaded areas in the figures) and the salary planning and budgeting processes in the left column.

Process	Impact		Implementation			Current State			Value	
	Number Affected	Client Level	Time to Market	Funding	Timing of Next Cycle	Client Satisfaction	Pain Level	Process Exist?	Benefit/ Return	Total Score
Salary planning										
Budgeting										

Figure 2-4 Process Prioritization Table Framework: Impact

▶ **Number affected** refers to volume, and it includes the number of employees affected by a business process. If a business process affects a large number of employees, it has a greater impact on the business than if it affects only a handful of employees.

For example, in a compensation and benefits department, how many employees are affected by a company's annual salary planning process compared to the budgeting process? Generally, you find a higher number of employees affected by the salary planning process because more employees receive a pay increase and fewer employees manage budgets. As a result, the salary planning process receives a higher score for this criterion because it affects a larger number of employees.

▶ **Client level** refers to the level of employees affected by the business process. As pointed out in Chapter 1, the term *client* denotes an internal customer in a company, whereas *customer* refers to a person external to the company who pays for a product or service. For demonstration purposes, let us categorize client levels as executive or senior level, midmanager level, professional level, and hourly level. Let us further decide that the higher the employee level is, the higher the score will be.

In the example, the employee level for the salary planning process can consist of all four levels because each category of employee usually receives a pay increase, whereas the employee level for budgeting probably includes only the executive and midmanager levels. As a result, the budgeting process receives a higher score for this criterion because of the senior-level visibility to the business process.

Remember to include any criteria in this category that defines the impact of the business processes on the business. You must also weigh political criteria, as in the level of employee example, against other criteria in terms of the overall effect on the business to achieve the proper end result.

Implementation

Implementation, the second prioritization category, refers to elements that measure the feasibility of a successful execution. Again, feel free to define additional criteria besides these three common ones: *time to market*, *funding*, and *timing of next cycle*. Figure 2-5 shows these three criteria added to the second row in the table framework.

Process	Impact		Implementation			Current State			Value	
	Number Affected	Client Level	Time to Market	Funding	Timing of Next Cycle	Client Satisfaction	Pain Level	Process Exist?	Benefit/ Return	Total Score
Salary planning										
Budgeting										

Figure 2-5   Process Prioritization Table Framework: Implementation

> ► **Time to market**, in marketing terminology, denotes the total time it takes to move from product conception to product availability. In business process work, it refers to how long it takes to proceed through the ten steps to business process improvement. Estimate the time on the basis of your understanding of the business process. Think about potential problems like:
> - The complexity of the process.
> - Whether you expect delays.
> - Anything unusual about the process that adds time.
> - The availability of knowledgeable resources to answer questions.
> - The number of people you have to include in the work.
>
> These factors all contribute to the length of time the work takes, and you should weigh them accordingly. For example, one group I worked with wanted to create a process map to explain how a particular business process worked, but it was a complex process that few people understood; so multiple gaps existed in the team's knowledge at different points in the process. As a result, it took a long time to draw the process map due to the complexity and lack of knowledgeable resources.
>
> The score that this criterion receives depends on your estimate of how long it will take to move through the ten steps. On this criterion, the shorter the time to market is, the higher the business process will score.

➤ **Funding** refers to whether you require a budget and its size. Although you may not know the exact cost associated with any technology investment, in most cases you do have an idea of the size of the investment (small, medium, large) and know whether you have to pay for additional services or resources. If you expect to require funding, this criterion receives a negative, low score because of the time-consuming nature of gaining budget approval.

➤ **Timing of next cycle** refers to the time lapse before the organization plans to use the business process again, that is, ongoing, almost daily, or cyclically (quarterly, semiannual, or annual). In the annual salary planning process example, this process receives a low score on this criterion if the annual process just occurred because it will not happen again for another year. On the other hand, an ongoing process receives a high score because any improvements immediately affect the business.

Current State

The third prioritization category, *current state*, refers to how well the business process works for the clients and for the internal department or area that owns the process. Three common criteria used to assess the current state are *client satisfaction*, *pain level*, and whether a *process exists*. Figure 2-6 shows these three criteria added to the table framework.

➤ **Client satisfaction** evaluates how well or poorly the business process currently works from the client's perspective—the effectiveness of the process. As you recall from

Process	Impact		Implementation			Current State			Value	
	Number Affected	Client Level	Time to Market	Funding	Timing of Next Cycle	Client Satisfaction	Pain Level	Process Exist?	Benefit/ Return	Total Score
Salary planning										
Budgeting										

Figure 2-6 Process Prioritization Table Framework: Current State

Chapter 1, we define effectiveness from the customer's/client's perspective. Answer the question, "How delighted are your clients with the current process?" If you score client satisfaction as low, this criterion receives a high score.

▶ **Pain level** refers to how well or poorly the business process currently works for the department responsible for delivering the process results. This criterion evaluates the efficiency of the existing process, and we define efficiency from the process owner's perspective. Answer the question, "How easily can the department manage the existing process?" If you score the process as an extremely manual one and feel that it requires too much work, this criterion receives a high score.

▶ **Process exist?** simply refers to whether a process exists or not. Even when no formal process exists and employees just do whatever it takes to get the job done, a process does in fact exist, albeit an informal one. If no formal process exists, this criterion receives a high score because the process should be documented.

Value

This final prioritization category can have a myriad of definitions. *Value* can denote economic value, personal value, or cultural value. A frequently accepted criterion for value is the size of the *benefit,* or return on investment, and this definition works well for business processes. Again, feel free to add more criteria to this category. Figure 2-7 shows this last criterion added to the table framework as well as a *total score* column.

Process	Impact		Implementation			Current State			Value	
	Number Affected	Client Level	Time to Market	Funding	Timing of Next Cycle	Client Satisfaction	Pain Level	Process Exist?	Benefit/ Return	Total Score
Salary planning										
Budgeting										

Figure 2-7 Process Prioritization Table Framework: Value

▶ **Benefit/return** refers to either a quantitative or qualitative measure of the value of improving the process:

■ **Quantitative** signifies a number or quantity, usually a measurement represented in numerical terms (like turnover rate or error rate).

■ **Qualitative** denotes quality, usually a measurement represented in softer terms (like responsiveness or the ability to make decisions).

Quantitative value often speaks louder to the business because it is associated with a number. However, in business process work, qualitative value becomes increasingly important because of the positive results that an effective business process can have on clients/customers.

This criterion requires further discussion to come to a common understanding and agreement about how to evaluate the benefit or return of a business process. Think about value relative to the status quo, which means leaving a business process in the existing condition. What merit do you associate with taking action versus doing nothing?

■ **Total score**, at the far right in Figure 2-7, shows the overall score for each business process once we populate the table with numbers.

Determining Scale

Now that we created the process inventory and defined the criteria, we have one more step before filling in the process prioritization table with the scores for each business process: determining the scale for the criteria. To determine the score for a business process, the first step is to settle on the scale to use for the criteria. You can use a 1–3 scale, a 1–10 scale, or any other scale that makes sense for the business. I generally like to use a small scale to reduce the degree of interpretation available to people. I use words like *small*, *medium*, *large*, and others to explain what the numbers mean in my example.

Figure 2-8 shows the process prioritization table, with the scale included on the third row. To avoid confusion, take a careful look at the scales used in Figure 2-8, and remember that the highest number is assigned to the item with the greatest im-

Figure 2-8 Process Prioritization Table: Framework

Row 1 = Category →
Row 2 = Criteria →
Row 3 = Scale →

Process	Impact		Implementation			Current State			Value	
	Number Affected	Client Level	Time to Market	Funding	Timing of Next Cycle	Client Satisfaction	Pain Level	Process Exist?	Benefit/ Return	Total Score
	3 = large number 2 = average number 1 = small number	3 = senior 2 = management 1 = other	3 = short 2 = average 1 = long	3 = small 2 = medium 1 = large	3 = close/ongoing 2 = intermediate 1 = far	3 = low 2 = medium 1 = high	3 = high 2 = medium 1 = low	1 = no 0 = yes	3 = high 2 = average 1 = low	
Salary planning										
Budgeting										

pact on making a decision. In *number affected*, the largest amount of people affected gets a 3 because in this case it has the greatest impact. Now look at funding. A score of 3 for funding goes to the business process that requires the least amount of funding because not having to go through an approval process to obtain a budget is a good thing.

So, in this example:

▶ If the number of employees affected by the business process (*number affected*) scores high, then this criterion should contribute more to the final total score: in this case, a score of 3.

▶ If we do not require much funding to improve the business process, then this positive fact should contribute more to the final total score: in this case, a score of 3.

While building the scale, make sure that it depicts what you intend. To clarify the importance of developing an appropriate scale, let us take a deeper look at the criteria in the four general categories to eliminate any confusion. I am using an intentionally simple explanation to help everyone follow along. If you happen to be a math enthusiast, you may want to use another method for scaling.

Scaling for Category 1: Impact

Remember that *impact* refers to the effect that the business process has on the organization, and Figure 2-9 shows the scale for this category.

▶ **Number affected:** For this criterion, the larger the number of employees affected by a business process, the higher the score the process receives. Figure 2-10 explains how the scale supports this decision.

▶ **Client level**: In this criterion, the higher the management level of the employees affected by a business process, the higher the score the process receives. Figure 2-11 provides an example of the application of the scale for this criterion.

Impact	
Number Affected	**Client Level**
3 = large number	3 = senior
2 = average number	2 = management
1 = small number	1 = other

Figure 2-9   Impact Category

Score	Description
1	The business process affects few employees.
2	The business process affects an average number of employees.
3	The business process affects a high number of employees.

Figure 2-10   Scores for Number Affected

Score	Description
1	The business process affects the *other* group, mostly composed of professional or hourly employees.
2	The business process affects the midlevel managers.
3	The business process affects the executive or senior-level employees.

Figure 2-11   Scores for Client Level

Once you develop the scale, as we just did for the impact category, apply it to the process prioritization table by giving each business process a score. To show how this works, Figure 2-12 shows the process prioritization table with the impact scale and scores applied to the salary planning and budgeting processes.

Figure 2-12 shows that the salary planning process receives a higher score for number affected because it affects a

Process	Impact		Implementation			Current State			Value	
	Number Affected	Client Level	Time to Market	Funding	Timing of Next Cycle	Client Satisfaction	Pain Level	Process Exist?	Benefit/Return	Total Score
	3 = large number 2 = average number 1 = small number	3 = senior 2 = management 1 = other	3 = short 2 = average 1 = long	3 = small 2 = medium 1 = large	3 = close/ongoing 2 = intermediate 1 = far	3 = low 2 = medium 1 = high	3 = high 2 = medium 1 = low	1 = no 0 = yes	3 = high 2 = average 1 = low	
Salary planning	3	2							5	
Budget	1	3							4	

Figure 2-12 Process Prioritization Table

larger number of employees than the budgeting process, which applies only to managers and above. The budgeting process receives a higher client level score than the salary planning process because of its visibility to the most senior-level employees in the organization, even though it pertains to fewer employees. After applying the scores for the impact category, the salary planning process seems to take precedence, relative to where to start an improvement effort, over the budgeting process because it has a total score of 5.

But we have three more categories to add to the table before making a final decision! The next three sections follow the same method used for the impact category to bring in the implementation, current state, and value categories.

Scaling for Category 2: Implementation

Now let us look at the scale for the *implementation* category, which refers to the feasibility of a successful execution. This category consists of three criteria: time to market, funding, and timing of next cycle. Figure 2-13 shows the scale for the implementation category.

Implementation		
Time to Market	**Funding**	**Timing of Next Cycle**
3 = short	3 = small	3 = close/ongoing
2 = average	2 = medium	2 = intermediate
1 = long	1 = large	1 = far

Figure 2-13 Implementation Category

- ► **Time to Market:** This criterion states that the longer you estimate it will take to improve the business process, the lower the score will be, and the low score negatively impacts the implementation category. Figure 2-14 shows the explanation of the scoring.

- ► **Funding:** As explained, a lengthy approval cycle lowers the score because it adds time to the work. Figure 2-15 reflects this scoring.

Score	Description
1	It will take a long time to examine and improve the business process, for whatever reason. This includes items like complexity, expected delays, uniqueness, lack of knowledgeable resources, and the number of employees involved in the work.
2	It will take an average amount of time to improve the business process.
3	The business process appears easy to improve. (When the process seems simple and does not involve many people, you will sometimes hear this referred to as a "quick win." Quick wins sometimes receive a higher score because they demonstrate progress.)

Figure 2-14 Scores for Time to Market

Score	Description
1	The business process requires significant funding.
2	The business process requires a reasonable amount of money that will not include a long approval cycle.
3	The business process requires little or no money.

Figure 2-15 Scores for Funding

▶ **Timing of Next Cycle:** The more frequently the business process is used, or if the process will be used soon (for cyclical processes), the higher the score will be because it becomes more critical to improve this business process over others. Figure 2-16 explains the scoring logic.

Now that we have defined the implementation scale, Figure 2-17 shows the updated project prioritization table, with the scale and scores from the implementation category added for the two business processes. Notice in Figure 2-17 on page 37 that the budgeting process now has the higher total score of 13 at this point, assuming the following:

Score	Description
1	The process is a cyclical one, and the timing of the next cycle for the business process is far out.
2	The process is a cyclical one, and the timing of the next cycle is not too close and not too far away.
3	The timing of the next cycle appears imminent or the process is an ongoing one.

Figure 2-16   Scores for Timing of Next Cycle

➤ It will take considerable time to work on the salary planning process because of its complexity and the number of people involved. (These considerations affect the time to market.)

➤ Technology will help improve both processes, but we assume that a software package to handle budgeting will not cost as much money as a tool to plan compensation. (This affects the funding criterion.)

➤ The annual process for salary planning has just ended. (Thus the timing of the next cycle is affected.)

➤ The budgeting process is ongoing because of the different pay programs available throughout the year. (Again, the timing of the next cycle is affected.)

As these assumptions show, any of the scores can change based on the evaluation of the criteria.

Scaling for Category 3: Current State

The *current state* category refers to how well the business process works for the clients and for the internal department or area that owns the process. Figure 2-18 on page 38 shows the scale for the current state category.

➤ **Client Satisfaction**: The more dissatisfied clients appear to be with the existing business process, the greater the impact this score has and the higher the score it receives. Figure 2-19 on page 38 reflects the scoring for this criterion.

Process	Impact		Implementation			Current State			Value	
	Number Affected	Client Level	Time to Market	Funding	Timing of Next Cycle	Client Satisfaction	Pain Level	Process Exist?	Benefit/ Return	Total Score
	3 = large number 2 = average number 1 = small number	3 = senior 2 = management 1 = other	3 = short 2 = average 1 = long	3 = small 2 = medium 1 = large	3 = close/ongoing 2 = intermediate 1 = far	3 = low 2 = medium 1 = high	3 = high 2 = medium 1 = low	1 = no 0 = yes	3 = high 2 = average 1 = low	
Salary planning	3	2	1	1	1					8
Budget	1	3	3	3	3					13

Figure 2-17 Process Prioritization Table

Current State		
Client Satisfaction	**Pain Level**	**Process Exists?**
3 = low	3 = high	1 = no
2 = medium	2 = medium	0 = yes
1 = high	1 = low	

Figure 2-18 Current State Category

Score	Description
1	Clients appear satisfied with how the business process works today.
2	Clients appear somewhat satisfied with how the business process works today.
3	Clients complain about how the business process works today.

Figure 2-19 Scores for Client Satisfaction

► **Pain Level**: Figure 2-20 shows that the higher the pain level for the department responsible for delivering the process results, the greater the need to increase efficiencies and therefore the higher the score will be.

Score	Description
1	The business process seems easy to implement and not cumbersome for the department to manage.
2	The business process requires an intermediate level of work.
3	The business process requires a significant effort because of the manual nature of the work.

Figure 2-20 Scores for Pain Level

► **Process Exist?** This criterion simply states whether a formal process already exists, and Figure 2-21 defines this criterion.

Score	Description
0	A business process exists.
1	No documented business process exists.

Figure 2-21 Scores for Process Exist?

Figure 2-22 shows the scale and scores from the current state category added to the process prioritization table, which continues to suggest that the budgeting process is the highest priority, since it has a total score of 20.

A review of the scores in the *current state* category, shown in Figure 2-22, reveals that:

➤ The budgeting process has lower client satisfaction.

➤ The pain level appears the same for both business processes.

➤ Because the budget process does not have a formal process in place today, it receives a higher score. One can assume that this fact probably contributed to the poor client satisfaction score.

Scaling for Category 4: Value

The final category, *value*, refers to economic, personal, or cultural value, and Figure 2-23 on page 41 shows the relevant scale.

➤ **Benefit/Return:** The more perceived value that the business expects to obtain from an improvement effort, the higher the score. Figure 2-24 on page 41 shows the explanation for this criterion.

Figure 2-25 on page 42 shows the scale and scores for the value category added to the process prioritization table. The scores listed for value presume that the business gains a higher value from improving the salary planning process because streamlining the process saves labor.

Figure 2-25 also shows the total score for each business process. After adding all the criteria scores together, we can see

Process	Impact		Implementation			Current State			Value	
	Number Affected	Client Level	Time to Market	Funding	Timing of Next Cycle	Client Satisfaction	Pain Level	Process Exist?	Benefit/ Return	Total Score
	3 = large number 2 = average number 1 = small number	3 = senior 2 = management 1 = other	3 = short 2 = average 1 = long	3 = small 2 = medium 1 = large	3 = close/ongoing 2 = intermediate 1 = far	3 = low 2 = medium 1 = high	3 = high 2 = medium 1 = low	1 = no 0 = yes	3 = high 2 = average 1 = low	
Salary planning	3	2	1	1	1	2	3	0		13
Budget	1	3	3	3	3	3	3	1		20

Figure 2-22 Process Prioritization Table

Value			
Benefit/ Return			
3 = high			
2 = average			
1 = low			

Figure 2-23 Value Category

Score	Description
1	The business process will deliver little expected value once improved.
2	The business process will deliver an average expected value once improved.
3	The business process will deliver a high expected value once improved.

Figure 2-24 Scores for Benefit/Return

that the budgeting process has a higher total score (22) than the salary planning process (16). Once you complete this analysis on your process inventory, you immediately know where to focus your improvement efforts. In our example, completing this analysis shows that the budgeting process should come first, for the following reasons:

➤ The budgeting process affects the senior level of employees in the company (client level).

➤ The improvement appears simple to design and implement (time to market).

➤ It requires minimal investment (funding).

➤ The process is used throughout the year (timing of next cycle).

➤ Both the clients (client satisfaction) and the department (pain level) do not appear happy with the process at the existing time.

➤ No formal process exists (process exist?).

Process	Impact			Implementation				Current State			Value	
	Number Affected	Client Level	Time to Market	Funding	Timing of Next Cycle		Client Satisfaction	Pain Level	Process Exist?	Benefit/ Return	Total Score
	3 = large number 2 = average number 1 = small number	3 = senior 2 = management 1 = other	3 = short 2 = average 1 = long	3 = small 2 = medium 1 = large	3 = close/ongoing 2 = intermediate 1 = far		3 = low 2 = medium 1 = high	3 = high 2 = medium 1 = low	1 = no 0 = yes	3 = high 2 = average 1 = low	
Salary planning	3	2	1	1	1		2	3	0	3	16
Budget	1	3	3	3	3		3	3	1	2	22

Figure 2-25 Process Prioritization Table

Notice that much of the differentiation between the two processes comes from the implementation category, suggesting that the budgeting process is more feasible to begin with than the salary planning process. The salary planning process received more significant scores than the budgeting process on only two criteria: number affected and benefit/return.

At this point, we have created the process inventory, developed prioritization categories, and defined how to measure the categories by introducing criteria and a scale. What happens now if your colleagues or sponsors criticize your approach because they feel that the return on investment should receive a higher weight than some of the other categories? In such a case, simply apply weighting to the prioritization categories. The next section explains how to do that.

Applying Weighting

To apply a weight to a category in the process prioritization table, start by deciding the importance of the category to the final result. Apply more weight to a category that you feel has a greater impact than another category. For example, make the score for the *impact* category contribute more to the total score by giving it a higher weight than one of the other categories.

If you decide to apply weighting, assign a weight to each category on a scale of 1 to 100. Decide which is the most valuable category, then decide where each of the other categories fall with respect to that most valuable one: half as valuable, a third, and so forth. Assign weights so that the total of all categories equal 100. For example, if we decided to apply a weight to the four general categories, we might use the following weights:

▶ 35 percent for the impact category
▶ 30 percent for the implementation category
▶ 20 percent for the current state category
▶ 15 percent for the value category

In this example, I defined the impact category as the most important, giving it 35 percent out of a possible 100 percent. Using these percentages, Figure 2-26 shows the addition of

Process	Impact (35%)			Implementation (30%)			
	Number Affected	**Client Level**	**Subtotal**	**Time to Market**	**Funding**	**Timing of Next Cycle**	**Subtotal**
	3 = large number 2 = average number 1 = small number	3 = senior 2 = management 1 = other		3 = short 2 = average 1 = long	3 = small 2 = medium 1 = large	3 = close/ongoing 2 = intermediate 1 = far	
Salary planning	3	2	5	1	1	1	3
Budget	1	3	4	3	3	3	9

Figure 2-26 Process Prioritization Table (with weights)

a *subtotal* column for each category in the process prioritization table and a new *total weighted score* column at the far right. (You will find it easier to calculate the weights if you use a spreadsheet application like Microsoft Excel.) To modify Figure 2-26, I created a formula in the *total weighted scores* cell that applied the appropriate weights for each subtotal column and that added all the subtotals together to determine the total weighted score for each business process. Figure 2-27 shows the calculation for the salary planning process.

You can choose to show the weighted score for each category in the table by adding another column after each subtotal column or just include the formula as part of the spreadsheet cell, as I did in this example. Figure 2-28 on page 46 shows the calculation if you use Microsoft Excel. Cell O5 in this figure shows the formula as:

$$= (D5*(35\%)) + (H5*(30\%)) + (L5*(20\%)) + (N5*(15\%))$$

Notice that, even after applying weighting, the budgeting process still surfaces as the most important business process to address first.

Weight ↓   Weight ↓

Current State (20%)				Value (15%)		
Client Satisfaction	Pain Level	Process Exist?	Subtotal	Benefit/ Return	Subtotal	Total Weighted Scores
3 = low 2 = medium 1 = high	3 = high 2 = medium 1 = low	1 = no 0 = yes		3 = high 2 = average 1 = low		
2	3	0	5	3	3	4.1
3	3	1	7	2	2	5.8

Subtotal ↑   Subtotal ↑

Formula:
Subtotal × Weight percentage = Contribution to total weighted score column

Example:

$$5 \times 35\% = 1.75 \quad \text{Impact}$$
$$3 \times 30\% = 0.90 \quad \text{Implementation}$$
$$5 \times 20\% = 1.00 \quad \text{Current state}$$
$$\underline{3 \times 15\% = 0.45} \quad \text{Value}$$
$$4.10 \quad \text{Total weighted score}$$

Figure 2-27 Weighted Score Calculation for Salary Planning Process

You can also decide to spread the weight further across the criteria in a category. For example, I could have split the 30 percent weighting for the *implementation* category as follows:

> ➤ **Time to Market:** 40 percent of the implementation category's 30 percent weighting

> ➤ **Funding:** 45 percent of the implementation category's 30 percent weighting

	Impact (35%)			Implementation (30%)				Current State (20%)				Value (15%)		
	# Affected	Client Level	Sub Total	Time to Market	Funding	Timing of Next Cycle	Sub Total	Client Satisf.	Pain Level	Process Exist?	Sub Total	Benefit/ Return	Sub Total	Total Score
	3=large # 2=average # 1=small#	3=senior 2=mgmt 1=other		3=short 2=average 1=long	3=small 2=medium 1=large	3=close/ ongoing 2=interm. 1=far		3=low 2=medium 1=high	3=high 2=medium 1=low	1=no 0=yes		3=high 1=low		
Salary Planning	3	2	5	1	1	1	3	2	3	0	5	3	3	4.1
Budgeting	1	3	4	3	3	3	9	3	3	1	7	2	2	5.8

Figure 2-28 Formula Example for Weighting

▶ **Timing of Next Cycle:** 15 percent of the implementation category's 30 percent weighting

After completing the process prioritization table, review it with your sponsor to see if he or she agrees with the results. As a result of the discussion, you may have to make some adjustments to either the criteria or weight, but you have a good start.

When I used this approach with Kendall Smith to help him decide which business process to start with, the results pointed to starting with the training process because of the acquisition that the bank just negotiated. As a result of the merger, bringing new employees on board fast hit several of the criteria that he and his management team had established.

You have to do some ongoing maintenance of the process prioritization table and rescore it regularly because the scores will vary depending on the time of year. For example, a business process may receive a low score for *timing of next cycle* in February, but it may receive a higher score six months later because the cycle is coming due.

Chapter Summary: Step 1

Building the process inventory organizes the business process work and demonstrates to your sponsor that you understand the business. It assists you in assessing how big a job you have on your hands, and it provides a tool to discuss the overall breadth of business processes. Your sponsor will probably add or subtract from the process inventory; so think of the inventory as a vehicle to encourage discussion between you and your sponsor.

After developing the business process inventory, identifying the prioritization categories, establishing criteria, developing a scale, and applying these items to each business process, you now have clear direction on where to start your improvement efforts. You can add more prioritization criteria to the four general categories of impact, implementation, current state, and value to meet your needs.

After applying the prioritization criteria to the process inventory, you have another occasion to discuss a meaningful topic with your sponsor. If the results do not reflect what the sponsor considers of utmost importance, determine why your work and the sponsor's viewpoint seem disconnected, and decide whether you have to change the criteria, scale, or weighting. Validate that you and your sponsor agree on the priorities before beginning any process improvement work.

Time Estimate

To help plan the time that it takes to work through this step, Figure 2-29 summarizes the time you should allow to complete the process inventory and process prioritization table.

Event	Time	Purpose
Build the business process inventory	90 minutes	■ List business processes.
Sponsor meeting	15 minutes	■ Gain approval on the list of business processes and how you grouped them. ■ Obtain preliminary insight on prioritization criteria.
Establish categories, criteria, scale, weighting	90 minutes	■ Identify categories and criteria. ■ Determine the scale for each criterion. ■ Determine weighting, if appropriate.
Complete process prioritization table	4 hours	■ Apply criteria, scale, and weight to each process listed in the process inventory.
Sponsor meeting	45 minutes	■ Gain approval on the process prioritization table results.

Figure 2-29 Time Estimate—Step 1: Develop Process Inventory

Build the Business Process Inventory

Start by listing any business processes identified either from your own knowledge or from your sponsor's knowledge. Then talk to other employees in the department or area about what they do, and translate their work into business processes. You can discover a lot of information by looking at an organization chart. If you work as an internal consultant in a company, talk to your colleagues instead of asking for job descriptions. Job descriptions can make the work seem more formal to people, and, at this point, all you want to do is build the process inventory.

Sponsor Meeting

Meet briefly with the sponsor to verify that he or she agrees with the business processes listed. If you grouped the processes around themes, validate that the sponsor agrees with the themes. You should also gain a sense at this point as to whether the sponsor has any ideas about the prioritization criteria. Share the criteria you plan to include, and get a sense as to whether the sponsor feels you are on track. This helps with the next step and shows the sponsor what to expect next.

Establish Categories, Criteria, Scale, Weighting

Think about the impact, implementation, current state, and value categories. Then, after your discussion with the sponsor, decide whether you want to add categories or change existing categories. Adjust the criteria under each category, add new criteria, or delete some. Decide how your scale should work and what weights to assign if you choose to use weighting.

Complete the Process Prioritization Table

During this time, build the table and score each business process listed in the left-hand column of the table.

A Second Sponsor Meeting

Review the results of the prioritization with the sponsor and ask whether he or she expected the results shown. Have a thorough discussion to ensure that you both agree on the priorities of the work.

What You Have Achieved

In this chapter, you have achieved the following:

► An understanding of the business because you see the business processes that a department or an area is responsible for delivering

► A grasp of what the business deems important because you identified and applied criteria to determine priorities

► Buy-in from the sponsor on the business processes to work on first, second, third

► And most important, the *power* to know where to focus your time

CHAPTER 3

Step 2: Establish the Foundation

Avoiding Scope Creep

Pete Hodges, regional sales manager for a computer parts distributor, expressed concern that his company's sales process did not generate enough new customers and that the overall process took too long. When I spoke with Pete and his sales team, each defined the problem a little differently. Pete identified the problem as closing the sale, one district sales manager cited identifying the customer needs as the issue, and the sales representatives said that they did not have enough leads.

How do you decide whom to believe? Pete asked me to look at their sales process from beginning to end, but how would an outsider begin to determine where their sales process starts and ends? Because the sales process varies with every company, I knew that I needed to start by identifying the boundaries. I also felt that I needed to understand how they measure success, or, put another way, how they know when their sales process is successful? They could define success as the number of new clients, as achieving a certain sales volume, or as something else entirely. I needed to establish a foundation that Pete and I could agree on so that we would be starting out on the same page.

As an analogy, think about building a house. What do you do first? Most people either hire an architect to help with design or find an existing house plan that they like. By starting with the design, you know the size of the house and have some idea of how much it will cost to build. A blueprint provides your contractor with step-by-step specifications to be followed throughout the building process.

The *scope definition document* guides you through the exercise of establishing the foundation for a business process. It becomes your blueprint. Once you develop the process inventory described in Chapter 2, and once you decide on the business process to focus on first, this document provides the baseline information you need about that particular business process. It guides you throughout your business process improvement effort.

In an ideal world, you would start out by creating a contract to establish a clear definition of what *is* and *is not* included in a BPI effort. Because we do not live in an ideal world, the scope definition document provides you with the next best way to keep the work on track. It serves the same purpose as a contract because it establishes boundaries, but it does so in a manner that appears far less intimidating to your colleagues, an important point when working as an internal consultant in your company. When you work with an external customer, as I did with Pete Hodges, it clarifies the scope of work similar to a statement of work, a common tool used by customers and vendors alike.

Taking the time to set the foundation helps to prevent scope creep, a risk in many projects. *Scope creep* is the veering away from the original purpose of the work without an increase in time, resources, or money. If you have ever built a house, then you have probably experienced scope creep. It occurs when you make changes after the contractor has started construction. Any change, such as adding an additional light fixture or changing the location of the stove, increases the cost of the house beyond what you originally agreed to pay.

Scope creep appears as a common problem in many areas of business. A software development company that I did work for shared a concern that their product development process took too long. It quickly became obvious that the continual addition of new functionality being added throughout the design and development process was the root cause of the problem. Although the new, additional functionality added to the value of the software product, it also increased the time and resources required to develop the product, thereby adding to the cost of the end product and increasing the time to market.

In business process work, scope creep weaves its way in because new ideas, demands, and needs surface as you get into the work, and the temptation is to continually expand the scope of a business process. Let me share an example.

At one company where I worked and acted as an internal consultant, a simple human error led to an embarrassing predicament at the company's executive level. After senior management chastised and embarrassed the department responsible for the error, I came in to work with them over the next six weeks to examine their business processes in order to ensure that internal controls existed. Internal controls, as we will see in Chapter 7, help minimize human errors.

I started by compiling the process inventory, described in Chapter 2, and discovered that the department had 22 business processes, far too many to evaluate in a six-week period. After convincing senior management that we should concentrate on one business process per week, we agreed that we would focus our attention on six key business processes. I started by working with the project team to develop the scope definition document for the union negotiation process, one of the business processes we would examine over the ensuing six weeks. After completing the document, I reviewed it with the sponsor and gained their agreement on the content.

Partway through the work, a project team member identified a missing subprocess and wanted to go back and include it in the scope definition. My evaluation showed that doing so would introduce a major increase in scope and add at least another 40 hours of work, placing my commitment to the six-week schedule at risk. My evaluation convinced me that the subprocess did not represent an important element and did not warrant further expense or delay—but now I had to persuade my sponsor of my assessment.

I asked the sponsor if she felt the subprocess was important enough to:

1. Eliminate one of the remaining business processes that I had committed to complete in the six-week timeframe.
2. Note the omission but remain on track to complete the remaining business processes on time.
3. Or extend the six-week timeframe to seven weeks.

The sponsor made the decision to stay on schedule because she agreed with my assessment that the subprocess's impact did not add significant risk and that the important consideration was to complete the remaining business processes.

As you can see, the sponsor owned making the decision, not me. I easily moved the responsibility for the decision to the sponsor for several reasons: We had clearly defined the process boundaries when we developed the foundation; the scope did not include the subprocess; and we had just determined that the subprocess did not introduce major risk. If the sponsor had not approved a scope definition document, we could have had a different situation, with scope creep rearing its ugly head.

The Eight Sections of the Scope Definition Document

Now let us take a look at a completed scope definition document for the human resource processes of a computer company I worked with, a company I will call Alistar Corporation (because of the proprietary nature of the work). Figure 3-1 shows the completed scope definition for their compensation department's budget process. I will discuss each of the eight sections of the scope definition document in detail.

Section 1: Process Name

This is the name of the business process, such as the hiring process, the sales process, the budget process, the software development process. For the Alistar Corporation it is the *budget process*, shown in Figure 3-2 on page 56.

Process Name : ___Budget Process___

Process Owner : ___Samantha James___

Client : ___President's Direct Reports___

Description (purpose):

To develop and manage the compensation budget, which is based on a fiscal year (July through June). The process covers the funding and ongoing spending of the following compensation programs:

- Executive compensation
- Manager and professional compensation
- Office hourly compensation
- Variable pay awards
- Open positions

Hourly compensation for plant workers is specifically *excluded* from the budget process.

Scope (boundaries):

Start ___Creating the business case for the annual budget___

End ___Year-end summary to corporate headquarters___

Process responsibilities:

1. Develop the business case for the annual budget.
2. Allocate the funds for each of the individual compensation programs.
3. Manage the budget balances.
4. Report ongoing spending to executives.
5. Ensure data integrity.

Client needs:

- "On demand" status of budget balances (including amounts spent, planned, and remaining)
- Ability to plan additional compensation in order to support pay-related needs throughout the year

Key stakeholders and interest:

Corporate headquarters	Accurate record of spending; compelling business case for budget proposal
Other executives (beyond president's direct reports)	Appropriate salary increases for their employees

Measurements of success:

1. "On demand" knowledge for the president's direct reports of their budget balances (the right information at the right time)
2. A process viewed as a reliable tool for use in employee-related activities like planning promotions and developing succession plans
3. Accurate tracking of spending
4. The ability to make better decisions on allocating funds

Figure 3-1 Scope Definition Document

Scope Definition

Budget Process

1

Process Name: Budget Process

Process Owner: _____

Client: _____

Description (purpose):

Client needs:
-
-
-

Key stakeholders and interest:

Scope (boundaries):

Start _____

End _____

Process responsibilities:
-
-
-
-
-
-
-

Measurements of success:
1.
2.
3.
4.

Figure 3-2   Process Name

Section 2: Process Owner

This is the person responsible for the overall process. You need to identify the *one* person who has ultimate responsibility for the process even if the process touches multiple departments. If you work on a single business process, you will often define the sponsor as the process owner because he or she has the authority to review and agree to your scope definition. If your work covers a broad set of business processes, you may have a separate sponsor and more than one process owner. As shown in Figure 3-3, for the Alistar Corporation it is *Samantha Jones*.

Section 3: Description

This is the definition or purpose of the process. Think of how to explain the process to a person new or unfamiliar with it.

Scope Definition

2

Process Name: _____

Process Owner: **Samantha Jones**

Client: _____

Description (purpose):

Client needs:
-
-
-

Key stakeholders and interest:

Scope (boundaries):

Start _____

End _____

Process responsibilities:
-
-
-
-
-
-
-

Measurements of success:
1.
2.
3.
4.

Figure 3-3 Process Owner

This step may seem simple, but my experience says that you will spend considerable time defining the business process. You need to define the scope when writing the process description, and, if something is specifically out of scope, you need to say so in section 3 shown in Figure 3-4.

Figure 3-5 on page 59 shows an example of a description for Alistar Corporation's compensation budget process. You can see that the scope *includes* five types of compensation programs and *excludes* one program (plant worker compensation). You can also see that the budget process includes two key areas:

1. The *funding* of compensation programs (how much money comes from and how much money goes to each program. For example, if an eight percent budget is received from headquarters, what percentage of that amount goes to each

Scope Definition

Process Name: _____

Process Owner: _____   Client: _____

Description (purpose):

Client needs:
-
-
-

Key stakeholders and interest:

Scope (boundaries):

Start _____

End _____

Process responsibilities:
-
-
-
-
-
-
-

Measurements of success:
1.
2.
3.
4.

Figure 3-4 Description

of the compensation programs (e.g., the executive compensation fund versus the office hourly compensation fund?).
2. The tracking of *ongoing spending* throughout the calendar
year.

One employee group intentionally omitted from this
process consists of the hourly employees who work in the company's plant locations. The reasons they are excluded can vary,
possibly because the funding comes from a different source or
because a union contract or labor law drives their pay increases.

The importance of getting the process description correct will become clear as the work progresses because you will
find yourself and others referring to this definition time and
time again as you create the process map. You may find it a
challenging exercise to write the description, especially if the
project team members have never done this kind of work. Like

Description (purpose):

To develop and manage the compensation budget, which is based on the fiscal year (July through June). This process covers the funding and ongoing spending of the following compensation programs:

- Executive compensation
- Manager and professional compensation
- Office hourly compensation
- Variable pay awards
- Open positions

Hourly compensation for plant workers is specifically *excluded* from the budget process.

Figure 3-5 Alistar Corporation Compensation Budget Process

most people, they may instinctively know about a process but have a difficult time explaining it to someone else.

When writing process descriptions, you may need to:

▶ Use unusual or technical terms in your description.
▶ Emphasize areas that are out of scope.
▶ Further define a term by giving examples.

The following scenarios cover these three situations, and these examples should help you to write clear and easy-to-understand process descriptions.

Scenario 1: Unusual or Technical Terms

Figure 3-6 shows a process description that contains one unfamiliar term (development promotions) and one unusual application of another term (client requests), so the description includes a further explanation of these terms. The first footnote in the figure defines a *development promotion* because it is differ-

---

Description (purpose):

This process covers:

Planned development promotions[1]
Unplanned salary adjustments based on client requests[2]

1 Development promotions are movements within a job family. There are typically two or more levels of the same type of job in a job family, with each level having increasing scope and responsibilities. Examples include:

- Financial analyst
- Human resource managers
- Engineers
- Programmers

2 Client requests, in this context, include only the following situations: retention adjustments, counteroffers, and unplanned projects.

Figure 3-6 Salary Adjustment Process

ent from a regular promotion. A development promotion means movement within the same job family. For example, the financial analyst job family is a typical job family in a company's finance department. It may consist of three levels:

➤ Financial analyst 1
➤ Financial analyst 2
➤ Financial analyst 3

A financial analyst at each of these levels performs the same basic job, but the overall responsibility or scope and the pay range increase with each level. An employee moves from one level to the next through a series of development promotions without moving to a new job. The definition needs to include an explanation of development promotions because they are paid for from a different budget than that used for regular promotions, which occur when an employee moves to a totally new job.

Defining such terminology as development promotion

becomes important if the words seem technical in nature or if they can have different meanings to different people. When a nine-year-old says her blouse is cool, she probably means she will wear it; when a 90-year-old says her blouse is cool, she probably means that she is freezing. To minimize confusion, you should continually listen for such words and clarify them when appropriate.

How often have you found yourself thinking a word meant one thing, while someone else had a totally opposite understanding of it? This becomes more of a problem when you work for a global company whose employees reside in different countries.

At Alistar Corporation, I worked on another human resource process: their hiring process. The global project team quickly became confused by the following terms: job seeker, applicant, qualified person, and candidate. To the members of the U.S.-based project team, the terms meant the same thing and could be used interchangeably. To the non-U.S. project team members, the terms had very different meanings, with each term denoting a change in the status of a person applying for a job.

From the non-U.S. team's perspective:

➤ A job seeker *may* turn into an applicant.
➤ An applicant *may* turn into a qualified person.
➤ A qualified person *may* turn into a candidate.

Figure 3-7 shows the result of a discussion I led with the global project team. From that point on, each term had the same meaning to everyone. You want to ensure that everyone understands the terminology in use before moving to step 3, mapping the process, in order to minimize confusion and keep the work moving smoothly.

So spend some time defining the terminology that you use while developing the process description. Gaining agreement on what a word means can be more important than whether it is technically accurate. You do not want someone months later saying, "Well, that's not what I meant when I said 'candidate.'" That kind of comment only places your work in question.

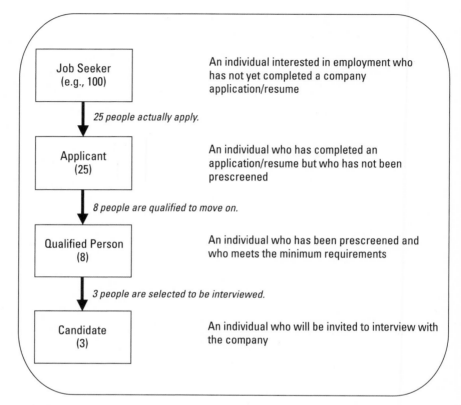

Figure 3-7 Recruitment Terminology

Scenario 2: Areas Out of Scope

If you feel that people need to understand that certain aspects of a process are out of scope, you should explicitly say so in the description. Figure 3-8 shows an example of a process description that intentionally excludes four types of employees. In this example, everyone may not understand the term *downgrade*, and you may need to further define it, as we did in scenario 1 for the term *development promotion*.

Scenario 3: Providing Examples

If confusion occurs around a term, Figure 3-9 shows another option to clarify what you mean by providing examples. In this figure, you can see that I clarified the employees *eligible* for a recognition bonus.

Description (purpose):

This process determines the rate of pay for an individual to fill a U.S.-based vacant position.

This process covers the following types of employees:

■ Managerial and professional
■ Office hourly

This process *does not cover* the following types of employees:

■ Executives
■ International local hires
■ Downgrades
■ Employees on an employment contract

Figure 3-8 *New Hire Pay Process*

Description (purpose):

This process is an ongoing cash reward program to recognize outstanding contributions beyond an eligible* employee's regular responsibilities.

*Eligible employees include:

■ All managerial and professional employees *not* eligible for any other bonus program.
■ All office hourly employees.

Figure 3-9 *Recognition Bonus Award Process*

You can use either footnotes or an asterisk to define specific terms. If you need to define only one term, as in Figure 3-9, an asterisk works fine. If more than one term needs defining, as in Figure 3-6, footnotes are more appropriate for distinguishing between multiple terms.

Section 4: Scope

Scope is the breadth or area covered by a process. It establishes the boundaries within which you will perform your work. This is when you define the starting and ending points of the business process, as shown in Figure 3-10.

Starting Point

In the Pete Hodges case, we defined the starting point as generating leads. We could have made the start of the process

Figure 3-10 Scope

establishing sale quotas, but after some discussion we decided to leave quotas as a separate process. We decided to keep the sales process focused on activities that the sales rep had control over.

In our Alistar compensation budget process example, the process starts with creating the business case in order to justify a specific budget from corporate headquarters, because headquarters has the responsibility for making the budgeting (or funding) decisions. This means that the process starts long before any money is spent or tracked. The decision to start the business process at this point makes the process a bit more complicated than simply tracking spending. (See Figure 3-11.)

Scope (boundaries):

Start: Creating the business case for the annual budget

End: Year-end summary to corporate headquarters

Figure 3-11 Alistar Corporation Compensation Budget Process

In the earlier hiring process example, we had to decide whether the process began:

▶ At the point where the business gained approval for the head count.

▶ When the recruitment department began sourcing the candidate.

▶ When the hiring manager selected the candidate.

▶ Or when the company hired the employee.

By simply reading the name of the process, the hiring process, you might say "when the company hires the employee." In our case, we began the process at the second point, when the recruitment department sourced the candidate.

Ending Point

In our compensation budget process example, the process ends after the compensation department completes a report at the end of the calendar year for corporate headquarters that shows the total dollars spent over the past year and where spending occurs by compensation program.

There is no right or wrong answer to where a business process begins and ends. It all depends on the project team's discussion and the sponsor's approval of the process boundaries, so that you can stay on track. The importance of setting boundaries will become evident when we move to step 3, mapping the process.

Section 5: Process Responsibilities

This is a list of the major tasks that the business process must deliver, and it constitutes another opportunity to validate the scope of the process. (See Figure 3-12.)

The discussion of this section with the project team may cause you to go back and change either the description or scope that you have already developed, and you should gladly make the changes. As people discuss the responsibilities of the business process, they naturally uncover new thoughts and ideas that you need to incorporate into the foundation so that team members become more engaged and bought into the scope definition. You want to document any changes now rather than after you begin step 3.

In the sales process example, establishing sales quotas came up at this point. If Pete and I decided to include this as a process responsibility, we would have had to go back and change the starting point of the business process from generating leads to establishing sales quotas because sales quotes are established in advance of any sales activity.

Figure 3-13 on page 68 shows a list of process responsibilities for our budget process example. Note that this figure includes a few process responsibilities we discussed earlier and a few new items.

Responsibility 1 shows that the process includes develop-

Scope Definition

Process Name: _____

Process Owner: _____   Client: _____

Description (purpose):

Client needs:
-
-
-

Key stakeholders and interest:

Scope (boundaries):

Start _____

End _____

Process responsibilities:
-
-
-
-
-
-

5

Measurements of success:
1.
2.
3.
4.

Figure 3-12 Process Responsibilities

ing the business case. Responsibility 5 refers to the integrity of the data: How does the compensation department ensure that it has an accurate tracking method?

The process responsibilities section identifies everything included in a business process. For our budget process example, it is not just about managing the budget; it is much more. The process includes developing the business case, determining the budget allocation, defining the method to generate reports to keep executives apprised of ongoing spending, and a method to double-check the accuracy of the compensation department's work.

Section 6: Client and Client Needs

These two sections identify the recipients of the outcome of the business process (the clients/customers) and what is im-

Process responsibilities:

1. Develop the business case for the annual budget.
2. Allocate the funds for each of the individual compensation programs.
3. Manage the budget balances.
4. Report ongoing spending to executives.
5. Ensure data integrity.

Figure 3-13 Alistar Corporation Compensation Budget Process

portant to them from the process (client/customer needs). (See Figure 3-14.)

When working as an internal consultant in your company, identifying the real clients will challenge the project team members, who may incorrectly think of their bosses or the sponsor as clients (see Figure 3-14). Because the boss evaluates your performance and has the authority to give you a raise and because the sponsor has responsibility for the successful implementation of the business process, you naturally want to keep them both happy. Do not confuse them, however, with the client, and remember to define the value of the business process from the customer's or client's perspective and no one else's.

In our compensation budget process example, the clients are the half dozen senior-level executives who report directly to the president. As Figure 3-15 on page 70 shows, they want to know at any point in time how much money they have spent on salary increases and how much they have remaining to spend. They also want assurance that sufficient money exists to reward employees throughout the year, especially when they want to promote them.

Section 7: Key Stakeholders and Interests

Although the customer/client is the main focus of business process improvement work, other areas or departments in

Scope Definition

Process Name: _____

Process Owner: _____   Client: _____ **6** _____

Description (purpose):

Client needs:
-
-
-

Key stakeholders and interest:

Scope (boundaries):

Start _____

End _____

Process responsibilities:
-
-
-
-
-
-
-

Measurements of success:
1.
2.
3.
4.

Figure 3-14   Client and Client Needs

Client: President's direct reports

Client needs:

- On-demand status of budget balances (including amounts spent, planned, and remaining)
- Ability to plan additional compensation in order to support pay-related needs throughout the year

Figure 3-15   Alistar Corporation Compensation Budget Process a company can either affect a business process or receive the downstream effect of a business process. We refer to the people in this group as *stakeholders*. (See Figure 3-16.)

In addition to listing the groups affected by the business process, you should also identify what the stakeholders care about or where their interest in the business process lies. Figure 3-17 shows the stakeholders and what they care about in our compensation budget process example.

Because the stakeholders at corporate headquarters determine how much money a business unit receives for any given year, they want to see a strong business case. They also want assurance that the compensation department has properly managed the budget over the past year. The other executives across

Figure 3-16 Key Stakeholders and Interest

Key stakeholders and interest:

Corporate headquarters	Accurate record of spending; compelling business case for budget proposal.
Other executives (beyond president's direct reports)	Appropriate salary increases for their employees.

Figure 3-17 Alistar Corporation Compensation Budget Process

the company care that they have sufficient money to appropriately reward their employees for good performance throughout the year.

In the Pete Hodges example, the sales department cares about closing the sale, but as a stakeholder, the legal department cares about the terms and conditions of the sale.

In Alistar's hiring process example, the recruitment department has responsibility for the hiring process; however, the compensation department, as a stakeholder, has responsibility for establishing pay rates.

Section 8: Measurements of Success

This section helps the project team identify what the business should measure. In terms of the client/customer and stakeholder needs that you just identified, the measurements of success should support what the client/customer and stakeholders define as important. (See Figure 3-18.)

You can also include internal requirements that a department may have for the business process. At this point, you do not need to worry about how to conduct the measurement; you just need to identify what you want to measure. Chapter 7 discusses how to develop the measurements.

As you can see from Figure 3-19, the first two measurements relate back to the client needs, the third measurement

Figure 3-18   *Measurements of Success*

supports both the client and stakeholder needs, and the fourth defines an internal metric for the compensation department.

Chapter Summary: Step 2

Discussing this baseline information with the project team at the start of the first meeting allows everyone to have input and assists the team in coming to a common understanding of the business process and any associated terminology. As you develop the scope definition document, remain flexible so that in the end you feel comfortable that everyone has had a chance to provide input to the scope of the work and that everyone understands what is and is not included in the business process. In my experience, involving people in developing or ap-

Measurements of success:

1. On demand knowledge for the president's direct reports of their budget balances (the right information at the right time)
2. A process viewed as a reliable tool for use in employee-related activities like planning promotions and developing succession plans
3. Accurate tracking of spending
4. The ability to make better decisions on allocating funds

Figure 3-19 Alistar Corporation Compensation Budget Process

proving scope causes them to better respect and honor the agreements made.

Once the project team has agreed on the content of the document, you need to review it with the sponsor and gain approval. The sponsor will appreciate the conciseness of the document, so keep it to a single piece of paper. You should view the scope definition as an easy read and a quick reference tool. The sponsor may want to make minor changes to the document after reviewing it or join your next meeting to discuss it with the project team. Either scenario works as long as the project team agrees with the proposed changes.

After everyone has reviewed and agreed to the scope definition, you have a document that works like a contract, one that you can revisit, as needed, to reinforce the agreements made. You should consider it "locked" to a certain extent. If you have spent sufficient time developing the content in the document, you should expect minimal changes. If you do need to change the scope after the next step has started—and changes occasionally happen—you can facilitate an honest discussion, reset expectations, and easily update the scope definition document.

You should feel free to change the scope definition document to fit your needs. Take components out and put others in to address any specific situations you may encounter. The document is meant to be flexible. The model I have used throughout this chapter should work 80 percent of the time.

Figure 3-20 shows an alternative that I used when I examined the processing of various employee transactions in Alistar's employee system of record. As this figure shows, I eliminated many sections of the scope definition document that did not apply and added other sections. Since the transactions did not belong to a single business process, I deleted the process name, process owner, process responsibilities, and the measurements of success sections of the template and adapted it for this specific case.

Time Estimate

To help plan the time that it takes to work through this step, Figure 3-21 on page 76 summarizes the amount of time you should allow to complete the scope definition document.

First Project Team Meeting

The first project team meeting should allow sufficient time to walk through the roadmap, introduced in Chapter 1, so that the team can see how the journey will unfold. At this meeting you also lead the team through a thorough discussion of all the sections of the scope definition document.

Give the project team a blank copy of the scope definition document at the first meeting and facilitate a discussion to complete the document together as a team. You should keep track of the discussion during the meeting on an electronic board, if available, so that everyone can see the document coming together.

An electronic board is a type of dry-erase board that has the capability to print a hardcopy of what you write on the board. You will find this helpful as the facilitator because it allows you to print a picture of the board contents simply by hitting a button or sending the board contents to a printer so

Key stakeholders and interest:

Recruitment	Quick, accurate information Filling the requisition in a timely manner Processing the hire in a timely manner
Compensation	Ensure the employee is paid correctly and is in the correct job Ensure funding is available Ensure that policy, if applicable, is followed
Central Services	Completeness, timeliness, and accuracy of data
Operations	Quick turnaround Accurate information from compensation and central services
Support Functions	Quick turnaround Accurate information from compensation and central services

Outside scope:

- Approval for creating a position
- Candidate selection
- Executive pay
- Third-party employees
- Union negotiations

Description (purpose):

To ensure that the following key transactions are accurately processed in a timely manner for all employees:

• Hires	• Relevels	
• Transfers	• Downgrades	
• Promotions	• Status changes	

Scope (boundaries):

Start   A candidate has accepted an offer.

End   Employee system of record is updated.

Within scope:

- Hiring an employee
- Transferring an employee
- Promoting an employee
- Downgrading an employee
- Changing an employee's status (e.g., full time, part time)

Figure 3-20 Alternative Scope Definition Document

Event	Time	Purpose
First project team meeting	90 minutes	■ Walk through roadmap (Chapter 1). ■ Complete scope definition document.
Sponsor meeting	30 minutes	■ Gain agreement on scope definition document.

Figure 3-21 Time Estimate—Step 2: Establish Foundation

that you do not need to take additional notes. You should use a dry-erase board in order to allow the project team to "see" the discussion as it unfolds and to keep them involved and interested in the work.

Sponsor Meeting

Before the initial project team meeting, you should have already scheduled time for a meeting with the sponsor for a date after the first meeting, where you will review the document and discuss any potential changes.

What You Have Achieved

In this chapter, you have achieved the following:

➤ A clear understanding of the business process you will start examining in step 3, mapping the process

➤ A common understanding of unusual terminology

➤ Buy-in from the sponsor on scope

➤ A pseudo contract—a document everyone believes in

➤ Most important, the *power* to keep scope creep at bay

CHAPTER 4

Step 3: Draw the Process Map

Flowcharting and Documenting

Ed Seinfeld, the manager of HRIS (human resource information systems) for Alistar Corporation, wanted to understand how technology projects secured funding and how system expenses hit Alistar's financial planning processes like the five-year capital plan, annual operations plan, and monthly forecasts.

While trying to collect the system costs charged to the human resources and information technology departments, Ed discovered that no clear process existed, causing him to ask for my help in understanding what he called the "technology funding process." When someone comes to me with this type of problem, I like to start by defining the process as we did in Chapter 3 and then draw a process map.

Drawing a process map is one of the best ways to help people understand any business process. It helps everyone involved in creating the process map learn how the process works, what activities constitute most of the work, where the handoffs occur between departments, and where the opportunities for improvement exist.

There are two schools of thought on how to approach this step depending on the technique that someone subscribes to: quality or reengineering. Both techniques are well-known process improvement methods:

▶ Reengineering focuses on the future state, driven by customer needs, and does not focus on the current process.

▶ Quality, also concerned with customer needs, examines the current process.

I have experience working with reengineering and understand why it became popular in the mid-1990s, but I find that most people have a difficult time becoming engaged in process work if you do not discuss how things work today. So, the technique I share in this chapter focuses on process mapping the current process, although you can use the techniques for any process-mapping exercise.

Let us start at the beginning with a simple definition of a process map and the introduction of some basic components used to draw a map.

Process Map Overview

A *process map* is a visual representation of a series of connected activities that, when strung together, deliver a meaningful outcome to the client/customer. To lead into the mechanics of building a process map, let me start by sharing a simple example.

Figure 4-1 shows the basic components of a process map. Each rectangle in Figure 4-1 represents an *activity* in a process that adds value to the next step in the process.

Each activity consists of a series of *tasks*, and each activity should start with an action verb that demonstrates doing or performing something. Examples of action verbs include words like *develop, approve, update, run,* and *communicate*. For example:

▶ **Develop** the business case.

▶ **Approve** an expense report.

Figure 4-1 Process Map Components

➤ **Update** the forecast.

➤ **Run** a report.

➤ **Communicate** the status.

An action verb is the first word in the activity box, followed by the action itself. For example, using the preceding action verbs, Figure 4-2 shows five different examples using each of the action verbs.

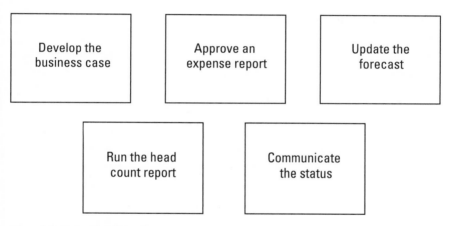

Figure 4-2 Action Verb Examples

You should have noticed the arrows in Figure 4-1 going from one box to the next. These arrows are known as *inputs* and *outputs*. Figure 4-3 shows an arrow leaving the first activity box and going to the second activity box. This arrow represents the *output* of the first box (activity 1) and the *input* to the next box

Figure 4-3 Output and Input

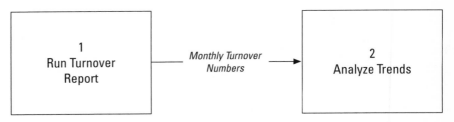

Figure 4-4 Start of Process Map

(activity 2). As the figure shows, the text on the arrow reads "Output from activity 1" and "Input to activity 2."

Whatever you write on the arrow must result from the actions taken in activity 1, and that output must then be used by activity 2 to accomplish its tasks. For example, if activity 1 states "Run a report," the output should identify what information results from running the report. Activity 2 would then state what to do with that information. If you added another activity (activity 3), you would follow this same logic and make sure that activity 3 used the output of activity 2.

Suppose that we defined the output of activity 1 as "monthly turnover numbers." Activity 2 would then show what happens to the turnover information. Does someone analyze trends, research why the numbers increased or decreased, or perhaps identify the departments with high turnover? Figure 4-4 shows what the beginning of this process map might look like.

Now if we look back at Figure 4-1, we see that the terminator symbol (see Figure 4-5) appeared at the end of the string of boxes to show that the process ends at that point. Process mapping includes numerous symbols, and I introduce them as I use them throughout this chapter.

Figure 4-5 Terminator Symbol

As explained earlier, almost everything we do is a process, and Figure 4-6 shows a simple process map for a parent's routine in the morning. As you can imagine, a number of tasks

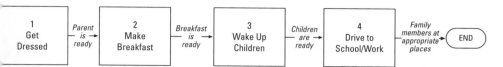

Figure 4-6 Morning Routine

occur within each of the four main activities shown. In this simple example, the parent seems to want to make sure that she showers and gets dressed before waking up the children. The parent also wants breakfast made before waking the children, suggesting that she wants a little quiet time, perhaps to enjoy a cup of coffee before the commotion begins. Eventually, we see that the parent drops the children off at school and then drives to work.

As this example shows, you can draw either a high-level process map without a great deal of detail or an extremely detailed process map. We could have included many more activities in Figure 4-6 if we wanted to develop a detailed process map to show the parent's entire morning process. You have to decide on the level of detail required to achieve your goals. If you cannot decide how detailed a process map to draw, use the criteria in Figure 4-7 to help with your decision to draw a process map at a high level, detailed level, or somewhere in between.

Detailed Level	High Level
Draw a detailed-level process map if the process: ■ Is used often by many people. ■ Experiences high turnover among process workers. ■ Is a subprocess of another business process.	Draw a high-level process map if the process: ■ Is undefined and little shared understanding exists in the organization of the end-to-end business process. ■ Is a complex process. ■ Is a highly variable process. ■ Has many subprocesses.

Figure 4-7 Level of Detail for a Process Map

Even if you start at a high level, you can always add additional details if the need surfaces. The amount of time you spend drawing a process map varies depending on the goals. Think about what level of detail you need to accomplish your goals, and do not go any deeper.

Drawing the Process Map

In step 2 of the roadmap you laid the foundation for the business process; now you can move to step 3, drawing and documenting the process map. But where do you begin? The first box always seems to be the most difficult one to fill in because you have to decide where to start.

To get started, use the scope definition document created in step 2, and reference the boundaries defined at that time. Look at where you said the process begins and ends, and use that information as the starting point.

Let us use Alistar Corporation's simple recognition bonus award process from Chapter 3 to demonstrate the building of a process map. Figure 4-8 contains a description of this business process. Since this process is about rewarding employ-

---

Description (purpose):

This process is an ongoing cash reward program to recognize outstanding contributions beyond an eligible* employee's regular responsibilities.

*Eligible employees include:

■ All managerial and professional employees *not* eligible for any other incentive program.
■ All office hourly employees.

Figure 4-8 Recognition Bonus Award Process

ees for good performance, our scope definition document lists the boundaries, as shown in Figure 4-9.

■ *Start:* Recommend employee for an award.

■ *End:* System of record is updated.

Figure 4-9 Boundaries

The entry point into the business process becomes the first data point to draw on the process map. In our example, we already identified the initial entry point when we established the boundaries in Figure 4-9. So we would write "Recommend employee for an award" on the process map and place an arrow going from this phrase to the first box. Figure 4-10 shows what the process map looks like at this point.

The next step is to decide what to write inside the first box on the process map.

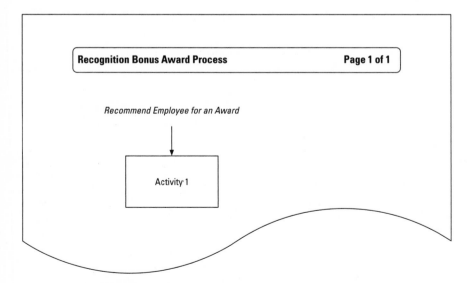

Figure 4-10 Recognition Bonus Award Process Map

Box 1

Once we defined "Recommend employee for an award" as the entry into the process, we start by asking the project team questions to get them talking and thinking about the process. In this example, the team consists of individuals from the human resource compensation department. To get the conversation rolling, you might say things like:

> OK, an employee was recommended for a recognition
> bonus award. What happens now?
> Or . . .
> Who recommends an employee for a recognition bonus award?
> Or . . .
> You've gotten a call from a manager who wants to give an
> employee a recognition bonus award. What do you do?

You can ask whatever question(s) you feel will get the project team talking. As the facilitator, you have to draw the information out of the team, rather than supplying the answers. In your role as facilitator, you should never give the answer, but you may need to rephrase statements made by the project team so that what you write on the process map is clear and concise.

By using the boundary start point as the entry into the business process, you will find it easier to draw the first box. In our example, we eventually learn that the first step in the process occurs when the manager fills out a form to request a recognition award for an employee. Draw a box on the electronic dry-erase board, write a number "1" at the top of the box, and write "Complete Recognition Bonus Award Form" inside the box. Figure 4-11 shows the beginning of the process map.

After writing the activity in the first step in the process, you then identify the person responsible for the activity and write the person's title below the box. Do not write the person's real name because the process map will become outdated as employees change jobs. Use their titles instead of their names because titles give the process map shelf life. For example, write "Manager" instead of "Bill Nguyen."

Does this seem too simple? Perhaps, but as we continue

Figure 4-11   Recognition Bonus Award Process Map

adding to the process map, you will see that, no matter how simple or complex your situation, the approach to drawing a process map is the same. I almost said the *process* to drawing a process map is the same, and there is that word *process* again!

As you look at Figure 4-11, notice several other items:

▶ The first activity starts with the word "Complete," which denotes an action—a task the manager must do. Always start each activity with an action verb.

▶ We use an icon to depict any tools used to accomplish the activity. In this case, the icon stands for a hardcopy form, as shown by the document symbol in Figure 4-12. All the symbols used in this chapter are available in Microsoft Visio.

Figure 4-12   Document Symbol

▶ Type the form name, if desired, either inside or outside the document symbol. Figure 4-13 shows the two alternatives.

If you include numerous documents throughout the process map, it helps to identify each one.

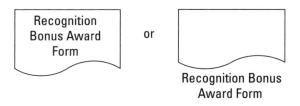

Figure 4-13 Document Symbol Examples

In Figure 4-11, notice that the arrow leaving activity 1 shows the output of that activity as a completed form. Sometimes process maps omit text on the input and output lines, but leaving out such information can cause confusion because the output of one activity feeds the next activity. For example, if we did not include an output from activity 1 in Figure 4-11 and you asked the project team to identify the next step in the process, the members may state an activity unrelated to the completed form. Yet whatever happens in activity 2 must have something to do with the form.

As I began working with Ed Seinfeld, the HRIS manager, we initially created the scope definition document for the funding process, stating the purpose of the process and the boundaries. That phase went well. The first dilemma surfaced when I asked the team to identify the initial step in the process. One person said, "Well, it could start when we identify the funding source." Another said, "I think the process starts when we determine whether it is capitalized or expensed." Yet a third person claimed we had to identify the type of system because of the different paths used to obtain funding for each system type. As the facilitator in this type of situation, how would you know where to begin drawing the process map?

I started the process map with a decision symbol, as shown in Figure 4-14. Whenever you hear people say, "Well, it all depends," you have a clue to start with this symbol. After some discussion, I got Ed and the team to agree to start the

Figure 4-14 Decision Symbol

process map by asking what kind of system we wanted to fund. Figure 4-15 shows the approach to handling situations like this when multiple conditions exist. In this case, I drew three outputs coming from the first activity to show one route for an enterprise system, another for a business group system solution, and a third that addresses a solution for a single strategic business unit within a group.

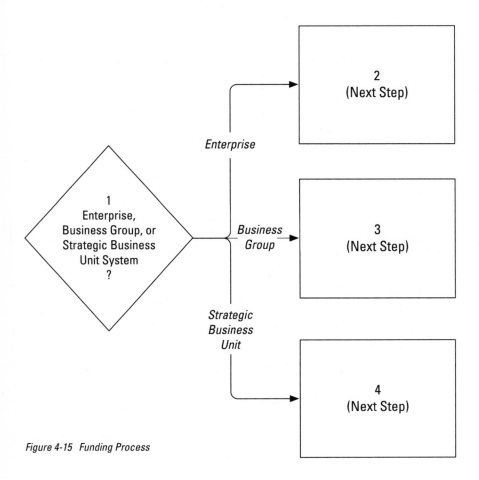

Figure 4-15 Funding Process

Another problem you may encounter when starting to draw a process map occurs when the business process has never been documented before or when no one on the project team has enough familiarity with the process. In either case, you might find yourself drawing a mix of the current process and a desired future state process. If you find yourself in this predicament, go with the momentum, while keeping track of the changes that have to occur to enable the new process to work. These changes become part of an impact analysis, which we discuss in Chapter 9.

Box 2

For the next box in the recognition bonus award process, we need to understand what happens to the form. Start by asking questions like:

Now that we have a completed form, what happens to it? If you have trouble getting an answer, ask more precise questions like:

Whom is the form sent to, how is it sent, and what do they do with it?

Do you get the feeling that you have to spend a good deal of time pushing things along? Well, you do. As the facilitator, you have to balance letting people talk and keeping the work moving.

In our scenario, let us suppose that after some discussion, it becomes obvious that in activity 2 another manager either approves or rejects the request. Figure 4-16 shows the continuation of the process map. As the figure shows, the second step in the process includes the next-level manager (manager 2) either approving or rejecting the request to give the employee a recognition award.

Notice that the project team's discussion caused other changes to the process map.

> ▶ The first activity changed to include mailing the form to the next-level manager. As a result, we added an interoffice mail symbol, as shown in Figure 4-17, to show how the next-level manager receives the form.

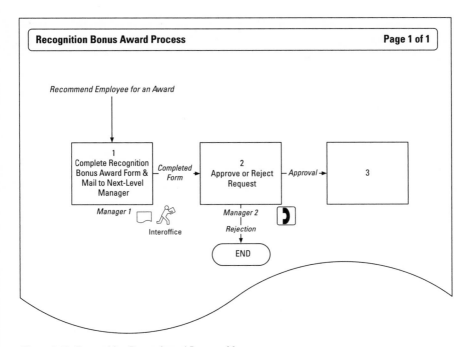

Figure 4-16 Recognition Bonus Award Process Map

Figure 4-17 Interoffice Mail Symbol

► Activity 2 can have two possible outputs. The next-level manager can either approve or reject the proposed bonus award:

■ If manager 2 approves the award recommendation, the process moves on to activity 3, and "Approval" appears as one output from activity 2 to activity 3.

■ If manager 2 does not approve the award recommendation, "Rejection" appears as the second output from activity 2, and the terminator symbol denotes the end of the process. Writing the word "End" inside the terminator symbol clearly communicates the end of the process and makes a process map easier to read.

You will find many different ways to draw multiple outputs from one activity, and the next few figures show some of the variations. Pick the one that works best for your situation.

▶ The alternative shown in Figure 4-18 requires additional real estate, or space, on a process map. So I do not use this approach when one output simply depicts the end of the process.

▶ Figure 4-19 shows another way to handle multiple outputs using the decision symbol. When using the decision symbol, the outputs can include "Yes/No" or anything else appropriate to the situation. You will find the decision symbol approach most useful when the two outputs denote obvious next steps instead of simply an end to the process.

▶ Figure 4-20 on page 92 shows another approach to using the decision symbol when how to handle a decision differs depending on the decision to be made. In the recognition bonus award example, assume the decision revolves around the size of the award because what occurs next may vary

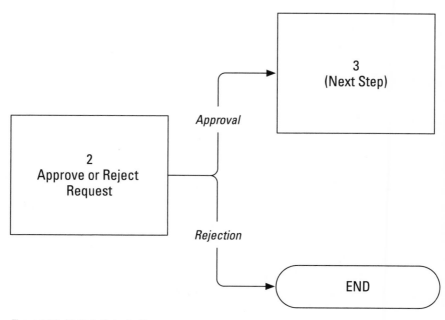

Figure 4-18 Multiple Outputs #1

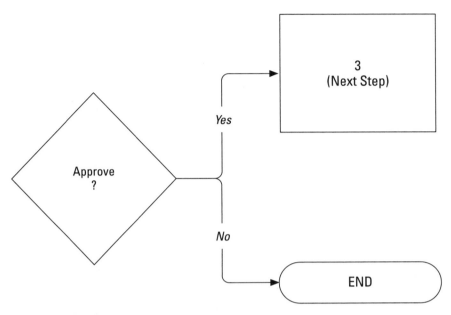

Figure 4-19   Multiple Outputs #2

depending on the dollar value of the award. The figure tells us that a different activity must take place when an award amount is less than or equal to $500 versus greater than $500 because of the two different paths leaving the "Award amount" decision symbol. The activity 1 and 2 boxes would contain an explanation of what happens in each case.

Now, let us go back to the recognition bonus award process.

Box 3

After activity 2 in the recognition bonus award process, we understand that the second manager either approved or rejected the award request. Let us assume that the next-level manager (manager 2) approved the award recommendation and that we must decide what to write in box 3. Ask questions like:

Now that management has approved the award, what happens?

Or . . .

Who gets the form next, and what do they do with it?

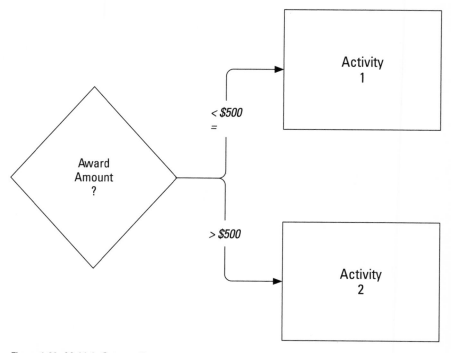

Figure 4-20   Multiple Outputs #3

In this example, we learn that, after the second manager approves the award, the form is sent to the compensation department. A compensation analyst reviews the eligibility of the employee, the justification for the award, and the dollar value of the award relative to the company's established guidelines. We then add activity 3 to the map, as shown in Figure 4-21. This figure shows a new concept associated with activity 3. The annotation symbol, as shown in Figure 4-22, is placed underneath an activity box to provide an area on the map to write key points associated with the activity.

You can easily overuse the annotation symbol and make the process map too busy, so include an annotation only when you might lose critical information.

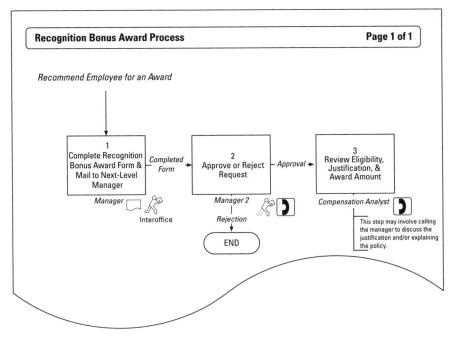

Figure 4-21   Recognition Bonus Award Process Map

Use the annotation symbol to
write key points about this step in
the business process

Figure 4-22   Annotation Symbol

Boxes 4–7

Figure 4-23 shows the final recognition bonus award process map. Notice that the "Final Approval" output from activity 6 causes two simultaneous things to happen: the manager's communicating the award to the employee face to face (activity 7) and compensation's updating the system of record with the award amount and effective date (activity 8). In this scenario, I drew the two activities resulting from activity 6 as one box on

Figure 4-23 Recognition Bonus Award Process Map

top of the other because they happen at the same time by different people.

Notice also in Figure 4-23 that I keep describing the tools used to perform activities by adding icons like:

► The telephone

Figure 4-24 Telephone

► Email

Figure 4-25 Email

► Face-to-face communications

Figure 4-26 Face-to-face Communication

► System of record

Figure 4-27 System of Record

The process map becomes more interesting and easier for someone to read by the addition of icons. The process map in Figure 4-23 shows the standard way to draw a process map, but other types of process maps may be useful.

The Cross-Functional Process Map

Figure 4-23 introduced two different groups of people responsible for the activities: managers and compensation analysts. The compensation analysts reside in a different department from the managers who request and approve the awards. When a process includes different departments, you may find it helpful to create a cross-functional process map. This kind of map, shown in Figure 4-28, draws its name from the cross-functional bands, or horizontal rows, used to show the departments involved in the process.

The cross-functional bands can represent as many functions as required. In Figure 4-28, the process map has two horizontal cross-functional bands: one for management and another

Figure 4-28 Cross-Functional Process Map

for the compensation department. When using this style, include a new functional band for each department or function involved in the process, and place activities in the appropriate bands depending on the department or area responsible for the activity. In Figure 4-28, activities 1 and 2, fall within the management band because managers perform these activities, whereas activity 3 falls within the compensation band for similar reasons.

Using a cross-functional process map makes it easy to see when responsibility for a step in a process moves from one department to another, something known as a *handoff*. Because handoffs often contribute to points in a business process where issues occur, use this technique to minimize such situations.

Cross-functional process maps can have two types of bands: the more common horizontal band, shown in Figure 4-29, or the vertical band, shown in Figure 4-30. The decision of which type of process map to draw depends on the goals of the work and the individuals involved. If the work involves a number of different departments, use the cross-functional process map; if the work includes only one department, then the standard process map will suffice. Those unfamiliar with reading a process map can easily get confused by the cross-functional bands.

Continuing the Work from Meeting to Meeting

More often than not, you will find it difficult to complete a process map in one meeting unless the work encompasses a simple business process or you plan a long meeting. Because

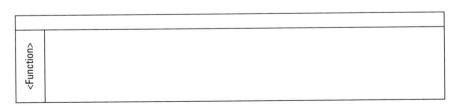

Figure 4-29 Horizontal Cross-Functional Band

Figure 4-30   Vertical Cross-Functional Band

everyone involved in helping to draw the process map returns to their normal jobs once the meeting ends, you will find that no one remembers the details of the process map you started creating when they come back together at the next meeting. As a result, to jump-start their memories at the next meeting, you have to accomplish several tasks between meetings.

➤ First, after each process mapping meeting, convert your hand drawing into a formal document using a software application like Microsoft Visio. If the project team does not finish drawing the process map in one meeting, document the work done to date so that the team members start the next meeting with a precise picture of where they left off. It helps to use an electronic dry-erase board so that you end a meeting with a copy of the project team's work. If not, copy the drawing on paper before leaving the meeting room. Another alternative that works well, if you have the available resources, is to have someone assist you who can draw the process map during the meeting using a laptop computer and the appropriate software application. I use Microsoft Visio because the software includes the normal flowchart shapes required.

➤ Second, once you completed drawing the process map from the first meeting, enlarge it to a poster size. If an enlarging machine is not available, locate a copy center, like FedEx/Kinko, who charges a moderate fee for black-and-white enlargements.

➤ Third, bring copies of the process map to the next meeting for the project team.

At the next meeting, hang the enlarged process map on the wall and begin the meeting by walking the team members through the partially completed process map to remind them all of what they accomplished at the first meeting. You should walk them through the process map box by box, highlighting what occurs at each step, naming the responsible party, identifying the tools used, and explaining annotations. Physically point to different sections on the process map, explain the output of each box, and describe how the output is used in the next step of the process.

Let us step through this process using the recognition bonus award process map from Figure 4-23.

Figure 4-31 shows sample dialog we might use to start the second meeting. Continue this type of dialogue until you reach the point where the project team left off at the last meet-

Pointing to "Recommend employee for an award

"We said in our last meeting that the process starts when an employee is recommended for an award and this leads to our first box. In box 1, we have the employee's manager completing a hardcopy form and justifying why the employee should receive an award. When the form is complete, the manager sends the form via interoffice mail to the next-level manager. So coming out of box 1, we have a completed form.

Pointing to box 1

Pointing to the output line

Pointing to box 2

In box 2, the next-level manager reviews the information on the form and, if they have additional questions, they call the requesting manager. Eventually, they either approve or reject the request. If they reject the award, then the process ends. If they approve the award, then the process moves to box 3.

Pointing to box 3

Pointing to the "Rejection" output from box 2

Figure 4-31 Sample Dialogue

ing. By physically pointing to the enlarged process map and walking the team through how they created the map, you engage the participants and enable them to picture the result of their work thus far. Think of this step as telling a story, reinforcing the salient points from the team's prior discussions.

You should allow and encourage the project team to stop and change the process map as you walk through it because it is the first time that they see the map in its clean state. Stop every time someone has a question and discuss the issue. If anyone has a question, it may mean that something on the process map needs to change. In addition, proactively watch the team members as you walk through the map to validate that they can follow along and encourage the team to discuss any unclear points. Physically write any changes directly on the enlarged process map using a thick marker so that everyone can see the map changing. You can also use a laptop and projector to display the process map on a screen, but you may find, as I have, that this is not as engaging or as flexible in a team setting.

After reviewing the enlarged process map hanging on the wall, switch back to the electronic dry-erase board and continue drawing the next steps in the process. When you leave the second meeting, you now have marked-up poster pages and new hand-drawn pages. After the second meeting, update the Microsoft Visio process map with the changes and incorporate them to prepare for the next meeting. Again, make copies for the project team, enlarge the updated process map, and walk the team through the updated map at the next meeting starting at activity 1. Go through these steps every time the team meets, regardless of the number of meetings, and always start back at activity 1.

In my experience, not many process maps result in a one-page document. Often, a single business process requires multiple $8\frac{1}{2} \times 11$-inch pages. As you add new pages to the process map, you will find yourself breaking up the flow, either on the same page or on another page. Use the connector symbols, as shown in Figures 4-32 and 4-33, to designate movement on the process map:

▶ Use the on-page connector, shown in Figure 4-32, when moving to another, nonsequential box on the *same* page of the process map. Inside the symbol, include the activity number that the reader should go to next.

Figure 4-32 On-Page Connector Symbol

▶ Use the off-page connector, shown in Figure 4-33, when moving to another box on a *different* page of a process map. Inside the symbol, include the page number and activity number that the readers should go to next.

Figure 4-33 Off-Page Connector Symbol

When you have a multiple-page process map, hang the enlarged process map pages around the conference room, moving from left to right.

Documenting the Process

Imagine that a new person joins your department and has to learn about one of the business processes. Do you just hand him or her a process map and walk her through the steps? You could, but a better way includes documenting the discussion that occurred during the drawing of the process map, thereby creating a business tool that the organization can use as a standard operating procedure for training new employees.

I call this tool the *detail document*, a narrative description of the process map, which should accompany the map. Because people have different learning styles, having both a graphical and text representation of the business process provides everyone with a choice on how to reference the process materials. Figure 4-34 shows the beginning section of the detail document for the recognition bonus award process, which begins when an employee is recommended for an award.

Write the design document after each meeting at the same time that you update the process map. Do not put off writing the design document until the process map is complete because waiting will cause you to forget some of the project team's discussion.

The detail document, combined with the process map, provides those who are unfamiliar with the business process the information that they require to understand the process, and it gives the process workers the information they need to do their jobs.

This documentation becomes important for step 6, when you move to improving the process, saving time as the project team attempts to recall the details of the process discussed weeks earlier.

Also start thinking about how to package the entire business process for future reference. In addition to storing the ma-

No.	Activity Description	Responsible Party	Tools	Output
1	**Complete the recognition bonus award form, and mail it to the next-level manager.** When a manager wants to recommend an employee for a recognition bonus award, he or she completes the recognition bonus award form. While completing the form, the manager has to look up the employee's record in the company's system of record to obtain their employee ID and other information required on the form. The manager also reviews the guidelines for recognition awards to determine the size of the award to propose. The guidelines show the minimum award amounts, based on the employee's annual salary as follows: ■ $100 if <$30,000 annual salary ■ $250 if between $30,000 and $50,000 annual salary ■ $500 if > $50,001 annual salary Having completed the form, the manager forwards it via interoffice mail to the next-level manager for approval.	Manager 1	Hardcopy form	**Completed form** A completed form is mailed to the next-level manager.
2	**Approve or reject request.** The next-level manager reviews the recognition bonus award form and decides either to: ■ Agree with the recommendation as presented. ■ Ask several questions about information on the form. ■ Or absolutely not agree that the employee should receive a recognition award. The approving manager refers to the guidelines for award amounts and reasons for giving a recognition award to make a decision whether to approve or reject the request. The approving manager may call the requesting manager to discuss either the dollar value of the award or justification. If the approving manager agrees, he or she forwards the signed form to the compensation department.	Manager 2 (approving manager)	Phone, interoffice mail	There are two possible outputs: *Approval:* The approving manager approves the request for an award. *Rejection:* The approving manager does *not* approve the request for an award and notifies the requesting manager of the decision.
3				

Figure 4-34 Recognition Bonus Award Process Detail Document

terials on a network drive or storage media, I like to create a binder because most people find it easier to read process information in hardcopy format. Up to this point, you have completed three pieces of process information that can comprise a binder, as depicted in Figure 4-35.

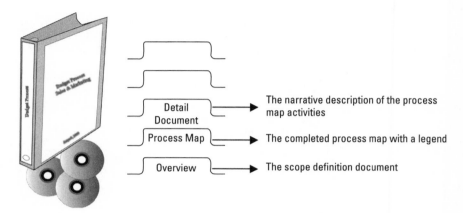

Figure 4-35 Process Documentation

The legend referenced in Figure 4-35 under the "Process Map" tab is a one-page sheet placed either in front of or behind the process map. It provides an explanation of symbols used throughout the process map. Figure 4-36 shows an example of a legend. All these symbols are available in Microsoft Visio. You probably understand most of the symbols in Figure 4-36 except perhaps for the internal control and cyclical/recurring symbols, shown in Figures 4-37–4-39.

Figure 4-36 Legend

Figure 4-37 Internal Control Symbol

► Use the internal control symbol (Figure 4-37) to denote that the activity constitutes a potential problem requiring additional attention. Chapter 7 covers internal controls.

► Use the cyclical/recurring symbol (Figure 4-38, also called the workflow loop symbol in Microsoft Visio), which originates from total quality management, when an activity repeatedly occurs throughout the year or because of its cyclical nature.

Figure 4-38 Cyclical/Recurring Symbol

Figure 4-39 shows the cyclical/recurring symbol placed around an activity box to denote that the activity occurs on a cyclical or recurring basis.

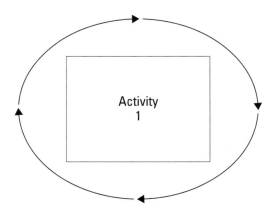

Figure 4-39 Cyclical Activity Sample

Chapter Summary: Step 3

Drawing the process map helps everyone involved better understand how the business process works, where handoffs occur between departments, and the background needed to apply the improvement techniques described in Chapter 6.

Decide on the type of process map to draw depending on your requirements: either a high-level or detail-level process map, and either the standard or cross-functional process map. You have great flexibility deciding how to flowchart and embellish the process map and document the process. Creating the process map and detail document provides the business with a tool that can be used as a standard operating procedure to train new employees.

Keep the project team involved from meeting to meeting by updating the process map and detail document between the meetings. Start each meeting by walking the team through the work done to date. As questions surface, stop and make changes with a thick marker on the enlarged process map.

The sample dialog shared throughout this chapter should help you develop confidence in leading this type of work. The techniques presented in this chapter work even if you work alone, to increase your understanding of a business process, or to lead a business process improvement effort with others. When you work alone, the blank template in Figure 4-40 provides some structure as you talk to colleagues about a business process.

I often use this template as I talk one on one with someone about a business process because it keeps me focused on my goal. If the person you talk to veers off on a tangent, having this template in front of you (either physically or mentally) helps you to remember to redirect the conversation back to the main topic.

Time Estimate

To help in planning the time that it takes to work through this step, Figure 4-41 summarizes the amount of time required to complete the process map and detail document.

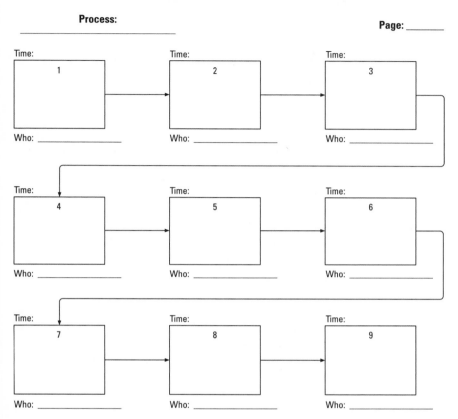

Figure 4-40 Blank Template

Event	Time	Purpose
Second project team meeting	3 hours	■ Review scope definition document and share sponsor feedback. ■ Begin mapping the process.
Postmeeting work	2 hours	■ Draw process map using Microsoft Visio or similar tool. ■ Create the detail document.
Follow-on project team meetings (until map is complete)	3–4 hours	■ Review enlarged process map to date (15–30 minutes depending on how far into the process map the team got at the last meeting). ■ Continue mapping the process.

Figure 4-41 Time Estimate—Step 3: Map Process

Second Project Team Meeting

This is the second time that the project team meets and the first time that you review the final scope definition document. Spend the first 20 minutes reviewing the scope definition document to help all members recall what they said the last time they met and to share the sponsor's feedback on the document. Because the project team will not have seen the scope definition document typed up before, it will appear more formal and the members may want to make adjustments. Once everyone agrees with the final version of the scope definition, move to building the process map, following the techniques outlined in this chapter.

Postmeeting Work

During this personal time, draw the process map using drawing software, such as Microsoft Visio, and document the discussion about each activity in the detail document. Write the detail document as you progress through the work instead of putting it off until the end because you may well forget portions of the rich discussion.

Follow-on Project Team Meetings

The first part of each future meeting should begin with a walkthrough of the enlarged version of the process map, moving activity by activity through the entire map. The greater the number of meetings you have, the longer this exercise takes. Although it may seem repetitive, this exercise is critical because it keeps the project team engaged, and it enables you to pick up where the team left off the last time they met. Remember that, even though you have worked on the process map and know it by heart, everyone else went back to their normal jobs and probably have not even thought about the business process.

As you walk through the process map, remain flexible and ready to make changes. Your flexibility ensures the ongoing improvement of the process map and keeps the team involved.

Remember to draw the changes directly on the enlarged copy of the process map using a marker so that everyone can see them.

Once you finish walking through the enlarged process map, switch to the electronic, dry-erase board and use it to continue drawing the process map from the point where the team left off the last time you met. You will find yourself referring to the wall hangings throughout the process mapping session as the project team discusses new topics, so leave the enlarged copies hanging up throughout the meeting.

You may find yourself in a predicament where the sponsor wants to do the work fast and suggests all-day work sessions. Unless you have a pressing reason, I recommend that the meetings on process work do not last longer than three or four hours. It gets harder to sustain the level of involvement required when meetings extend beyond this timeframe because of the mental strain of the work. In general, I find two hours too short and longer than four hours too tiring for everyone involved.

What You Have Achieved

In this chapter, you have achieved the following:

➤ Agreement by the project team on the scope definition

➤ An understanding of when to draw a high-level or detail-level process map

➤ The importance of inputs and outputs

➤ A grasp of how to create a standard and cross-functional process map

➤ Knowledge of many of the standard flowcharting shapes

➤ Insight into how to lead a team through the work and keep them interested

➤ Most important, the *power* to uncover the opportunities for improvements

CHAPTER 5

Steps 4–5: Estimate Time and Cost and Verify the Process Map

Introducing Process and Cycle Time and Gaining Buy-In

Alistar Corporation's compensation department understood its business process for granting recognition bonus awards to employees, but Stuart Wang, the director of compensation, wanted to know what it cost to administer the business process. This step identifies what a single business process costs an organization. Throughout this chapter you will see how I answer Stuart's question using simple formulas that you can use.

The process map you drew in step 3 provides you with the information required to handle this step. At the end of this step you will know how long the process takes and how much it costs.

Business Process Timing

You often hear two types of time related to business processes: process time and cycle time.

► **Process time** is the time required to complete a single activity in a process. For example, in the morning routine process covered in Chapter 4, this means how long it takes for activity 1, getting dressed, to be completed.

► **Cycle time** is the time required to complete an entire process, from its first to its last step. You may also hear this referred to as elapsed time. In the morning routine example, it is the measure of time from when the parent began getting dressed in activity 1 until everyone arrived at work or school. You cannot calculate the cycle time by just adding up the process times for each activity because cycle time includes waiting time, which adds considerably more time to the total.

So let us start our discussion by focusing on process time.

Process Time

To establish an improvement target, you first need to define how long the process takes today. You do this by going through the process map and identifying how long each activity takes. This is your baseline time. Without a baseline, you cannot establish an improvement target.

Project team members may feel uncomfortable starting off with this step because they do not like estimating and prefer using a more formal technique to measure process time. You can use one of the formal quality control methods, like a time study, where you observe and measure the time it takes an employee to complete each activity in a process. Although this technique and others provide a definitive analysis of time, you will find that most formal techniques are extremely structured and time-consuming and that they often require a skilled person to effectively apply them. Sometimes you require this level of detail, but it is often not necessary with the more administrative processes. You can also look at historical data or test a sample in lieu of a full-blown analysis.

An effective alternative to the formal methods is simply to ask the project team how long each activity takes. Generally, estimating works well for the administrative type of processes used as examples throughout this book. This timing provides useful directional information, and you can always supplement it with a formal technique if you find the need for more statistical data at a later date. I experimented with both approaches for a business process I worked on to see whether any significant difference in the numbers would surface. First, I estimated the process timing with the project team and then conducted a time study of my own. I found the results so close that it suggested the time study was not worth the extra time required. When working with a manufacturing process, however, you may find that you have to use one of the more formal quality control tools.

Most people have a fairly good idea of how long it takes to complete the tasks that comprise a business activity. Although some may have trouble initially with this exercise, it gets easier with time, and participants will become more comfortable with estimating. To identify the process time estimates, proceed box by box on the completed process map, adding the information to the process map above each activity box in the upper left-hand corner.

To demonstrate how to complete this step, let us use Stuart Wang's recognition bonus award process map from Chapter 4, Figure 4-23. To get started, I said:

> In activity 1, we said that the manager completes the recognition bonus award form and mails it to the next-level manager. How long do you think it typically takes a manager to complete the form?

Of course, the project team felt uncomfortable giving an estimate because they said the managers perform this step, not them. So I rephrased the question:

> How long do you think it would take you to complete the form?

If I still had trouble getting a time estimate, I would have asked one of the team members to fill out the form. Your main goal at this point is to keep the work progressing.

If the project team members want to confirm the time estimates after the meeting, let them do that. I generally find very little change between the estimates a team gives me and the later confirmation. If the team simply cannot give you an estimate because the first step in the process does not involve them, you can always come back to activity 1 later. Just move on to an activity where the team owns responsibility and can provide an answer. Return to the earlier activity at a future date with accurate information. Eventually, you will get answers, and sometimes the team may give you a range instead of a single time. For example, the team may feel more comfortable saying that it takes 10–15 minutes instead of a single number, and you should simply accept a range. Rest assured that, after the first box, the process does move more quickly.

Record the time estimate above each activity on the process map. Keep moving through the map, adding process time estimates until you have walked through the entire process. When I update the process map using Microsoft Visio, I use a white clock symbol, as shown in Figure 5-1, to denote process time.

Figure 5-1   Process Time Symbol

Figure 5-2 shows the recognition bonus award process map with process times added above each of the activities on the left-hand side of the box. Naturally, I do not draw clocks during the meeting; instead, I simply write the time as, say, "20 minutes" above the activity on the left-hand side of the box. Figure 5-2 also shows that three of the activities (2, 3, and 8) state a range of time because the project team had a difficult time providing a single number.

When you add up all the activity times, as depicted in Figure 5-3 on page 115, it becomes clear that the entire business process requires between 70 and 87 minutes, roughly between 1 and 1½ hours, assuming that compensation approves the award in activity 4. I derived this estimate by totaling the minutes in the low end and high end of the range.

After completing this summary, you have an estimate of the time employees spend performing the activities that com-

Recommend Employee for an Award

process time

20 minutes

1 Complete Recognition Bonus Award Form & Mail to Next-Level Manager

Manager

Interoffice

Completed Form

5–10 minutes

2 Approve or Reject Request

Manager 2

Approval

Rejection

END

20–30 minutes

3 Review Eligibility, Justification, & Award Amount

Compensation Analyst

This step may involve calling the manager to discuss the justification and/or explaining the policy.

Approved Justif. & Amount

4 OK to Proceed?

Yes

No

5 minutes

5 Send Authorization to Payroll

Compensation Analyst

Payroll Notification

5 minutes

6 Notify Requesting Manager

Compensation Analyst

E+

Denied Request

Final Approval

5 minutes

7 Communicate Award to Employee

Manager

Award Communicated

END

Final Approval

10–12 minutes

8 Update Employee System of Record (SOR) & Retain Hardcopy

Compensation Analyst

SOR

System Updated

END

Figure 5-2. Recognition Bonus Award Process (with Process Time)

Activity Number	Low End	High End
1	20 minutes	20 minutes
2	5 minutes	10 minutes
3	20 minutes	30 minutes
4	n/a	n/a
5	5 minutes	5 minutes
6	5 minutes	5 minutes
7	5 minutes	5 minutes
8	10 minutes	12 minutes
Total	**70 minutes**	**87 minutes**

Figure 5-3 Process Time Summary: Recognition Bonus Award Process

prise the recognition bonus award process. At this point, however, you do not know the cycle time.

Cycle Time

Cycle time is the measure of the overall time it takes for the entire process, or, in our example, how long it takes from the time the initial manager initiates the request for a bonus through the time that he or she can communicate the bonus to the employee.

To estimate the current cycle time for Stuart's case, I included waiting, or delay, time. After the manager in activity 1 completed the form, we had to determine the time lapse before manager 2 would approve or reject it in activity 2. The timing between activities 1 and 2 varies depending on the managers involved, and we uncovered a variety of reasons for the delay in completing activity 2.

To get the project team to state cycle time, you have to lead them through another discussion by saying something like:

We know that it takes the manager in activity 1 about 20 minutes to complete the form and send it to the next-level manager, but I want you to think now about interruptions that the manager may have or additional tasks, unrelated to completing the form, that the manager may have to handle before finishing the form. The phone may ring, a colleague may walk into the office, or their boss may request something unexpectedly. With all these interruptions, how long do you estimate it takes to finish the form and send it on its way?

In Stuart's case, we estimated a one-hour cycle time for activity 1, so I recorded the cycle time estimate on the process map above activity 1 on the right-hand side of the box. I used a dark clock symbol, as shown in Figure 5-4, to denote cycle time when I updated the process map.

Figure 5-4 Cycle Time Symbol

Figure 5-5 shows the recognition bonus award process map with a cycle time added above each of the activities on the map. The figure shows that the team suggested a modest one hour for activity 1, but look at activity 2, where the process map suggests that approving or rejecting the award may take five days. Include notes around the cycle time in the detail document so that you have that information available when you move to the improvement step.

Figure 5-6 on page 118 shows the overall cycle time estimate for this business process at 11 days (or 92 hours), assuming that compensation approved the award in activity 4. Since I wanted to work with *days* when discussing cycle time, I translated the project team's hours into number of days in Figure 5-6 by dividing the hours by eight, the normal number of working hours in one day.

Figure 5-7 on page 118 shows the formula used to translate hours to days for activity 1.

When you compare the process and cycle times for this business process, you can see a significant variance between the numbers. Although the physical work involved in this business process requires only 1 to 1½ hours, the time it takes to com-

Recognition Bonus Award Process

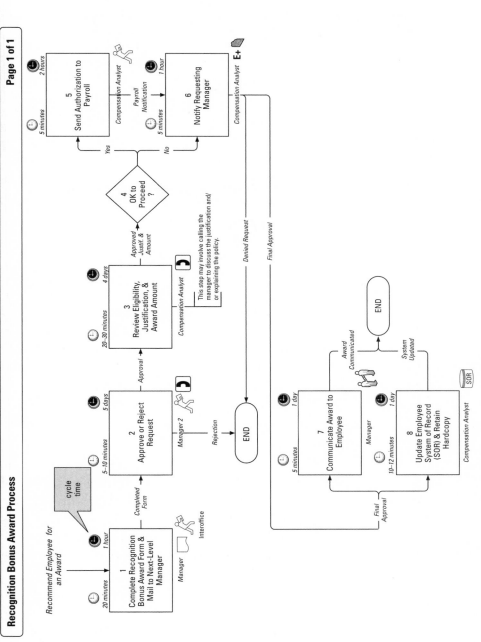

Figure 5-5 Recognition Bonus Award Process (with Process Time)

Activity Number	Number of Hours	Number of Days
1	1 hour	0.125 day
2	40 hours	5 days
3	32 hours	4 days
4	n/a	n/a
5	2 hours	0.25 day
6	1 hours	0.125 day
7	8 hours	1 day
8	8 hours	1 day
Total	**92 hours**	**11.5 days**

Figure 5-6 Cycle Time Summary: Recognition Bonus Award Process

Formula:

$$\frac{\text{Number of hours}}{8 \text{ hours}} = \text{Number of days}$$

Example:

$$\frac{1 \text{ hour}}{8 \text{ hours}} = 0.125 \text{ day}$$

Figure 5-7 Hours-to-Day Translation

plete the entire process from beginning to end can be as long as 11 days. From this comparison, it became apparent that the greatest opportunity for improvement lies with the cycle time, not with the process time. Generally, clients see only cycle time because they cannot see the steps involved in a department's internal processes. When a client complains about the turn-around time of a business process, it usually points to a problem with the cycle time.

I suggest that you do not add the process and cycle times to the process map until *after* you have finished drawing the map in its entirety for two reasons:

1. The project team has gone through the process map multiple times, and they will feel comfortable with the steps involved in the process.
2. If you attempt to collect this information as you draw the process map, the project team will begin thinking about how long an activity takes instead of getting the activities right. The team should initially focus on getting the steps accurate and not worry about the timing.

Process Cost

Now that we know how long each activity in the process takes to complete, we can determine how much the process costs the business. At this point, Stuart Wang recognized that it took his staff 1 to 1½ hours to process a single bonus award, but he still did not know the cost of the process. At this point, we have all the information we need to calculate the cost. Figure 5-8 shows the three components that comprise the total cost:

1. The cost of the people who do the work
2. The cost of technology tools used in the process
3. The cost of overhead such as space, air conditioning, and the like

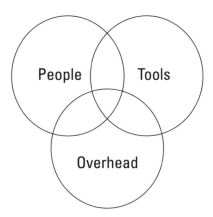

Figure 5-8 Process Cost Components

People Costs

The first component consists of employee costs. Any improvement in process time generates an employee-related cost savings because the employees spend less time on the process. You can define cost savings as either *hard* cost savings or *soft* cost savings:

> ► **Hard cost savings** equate to a reduction in head count, or the number of employees that support the business process, thus lowering the labor cost. This quantitative measure means that, for example, you reduce your employees from a number like 20 to perhaps 18 in a department. The reduction may result from a layoff or attrition, but the overall number of employees supporting the business process declines and thereby lowers costs.

> ► **Soft cost savings** signify a reduction in the number of employees who support the business process, but in this case the affected employees do not leave their current department. Instead of laying them off or moving the employees to different jobs, these employees shift their workload to more value-added work. The cost leaves the process, but not the department.

In working with administrative business processes, I have found that sponsors often look for improved efficiency in their business processes so that they can take on additional work with the same number of employees. Particularly during economic downturns, it is hard to gain approval for additional head count, yet the work never seems to stop; so you need your employees to accomplish more work in the same amount of time.

Determining the People Costs

Estimating the labor cost of a business process takes four steps:

1. List process activities and times in a spreadsheet.
2. Identify the annual volume.

3. Determine the FTE (full-time equivalent) number to use.
4. Determine the salary and employee benefit rate to use for the employees or process workers.

Now let us take a look at how I identified the costs associated with the employees involved in the recognition bonus award process.

Step 1: Process Activities and Time

Figure 5-9 shows the first step, creating a spreadsheet that includes all the activities listed on the process map. The activity number and description appear in the first two columns of the spreadsheet, the total process time required by all employees appears in column three, and only the compensation department's process time appears in column four. This figure shows that each recognition bonus award takes 78.5 minutes, or 1.3 hours, of processing time to complete and that compensation has responsibility for only 46 of those minutes. The figure also shows how to handle a process time range. When the project team gave me a range of five to ten minutes for activity 2, I used the midpoint of the range (7.5 minutes) in the spreadsheet.

If multiple departments are involved in the work, you can add more columns to Figure 5-9 to accommodate as many departments as necessary.

Activity Number	Description	Total Time	Compensation Department Time
1	Complete recognition bonus award form and mail to next-level manager	20.0 minutes	—
2	Approve or reject request	7.5 minutes	—
3	Review eligibility, justification, and award amount	25.0 minutes	25.0 minutes
4	OK to proceed?		
5	Send authorization to payroll	5.0 minutes	5.0 minutes
6	Notify requesting manager	5.0 minutes	5.0 minutes
7	Communicate award to employee	5.0 minutes	—
8	Update employee system of record and retain hardcopy	11.0 minutes	11.0 minutes
	Total minutes/award	**78.5** minutes (1.3 hours)	**46.0** minutes (.8 hours)

Figure 5-9 Recognition Bonus Award Process: Process Timing

Step 2: Annual Volume

The second part of the formula includes the volume of recognition bonus awards. How many recognition bonus awards does the compensation department process in a year? Let us assume that compensation processes 1,500 awards annually.

To calculate the total labor hours spent on this process, multiply the number of awards per year (annual volume) by the process time required for each award. Assuming we are interested only in the compensation department's labor, Figure 5-10 shows how to calculate the department's total time dedicated to the process.

Formula:
Annual volume × Minutes per award = Total annual minutes

Example:
1,500 awards × 46 minutes = 69,000 total annual minutes

Figure 5-10 *Annual Process Time (in minutes)*

To calculate the number of hours that the compensation department spends administering the recognition bonus award process annually, simply divide the total minutes from Figure 5-10 by 60, as shown in Figure 5-11.

Formula:
$$\frac{\text{Total minutes}}{60 \text{ minutes}} = \text{Total annual hours}$$

Example:
$$\frac{69,000 \text{ minutes}}{60 \text{ minutes}} = 1,150 \text{ total annual hours}$$

Figure 5-11 *Minutes-to-Hours Translation*

The compensation department spends 1,150 hours a year administering the recognition bonus award process. The next step includes translating the 1,150 hours into the number of employees, or head count, that those hours represent.

Step 3: FTE Formula

Use of the term *FTE* (*full-time equivalent*) varies from one business to another, but it usually describes the total number of hours that an employee can be paid for in a work year. Assuming that an employee works 40 hours in a week, one FTE equates to 2,080 hours in a year (40 hours × 52 weeks).

Using the FTE concept, the third step translates the 1,150 hours spent on the recognition bonus award process into the number of employees those hours represent. Without the FTE concept, you might wonder whether 1,150 hours constitute one employee, two employees, or more employees. If we use the FTE concept, though, we can see that one FTE may mean:

▶ One employee working 2,080 hours a year.

▶ Or two employees working part time at 1,040 hours each.

Using the FTE concept enables you to account for percentages of an employee's time spent on a business process.

You normally never use the standard 2,080 hours as your baseline because employees take vacations and earn holidays. Talk to your sponsor to identify what baseline you should use in your labor calculation. With Stuart's input, I used 1,880 annual hours as the baseline for the recognition bonus award process. Figure 5-12 shows how I calculated this number.

Labor Calculation Used: 1,880

Annual hours	2,080*
Less 2 weeks vacation	80
Less 1 week sick	40
Less 10 days paid holidays	80
Total	**1,880**

*40 hours per week × 52 weeks in a year

Figure 5-12 Calculating the Baseline

As Figure 5-12 shows, I subtracted vacation, sick, and holiday hours from the standard 2,080 hours to arrive at my baseline of 1,880. If the group you work with has many employees with a lot of seniority, you may have to increase the hours subtracted for vacation to three or four weeks. Likewise, if your company has more or fewer holidays, you may have to adjust this number.

The next step is to divide the total hours spent on the business process by the baseline so that you can determine the number of employees required to support the process. Figure 5-13 shows this calculation. As the figure shows, the recognition bonus award process requires 0.611 of an employee, which equates to slightly more than half an FTE, or half a person, annually. Any improvements you introduce to the process that decreases the process time also decreases the FTE, or number of employees, required to support the business process.

Formula:

$$\frac{\text{Total process hours}}{\text{Baseline}} = \text{Total number of FTEs required to support the business process}$$

Example:

$$\frac{1,150 \text{ hours}}{1,880 \text{ hours}} = 0.611 \text{ FTE}$$

Figure 5-13 Calculating the Number of FTEs

Step 4: Employee Salary and Benefit Costs

The fourth step involves calculating the cost of the 0.611 FTE. First, identify the employees to include in the cost estimate by looking at who performed each activity on the process map. If your client is a single department, as in Stuart's case, the sponsor may want to understand only what the process costs that particular department. In this case, identify only the employees who work in the compensation department, even though the other departments may have some responsibility for the process.

The only compensation department employee on the process map is the compensation analyst. Assuming that this level of employee earns $50,000 per year, Figure 5-14 shows the formula to identify how much of this employee's salary to apply to the recognition bonus award process. The figure shows that $30,550 of the employee's $50,000 annual salary is charged to the recognition bonus award process.

Formula:
Annual salary × FTE = Employee labor cost dedicated to business process

Example:
$50,000 × 0.611= $30,550 labor-only employee cost

Figure 5-14 *Employee Labor Cost*

But we have not finished the employee labor cost calculation. Next, we add the employee benefit rate to the employee's salary because employees cost a company more than just their salaries. You may have heard the employee benefit rate referred to as the EB rate. This rate adds the cost of company-sponsored benefits to the employee's salary to come up with a total employee cost. Use your company's standard EB rate to perform this calculation. In Figure 5-15, we use a 30 percent EB rate to show the formula for calculating the labor plus EB cost.

Formula:
Employee labor cost × (100% + 30% EB rate) = Total employee cost dedicated to business process

Example:
$30,550 × 130% = $39,715 total employee cost dedicated to business process

Figure 5-15 *Calculating the Total Employee Cost*

At this point, we have determined that it costs Stuart Wang 0.611 of an employee, at an employee cost of $39,715, to support the 1,500 annual volume of recognition bonus awards.

In summary, the four components of people cost for Stuart Wang are:

1. Process activity time: 46 minutes
2. Annual volume of awards: 1,500 awards
3. FTE: 0.611
4. Labor cost: $39,715

To explain how to calculate the labor cost for a business process, I used a simple example on purpose. You would use the same method to calculate the labor when a process includes many different types of employees whose rates of pay vary. In the recognition bonus award process, for example, the process could have included a compensation manager, compensation consultant, and compensation analyst, all with different rates of pay. The same formulas work, but you would have to include more columns in the spreadsheet. The case study in Chapter 12 shows an example that includes multiple types of employees performing process activities.

Tool Costs

The second cost component includes the tools used by the business process. This category may include technology tools, like software applications, or internally developed tools, such as a reference guide.

Determining Tool Costs

To estimate the tool costs, identify the tools used by employees who support the business process. This list can become extensive and vary depending on the complexity of the process. To capture this information, you can either create a separate spreadsheet that includes the details for the tools used or just add columns to the process timing table in Figure 5-9. Figure 5-16 shows an updated table with two additional columns to include the tools used and their cost.

Activity Number	Description	Total Time	Compensation Department Time	Tools Used	Tool Cost
1	Complete recognition bonus award form and mail to next level-manager	20.0 minutes	—		
2	Approve or reject request	7.5 minutes	—		
3	Review eligibility, justification, and award amount	25.0 minutes	25.0 minutes		
4	OK to proceed?	—	—		
5	Send authorization to payroll	5.0 minutes	5.0 minutes		
6	Notify requesting manager	5.0 minutes	5.0 minutes	Outlook	$75
7	Communicate award to employee	5.0 minutes	—		
8	Update employee system of record and retain hardcopy	11.0 minutes	11.0 minutes	System of Record	$350
	Totals	**78.5** minutes (1.3 hours)	**46.0** minutes		**$425**

Figure 5-16 Recognition Bonus Award Process: Process Timing and Tool Cost

The current recognition bonus award process appears extremely manual because it uses hardcopy forms and interoffice mail. The only technology-related tools include Microsoft Outlook, the company's email system used to notify the requesting manager of the award status and the company's employee system of record to document the award amount. The software license costs for the two applications become the only tool costs to include in the spreadsheet and, with a volume license discount, totaled $425. This, however, is not the actual cost because the employee uses the software applications to perform other tasks not associated with this business process. As a result, we have to multiply the $425 by the 0.611 FTE to apply the portion of the license fees attributable to supporting this one business process. You may decide not to even include this figure since it is so small and only a *portion* of the business process uses it. Figure 5-17 shows the formula to perform the calculation.

Formula:
Tool costs × FTE = Total tool cost dedicated to business process

Example:
$425 × 0.611 = $260 tool cost dedicated to business process

Figure 5-17 Calculating the Tool Cost

Once you improve a business process, you will probably use additional technology, and this component of cost often increases. So far, though, we have identified the following costs for the recognition bonus award program:

1. Labor (salary + EB): $39,715
2. Tools: 260

    Total: $39,975

Overhead Costs

The third component of cost includes *overhead*, which refers to the ongoing expenses associated with running a business. It includes things like the physical office space an employee occupies, utilities, supplies, taxes, insurance, and computer equipment.

Calculating overhead varies by company. You may find that your company considers all administrative business processes as overhead costs because they do not deliver a product sold to external customers.

Determining Overhead Costs

Companies generally use a standard overhead rate, so use that number for your calculation. For example, a 150 percent overhead rate means that for each $1.00 of direct labor, an additional $1.50 is added for overhead costs. To calculate overhead rates, divide overhead costs by direct (e.g., labor) costs. You should not have to calculate the rate if you use your company's standard overhead percentage.

Figure 5-18 applies Stuart Wang's standard overhead rate of 110 percent to the process-related employee cost.

Putting It All Together

The administration of the recognition bonus award process costs Stuart Wang $123,542 a year, calculated by adding the three cost components together:

Formula:
Employee labor cost + (Overhead rate × Employee labor cost) = Process overhead cost

Example:
$39,715 + (110% × $39,715) = $83,402 process overhead cost

Figure 5-18   Calculating the Overhead Cost Formula

1. Labor (salary + EB): $39,715
2. Tools: 425
3. Overhead: 83,402
   _____
   Total: $123,542

You may also hear the term *fully loaded* with reference to the total employee-related costs that include employee benefits and overhead.

In the recognition bonus award process example, if we included employees outside the compensation department, we would realize a higher overall process cost because we would have to add the labor and overhead costs associated with managers.

Alternative Cuts of the Data

You may want to break down the cost summary into additional detail, depending on your situation. For example, you may want to know the cost for administering a single bonus award. To calculate the cost for each recognition bonus award, simply divide either the labor cost or total cost by the 1,500 annual volume number. Figure 5-19 shows the calculation used to determine that a single bonus award costs Stuart $26.48 when he looks only at labor.

When Stuart looks at the total cost per award, Figure 5-20 shows that a single bonus award costs $82.36 when you consider all costs.

Formula:

$$\frac{\text{Employee labor cost}}{\text{Volume}} = \text{Individual award cost}$$

Example:

$$\frac{\$39{,}715}{1{,}500 \text{ awards}} = \$26.48 \text{ per award (labor only)}$$

Figure 5-19   Cost per Award (using labor costs only)

Formula:

$$\frac{\text{Total process cost}}{\text{Volume}} = \text{Individual award cost}$$

Example:

$$\frac{\$123{,}542}{1{,}500 \text{ awards}} = \$82.36 \text{ cost per award}$$

Figure 5-20   Cost per Award (using total costs)

To further analyze the data, you may find it helpful to summarize the process information in a single spreadsheet like the one shown in Figure 5-21. This table combines the time and cost estimates for the compensation department and provides summary information in one place. Activities performed by employees outside the compensation department (i.e., managers) are grayed out. If you wanted to include costs for the entire company, you would then have to identify a standard salary for managers and apply the same formulas introduced in this chapter to determine the people, tool, and overhead costs for the managers.

In looking at Figure 5-21, we see that:

➤ It takes 46 minutes for compensation to process one award.
➤ It takes 5.4 days to complete the overall cycle.
➤ Each award costs $26 in labor costs, $0.05 in tool costs, and $55 in overhead costs, for a total cost of $82.

Activity Number	Description	Time Estimate		Cost Estimate			
		Process Time (minutes)	Cycle Time (days)	Labor ($)	Tools ($)	Overhead ($)	Total ($)
1	Complete form/mail						
2	Approve/reject request						
3	Review form	25.0	4.0	14.40		30.25	44.65
4	n/a						
5	Send authorization	5.0	0.3	2.88		6.05	8.93
6	Notify manager	5.0	0.125	2.88	0.01	6.05	8.94
7	Communicate award						
8	Update employee system of record	11.0	1.0	6.34	0.04	13.31	19.69
	Totals	46.0	10.3	$26.49	$.05	$55.66	$82.21

Figure 5-21   Recognition Bonus Award Process Summary

▶ Activity 3 seems like the most expensive step in the process because it contributes $44.65 to the total cost per award.

You should be familiar with the time estimates in Figure 5-21 because they came from our earlier work back in Figures 5-6 (cycle time) and 5-9 (process time).

Analyzing the Cost Estimate Columns

Now let us take a closer look at the cost estimate columns in Figure 5-21. Under cost estimate, you see four columns for labor, tools, overhead, and total. The next section explains how to break down these cost estimates by individual process activities because this helps you easily notice where an opportunity may exist to reduce the process time. For example, just looking quickly at the *total* column in Figure 5-21, we can tell that the most expensive step in the process is activity 3, reviewing the form, because it costs $44.65 each time compensation processes an award.

Now let us look at each of the cost estimate columns.

Labor Cost Estimate

Two components that contribute to the labor cost are process time and the employee's labor cost. Because we show process time in minutes in Figure 5-21, we have to convert the employee's annual salary into minutes, so that we know what each activity costs. The next two figures show how this is done.

Figure 5-22 shows how we converted the compensation analyst's annual hours to minutes. Once we know the annual minutes worked, we apply a simple formula to calculate the cost per minute. Figure 5-23 shows the formula to use to calculate the employee's rate of pay per minute.

Formula:
Annual hours worked × 60 minutes/hour = Annual minutes worked × FTE rate = Annual minutes worked on business process

Example:
1,880 hours × 60 minutes/hour = 112,800 minutes × 0.611 = 68,921 annual process minutes

Figure 5-22 Annual Minute Calculation (Labor Cost)

Formula:
$$\frac{\text{Employee labor cost}}{\text{Process-related annual minutes}} = \text{Pay per minute}$$

Example:
$$\frac{\$39,715}{68,921 \text{ minutes}} = \$0.576 \text{ per minute}$$

Figure 5-23 Employee's Rate of Pay per Minute

So, what does it cost for the compensation analyst, who earns $0.576 per minute, to review the form in activity 3? By simply multiplying the $0.576 rate of pay by the 25 minutes it takes to review the form, we find it costs $14.40 in labor cost.

Figure 5-24 shows the formula to calculate the cost per process activity.

Formula:
Process time × Pay per minute = Cost per process activity

Example:
25 minutes × $0.576 = $14.40 per form

Figure 5-24 Process Cost by Activity (Labor Cost)

In this example, I added the $14.40 to the labor column in Figure 5-21 for activity 3. Apply this same formula to the other process activities listed in Figure 5-21 to determine the labor cost for each step in the process, and you see that sending the authorization and notifying the manager (activities 5 and 6) cost $2.88 each, and updating the employee system of record (activity 8) costs $6.33.

Tool Cost Estimate

To calculate the tool cost for each process activity, divide the tool cost for the entire process ($260) by the annual minutes spent on the process (68,921 minutes from Figure 5-22) to arrive at the tool cost per minute for the process. Figure 5-25 shows the calculation for determining tool costs for an activity that uses tools (in this example, activity 6). We add 0.01 in the tool column in Figure 5-21 for activity 6. Apply the same formula to the other process activities listed in Figure 5-21 that use tools to accomplish tasks.

Overhead Cost Estimate

To calculate the overhead cost, apply the overhead rate to the employee's pay per minute. In Figure 5-26 we add Stuart's 110 percent overhead rate to the employee's salary.

Now that we know that each activity adds $1.21 in overhead expense, Figure 5-27 shows applying the per-minute overhead cost to the reviewing-the-form activity to show that this activity 3 costs $30.25 on top of the labor cost.

Formula:

$$\frac{\text{Tool cost}}{\text{Total minutes spent on process}} = \text{Total cost per minute} \times \text{Process time} = \text{Tool cost per process activity}$$

Example:

$$\frac{\$260}{68{,}921 \text{ minutes spent on process}} = 0.003772435 \times 5 \text{ minutes} = \$0.012 \text{ per manager notification}$$

Figure 5-25 *Process Cost by Activity (Tool Cost)*

Formula:
Pay per minute + (Pay per minute × Overhead rate) =
Overhead cost per activity

Example:
$0.576 + ($0.576 × 110%) = $1.21 overhead cost per activity

Figure 5-26 *Overhead Cost per Activity*

Formula:
Minutes × Overhead cost per minute = Overhead cost per process activity

Example:
25 minutes × $1.21 = $30.25 overhead cost per form

Figure 5-27 *Process Cost by Activity (Overhead Cost)*

Apply this same formula to the other process activities listed in Figure 5-21 to determine the overhead cost for each step in the process, and you see that sending the authorization and notifying the manager (activities 5 and 6) cost $6.05 each, and updating the employee system of record (activity 8) costs $13.31.

You should now understand how to calculate each number in Figure 5-21, and you can tell from this analysis that the most costly activity in the business process is reviewing the form, followed by updating the employee system of record, and, finally, notifying the manager and sending the authorization.

By the end of this step, you have completed the process map and added the process and cycle times to it. Before moving on to the improvement stage, there is one more step.

Verify the Process Map

After you complete the process map, review it with interested parties to confirm that it accurately reflects the existing process. This step helps you prevent someone's claiming, to downplay your improvements, that you started with a flawed process.

This step may happen fast or it may take weeks depending on the knowledge of your project team and the number of people that have to review the process map. You may want to validate the accuracy of the process map with three groups of employees:

➤ Process workers
➤ Stakeholders
➤ Sponsor

Process Workers

Process workers are the employees who perform the activities depicted in the process map, such as the compensation analyst in the recognition bonus award process. If you had a compensation analyst on the project team, then this step is easy. If not, then this step takes longer to complete.

Although the recognition bonus award process is an intentionally simple example that consists of only two groups of process workers (managers and compensation analysts), in a complex process you will probably have to incorporate a dozen different process workers in this step. You do not have to meet with all of them, just those most responsible for the process activities or others crucial to the business process. Review the scope definition document created in step 2 to help decide on whom to include. If an employee has ownership for delivering one of the process responsibilities you identified, include that individual in the process verification.

If you have a large number of process workers to interview, allow your project team to help. Delegation not only offloads a portion of the work from you, it also engages the team and strengthens the members' sense of ownership. Everyone involved in the validation should focus on the:

➤ Accuracy of the process map
➤ Points requiring clarification
➤ Accuracy of the time estimates

After finishing the verification, the project team should reconvene and decide whether to make changes to the process map.

Stakeholders

Depending on the foundation you established in step 2, you may or may not choose to walk your *stakeholders* through the completed process map. Take a look at what you said the stakeholders care about, and decide whether you sense that a stakeholder may not agree with something in the process map.

If you decide to meet with a stakeholder, schedule the meeting after completing the validation with the process workers and after incorporating any changes to the process map so that you share an accurate, up-to-date version. You should perform the validation with the stakeholders yourself and not delegate the responsibility to another project team member because you have the best overall knowledge to correctly position the work. Meeting with the stakeholders also provides you with a good networking opportunity.

Sponsor

The *sponsor* should also validate the process map before you move to the next step. The sponsor may have a point of view that you have not considered. Before jumping in and walking the sponsor through the process map, go back and review the scope definition document you created in step 2 with him or her. Even though the sponsor approved the scope definition document, the review refreshes the memory and provides a transition tool. Highlight the boundaries from that document as a transition to the entry point into the process map.

Once you have completed the reviews and you have made the changes to the process map, you can move to step 6, applying improvement techniques.

Chapter Summary: Steps 4–5

In step 4, you learned the difference between process and cycle times. Whereas process time helps you to summarize the labor required to deliver a business process, cycle time identifies how long the process takes from beginning to end, a key metric that clients/customers often list as a top concern.

Identifying the people, tool, and overhead costs associated with a business process brings a financial component to your work and positions you as a businessperson who understands how processes and costs relate to each other. The full-time equivalent (FTE) formula identifies the percentage of employee time spent supporting a business process. Learning to apply the overhead rate gives you a total employee cost perspective. Sometimes the sponsor cares only about a subset of numbers, such as the labor costs associated with a business process, in which case your job gets easier.

After completing the calculations described in this chapter, you can cut the data numerous ways to meet your needs, stating the cost for each step in the process, the cost per transaction, the time from beginning to end, where to focus your time in the improvement stage, or any other statistic that you want to share.

In step 5, you verified the accuracy of the process map with the process workers, stakeholders, and sponsor so that you can move to step 6, improving the process, and feel comfortable that any improvement targets you set have the appropriate support from these groups.

In conducting the verification, focus on the accuracy of the process flow and on the validation of the time estimates that the project team defined; also include a list of points of confusion or concern.

Time Estimate

To help plan the time that it takes to work through the two steps covered in this chapter, Figure 5-28 summarizes the amount of time you should expect to spend on steps 4 and 5 (estimating the process and cycle time, calculating the costs, and verifying the process map).

Project Team Meeting

This meeting is a continuation of the project team meetings. I like to start this task as part of an existing meeting because doing so makes the work look like a natural continuation of the process mapping work. The time required for this step depends on the complexity of the process map. You may start off slow, but you will gain speed as the team becomes comfortable with this step.

Event	Time	Purpose
Project team meeting: estimate process and cycle time	1–2 hours	■ Add process and cycle time to the process map in preparation for the improvement phase. ■ Identify volume.
Postmeeting work: calculate costs	16 hours	■ Identify the people, tool, and overhead costs associated with the business process.
Sponsor meeting	1 hour	■ Review the process summary.
Verify process map	5 hours (over 2 weeks)	■ Verify the accuracy of the process map before moving to the improvement phase.
Postvalidation work: update process map	4 hours	■ Make changes to the process map and documentation based on feedback.

Figure 5-28 Time Estimate—Steps 4–5: Estimate Time and Cost and Verify Process Map

Postmeeting Work

This time provides you with personal time to perform the calculations covered in this chapter and includes:

➤ Identifying the FTE number to use

➤ Calculating the FTEs required to support the business process

➤ Calculating the people costs, including the employee benefit rate

➤ Calculating the tool costs

➤ Calculating the overhead costs, using the overhead rate

➤ Determining the cost per transaction (in our example, per award)

➤ Summarizing the process times and costs

Verify the Process Map

This time provides you with the occasion to meet with process workers, stakeholders, and the sponsor to verify the accuracy of the process map you have drawn. For my example, I estimated five hours over a two-week period.

Postvalidation Work

This time includes a meeting with the project team to discuss the results of the verification with the process workers, stakeholders, and sponsor. This work provides you with personal time to make the appropriate changes to the process map and documentation.

Sponsor Meeting

When you find yourself close to completing the analysis, schedule time with the sponsor to review the summary information you compiled. The sponsor will have a keen interest in your summary, and this meeting provides you with the chance for increased visibility.

What You Have Achieved

In this chapter, you have achieved the following:

➤ An estimate of how long the process takes to deliver the results

➤ An understanding of the labor required by the process

➤ Knowledge of the total cost for the business process

➤ An understanding of the cost of a single transaction

➤ Agreement on the validity of the process map

➤ Buy-in from the sponsor on the process map

➤ Recognition from your sponsor on your financial evaluation

➤ Most important, the *power* to know where to focus your efforts in the improvement stage

CHAPTER 6

Step 6: Apply Improvement Techniques

Challenging Everything

On the basis of his prioritization results, Kendall Smith, the banking vice president from Chapter 2, picked the process he wanted to start with. First, I helped him develop the scope definition document on the training process for newly hired employees; then we created the process map, including the time estimates. We validated the process map and set our improvement target as a 50 percent reduction in cycle time for the course development process.

As a result of drawing the process map for your current business process in step 3, you saw how the process works; then in step 4, you identified how long the process takes and how much it costs. Now we look at how to make the process more effective, efficient, and adaptable.

While listening to the project team talk about your process throughout the previous steps in the roadmap, you probably already have thoughts on how to improve the process. This knowledge, combined with the information in the scope definition document, prepares you for this step. If you think about the very manual recognition bonus award process we used as an example over the last several chapters, you undoubtedly have ideas on how to improve that process. Clearly, we can find ways to reduce the 11 days of cycle time.

The improvement technique wheel in Figure 6-1 shows

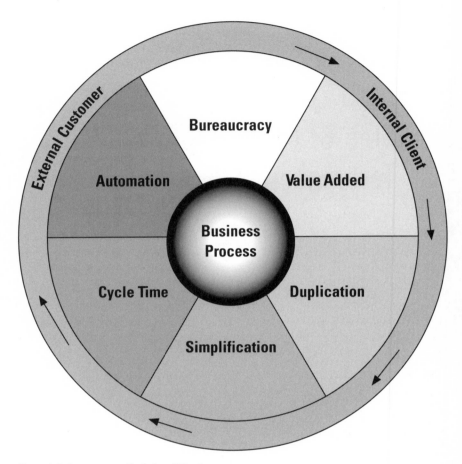

Figure 6-1 Improvement Technique Wheel

the business process at the center of the wheel, the six techniques used to improve business processes wrapped around it
in the middle circle, and the client/customer on the outer circle
as a reminder of why we want to improve the business process
in the first place. This chapter discusses each of the techniques
and how to use them in business process improvement.

To use the improvement technique wheel, start at the top
with bureaucracy, the first improvement technique, and move
clockwise around the spokes of the wheel, ending with automation. The wheel depicts the automation technique last because
we want to focus on automating an efficient rather than an inef-

ficient business process. Applying the other five techniques first ensures that we remove the process inefficiencies before moving to automation.

Use each of the techniques one at a time during a project team meeting. I like to start this exercise at a new meeting, when the team has a fresh perspective, rather than at the middle or end of another team meeting. This work is difficult and it helps to have an alert group.

The project team members should feel a bit uncomfortable during this step in the roadmap because your role is to challenge the status quo and push them to think strategically. Strategic thinking sounds complex, and some people feel that only a few people possess this skill, but it simply means an ability to conceptualize and see the big picture. Like anything else, you can improve the skill with practice.

To get started, introduce the improvement technique wheel, define each of the techniques, and explain how you will accomplish the work. Then walk through the process map that you created and focus on a single technique, applying it as thoroughly as possible before moving to the next technique. Focusing on one technique at a time ensures that you thoroughly apply each in its turn. As you move along the improvement technique wheel, you will start to see the relationship of one technique to another. For example, in most cases, simplifying an activity or eliminating bureaucracy also reduces cycle time.

During this phase of the work, enlarge the completed process map to a poster size, as you did in step 3, so that everyone stays interested and can follow along as the team moves through the activities on the process map.

Eliminate Bureaucracy

Tamara Chase, a buyer who specializes in purchasing merchandise for the home and garden line of a nationwide retailer, became frustrated when time after time her orders were not filled in a timely manner. Tamara works under pressure because of the competitive nature of her market, and she did not like having to wrestle with an internal process that negatively affected her ability to bring product into her stores.

The order processing cycle time, overburdened with multiple layers of approvals, seemed to be getting longer and longer. Tamara needed approval before she submitted an order to her central purchasing group, and then purchasing had to obtain additional approvals. The bureaucracy made it difficult for her to buy and distribute products to her retail stores in time to beat the competition, and Tamara increasingly heard complaints from the store managers.

In a business process, bureaucracy requires following a complex series of activities that hinders an effective and efficient process. The process gets bogged down in red tape, sometimes for no apparent reason. Everyone knows bureaucracy when they see it. Red tape and inflexibility go hand in hand with bureaucracy.

You can normally trace the cause of bureaucracy to either the need for excess control, the fear of making a mistake, the desire to cover our backs in case something goes wrong, or simply something that grew over time. You might wonder, because bureaucracy seems so counterproductive, how it can have any advocates. Even though no one outwardly admits to supporting bureaucracy, you will run into resistance as you work to eliminate it because of the fear of the unknown and the inclination of human nature to just carry on doing things in the same old way. In Tamara's case, I started by asking what would happen if the company eliminated some levels of approval. Would the world fall apart? Was Tamara incompetent? Would the next approval level not catch any possible errors?

Jack Welch, former CEO of General Electric, is well-known for his dislike of bureaucracy. He calls it "productivity's enemy." Think about bureaucracy from this perspective: as the enemy!

Even the federal government, as bureaucratic as many concede it is, has a strategic vision to be "citizen-centered, not bureaucracy-centered." Although it may never change the way it does business, by thinking of the people as their customers, at least the government seems to have the right perspective.

It takes extra work to search for bureaucracy because it has become so commonplace, but the project team members will find countless steps in a business process that introduce bureaucracy—and they should strive to eliminate them. To accomplish this task, begin by walking through the process map box by box and challenge the project team to identify bureaucracy. Mark the activities identified as bureaucratic with a colored highlighter on the enlarged process map posted in the room. Use different-colored highlighters for the six improvement techniques. For example, use a green highlighter for bureaucracy, a pink highlighter for value added, and so forth.

In Alistar's recognition bonus award process, recall that activity 1 involved completing a form and sending it to the next-level manager. Do you see any potential bureaucracy in this step? You might ask:

Why is the form sent to the next-level manager?

This question helps the project team determine whether the requirement to gain another manager's signature adds value to the process or just adds a bureaucratic step. Who owns the budget? If manager 1 owns the budget, why does manager 2 have to approve an award? You may uncover other problems with the business process that do not relate to bureaucracy, but hold off on those issues and stay focused on bureaucracy to keep the team moving and on track.

Typically, you see a relationship between multiple approvals and bureaucracy, as in Tamara's case. If the reason for a second or third approval adds no value, eliminate the multiple approvals. The scope definition document you created in step 2 guides you through the exercise of eliminating bureaucracy. If an activity does not support the statements made in the scope definition, get rid of it.

In Tamara's case, the process required four approvals before purchasing sent the order to the vendor. After some discussion, we reduced the bureaucracy by keeping only two levels of approvals: central purchasing and finance. Although we focused on eliminating bureaucracy and reduced the number of approvals required, we also reduced the cycle time as a result. You can start to see the connection among the six techniques because reducing bureaucracy also reduces cycle time.

Another filter that you can use to eliminate bureaucracy is evaluating whether an activity supports a SALT requirement of a business process. SALT stands for:

> Statutory
> Audit
> Legal
> Tax

▶ **Statutory** denotes that the activity supports legislation or a government statute, such as imposing statutes of limitations, whether enacted by a national or state legislative governing body.

▶ **Audit** means examining records or transactions to check for accuracy or compliance with preestablished guidelines or rules.

▶ **Legal** signifies that the activity supports a law, like the labor laws that control minimum wage levels and overtime pay.

▶ **Tax** denotes a financial charge or fee paid to a government body, like a sales tax or income tax.

If an activity supports SALT, it probably should remain, except perhaps for audits because we often audit too frequently. Validate the reason for an audit to determine whether it should continue. If an audit does remain, ask whether a spot audit can replace a normal audit to reduce the time required to conduct it. You run a spot audit on a subset of data or transactions. Spot audits do not cost as much as normal audits because they do not take as long to complete, yet they generally find the errors.

A recent study by Tom Terez (www.betterworkplacenow .com) stated that the number one complaint employees had about their jobs was "too much workplace bureaucracy." Their survey also found that employees spend about ten hours every week tangled in corporate red tape and cumbersome workplace rules.

Here are some questions you can ask the project team as you work to eliminate bureaucracy:

- How many approvals do we have in place? Why?
- Can we reduce the number required?
- Do we make decisions at the right place?
- Do we generate unnecessary paperwork?
- How many copies of each document do we make?
- Why do we keep hardcopies?
- Do people receive information that they do not need?
- Do we understand what people do with the information or reports that we send them?
- Does one person check the work of another? Why?
- How do we use the information requested on a form in making decisions?
- Can we eliminate any forms? Do we absolutely need them?
- Do we have unnecessary rules?
- Does a policy or procedure get in the way?
- What will happen if an employee makes a mistake? Does the added scrutiny seem worth the expense?

Help the project team conceptualize the business process without bureaucracy. Ask them to show how an activity contributes to addressing the client's/customer's needs. If an activity does not contribute to client/customer satisfaction, if it negatively affects cycle time, or if it increases cost, then eliminate it.

Value Added

Tina Hernandez, marketing director for the consumer product division of a global company, felt that her company experienced an unusually long time to market. As Tina described the situation, time to market includes everything from idea conception through customer availability.

After I completed a value-added analysis, it became apparent that the problem lay with the distribution component of their marketing strategy. We identified activities in the distribution process that did not add value for the customer. Because every activity in a business process adds to the cost of the end product or service and because every step adds labor, overhead, or other expenses, you should spend time evaluating each activity to determine whether it adds value. Would customers willingly pay for a step in the business process if they were aware of the step?

The value-added analysis examines how each activity in a business process contributes value to the client/customer. Because clients/customers define value, review the scope definition document from step 2 to review what they consider valuable, and ask whether each activity in the process contributes to delivering what you listed as client/customer needs. Then ask whether the clients/customers would agree that an activity adds value and whether they would pay for that step if you based your charges on a cost-per-activity fee.

In Alistar's recognition bonus award process, activity 3 had the compensation analyst reviewing the eligibility of the employee for a bonus award, ensuring that the manager provided appropriate justification, and validating that the award amount falls within the guidelines. Do you think that manager 1 would agree that these tasks add value to the process? You might ask questions like:

Whose decision is it to determine when an employee deserves recognition?
Why can't the manager be trusted to know whether
an employee is eligible for an award?
What happens if a manager exceeds the award guidelines?
Do managers have a budget that they control?

These questions help determine whether the process should include the compensation department in this step. Why does the compensation analyst perform these tasks? Is the reason to check on the managers? Are the managers incompetent? If you look at the time that this step requires, you can see that it takes 20 to 30 minutes of process time and four days of cycle time. If the activity does not provide added value to the client/customer, you should try to eliminate it.

Notice again the close relationship between the improvement techniques—in this case, between the bureaucracy and value-added techniques. If we eliminate activity 3 from the recognition bonus award process because it does not add value for the client/customer, we also remove a degree of bureaucracy from the business process. However, we would have encountered resistance from the business if we tried to eliminate this activity when we discussed bureaucracy because the business would defend the need for the step. Once the project team members discuss the same activity from the client's/customer's perspective as part of the value-added technique, they might have a harder time making the case that the step adds value to the client/customer.

With that said, what about the business or the operation? Should you always delete a step in the process just because it does not add value to the client/customer? The answer is yes, but now office politics come into play. While activity 3 in the recognition bonus award process does not add value from the client's/customer's perspective, does it add value from the business's perspective—in this case, the compensation department? Even if a process step does not contribute to the client's/customer's value perspective, the step may still appear crucial to the business. How would the compensation department feel about eliminating this step? It will probably claim that the step adds value; how else can they guarantee compliance or consistency across the company?

This may seem like a genuine concern because Alistar's compensation department owns responsibility for the consistent application of the company's pay programs. However, if you attribute the value of an activity to the business and not to the client, then you should challenge the thinking and push for a candid answer to the question, "Why?" If you cannot eliminate the step, you can probably minimize it.

Just as we saw when we examined bureaucracy, numerous steps in a business process do not add any value to the final output; so you should eliminate these activities as well. Walk through the process map again box by box, this time challenging the value-added contribution of each activity. Mark the activities that have value to the client/customer in one color, those with value to the business in another, and those with no value in a third color. Your process map should start looking like an artist's palette!

You can use the value-added analysis table shown in Figure 6-1 as an alternative to color coding the process map for value-added activities. If you choose to use the table, simply list the business process activities in the left column and add three additional columns for client/customer value added, business value added, and non–value added. Put an "X" in the appropriate column for each activity. Figure 6-2 shows what the analysis might look like for Alistar's recognition bonus award process.

Although color coding brings more visual clarity to the work and allows everyone to stay involved, the value-added analysis shows the same information and may work better for complex processes. Even if you color-code the map, use the value-added analysis as a way to summarize the project team's final decisions.

In my experience, the hardest activities to eliminate are those that the business considers valuable for their own reasons because the temptation to say an activity adds business value, instead of being a bureaucratic step, is far too easy. You have to show courage when talking about business-value-added activities. Remember to think strategically and keep the big picture in mind. Make the project team uncomfortable by challenging the status quo. The main question to ask when applying the value-added technique is, "Would the client/customer pay for this activity?"

Eliminate Duplication

Wendy Chan, manager of the workforce analysis group for a software company, has responsibility for running the com-

Number	Activity	Client/Customer Value Added	Business Value Added	Non–Value Added
1	Complete recognition bonus award form and mail to next-level manager		X	
2	Approve or reject request			X
3	Review eligibility, justification, and award amount		X	
4	Send authorization to payroll	X		
5	Notify requesting manager		X	
6	Communicate award to employee	X		
7	Update employee system of record and retain hardcopy		X	

Figure 6-2 Recognition Bonus Award Process: Value-Added Analysis

pany's monthly head count reports to track turnover and other employee-related statistics. Departments on the operational side of the business also track their own head counts, instead of relying on Wendy's data, so that they have the information available to conduct additional analysis.

Duplication, or redundancy, occurs when multiple groups get involved in a business process and silos are formed with no integration between them. Each group or department maintains a separate set of data because they want to have all the information they require in order to tell their story as they want it heard. Sometimes the duplication appears innocent because one group or department simply does not understand what the other group is doing; at other times, one group may not believe in the other's competence, or worse, the groups compete.

In Wendy's case, the workforce analysis group did not provide the level of detail that the operational groups wanted, and so operations duplicated the work instead of asking the workforce analysis group to change their report to meet the operation's business need. The workforce analysis group would have gladly changed the report if told about the operation's dissatisfaction. This example both demonstrates a lack of awareness of client/customer needs by the workforce analysis group and shows how easy it is for duplication to occur.

Each time a step in the business process moves from one department to another, a handoff occurs. Handoffs can easily lead to duplication of efforts, errors, and redundancy of information, so you should pay attention to any activity on the process map where a handoff occurs. The federal government recognizes "that redundant and overlapping agency activities have been major impediments to creating a citizen-centered electronic government."

You can spot the duplication of efforts when you find multiple employees keeping copies of the same documents. Think of your own company, and you can probably identify cases where more than one person files a copy of a document for some reason. Look at Alistar Corporation's recognition bonus award process:

➤ Manager 1 retains a hardcopy of the completed form when the bonus award is requested.

➤ Manager 2 keeps a hardcopy of the signed form when approving the bonus award.

➤ Compensation files a hardcopy in its recognition bonus award file.

➤ Personnel retains a hardcopy in the employee's personnel file.

Does everyone need a copy of the document? When multiple employees maintain the same data, they increase the cost to the company. It takes time for an employee to copy and file a document, and a cost is associated with the employee's labor.

Copies take up storage space, and a cost is associated with the increased storage requirements. Although the space required may seem small, think about it on a company-wide scale and imagine the cost multiplied across your entire company. Also consider the legal implications of maintaining documentation, and answer the question, "Where should the company's official documentation be stored?"

A big challenge exists when a company does not define a single source of data. In Wendy's case, which head count report is correct? Do the operations and the workforce analysis group count head counts differently? Do the groups use different sources of data? Data errors can easily occur when different groups use different sources. As a result, you begin to doubt the integrity of the data. *Data integrity* means consistent, correct, and accessible data. Problems with data quality, or data integrity, costs companies billions of dollars a year. Working to confirm that you have a single source of data helps to reduce costs and errors.

When you completed step 5 and verified your process map with the process workers, stakeholders, and the process owner, the project team made the appropriate changes so that the map accurately reflected how the process works. During the validation meetings, confirm where handoffs and possible duplications occur. In addition to the steps in the process, look for duplication in data and reports generated from the process because employees often duplicate data or reports.

You may have to talk to other departments to uncover redundancy if your process map focuses only on one department. Find out what happens at the other end of an activity after you hand something off to another department. Look for occasions where you can:

➤ Establish a single source of data.

➤ Eliminate two employees doing the same work, like generating similar reports.

➤ Eliminate two people maintaining the same data.

➤ Eliminate the dual entry of information.

➤ Minimize document storage.

Simplification

The inefficient warehouse process uncovered by Tina Hernandez caused her marketing team to reevaluate their distribution strategy. Tina admitted that her marketing team spent more time developing the product, price, and promotion components of their overall strategy than they did the fourth "P" (placement). They did not think too long about distribution decisions and instead continued with business as usual. With her concern about time to market, Tina's team reconsidered and agreed that they needed to make a change. Tina now felt that her team could identify more streamlined distribution options to further improve their product's time to market.

Simplification, or streamlining the process, means reducing or eliminating the complexity of an activity in a business process so that the process becomes easier to understand and more efficient. When you keep a process simple, it gets easier to sustain and more flexible in responding to client/customer needs. Keep one of the Dalai Lama's quotations in mind as you work to simplify a business process: "Simplicity is the key to happiness in the modern world." Albert Einstein came up with his own observation: "Simplicity means the achievement of maximum effect with minimum means."

Over time, our business processes become increasingly burdensome as we accommodate changes in the business. We cause our processes to become bloated by continually adding complexity. Looking at your process map, identifying where complexity exists, and simplifying the related activities become your main focus with this technique.

In the recognition bonus award process, we started by looking at the form used in activity 1. Since we decided we could not eliminate the form, we simplified and redesigned it to keep the information required to a minimum, while ensuring that managers could easily obtain the required data without having to go to a myriad of sources to obtain it. To simplify the form, I asked the project team questions like:

Is any unnecessary information requested on the form?
Where does the manager obtain the information requested on the form?
Is the information readily available?
How often do managers call compensation with questions on how to complete the
form, and what kind of questions do they ask?

When you start looking at your company's forms, you will find most of them more complex than necessary and, as a result, take longer to complete. Streamline all your forms so that they include only the information essential to making a decision. Look for chances to simplify all reports and documentation.

You can find countless examples of unnecessary complexity in business processes, so keep the old KISS engineering philosophy in mind: Keep it simple, stupid. (If you find *stupid* offensive, you can say, "Keep it simple, silly" or "Keep it short and sweet" or "Keep it sweet and simple." You get the idea.)

In activity 3 in the recognition bonus award process, how often does compensation have to call the manager, or vice versa, in completing the tasks associated with this step? Think about the number of times a phone call is made to ask a process question. Eliminate unnecessary calls by simplifying the language on forms and providing any required information directly on them.

Here are other questions you can ask the project team as you work to simplify the process:

➤ Can we streamline any step in the process?

➤ Can we streamline or simplify any of the forms?

➤ How many emails are sent at any point in the process? A substantial number of them should signal that unnecessary complexity exists.

➤ Where do employees go to obtain information to complete any step in the process?

➤ Do you see any roadblocks?

➤ Do you see unnecessary handoffs?

➤ Can we standardize a step, a report, or a form to make it easier to understand?

▶ Do we know the number of errors we make and why?

▶ Can we eliminate or combine any steps in the process?

▶ Must process workers call other people to complete any step in the process?

▶ Does everyone understand the process?

▶ How do we use data and reports throughout the process?

You should also consider redesigning the process to make it simple for the client/customer. Even if you do not use every one of the ideas to improve your business process, the clues help you simplify the process.

As you apply the improvement techniques, you will start uncovering cultural changes that have to occur in the organization, and these types of changes are often difficult to implement. Nevertheless, keep track of them, even though they may take a long time to accomplish. In Chapter 9, I discuss the *impact analysis* as a tool to capture changes that need to occur to implement a new, improved business process. Do not exclude a change from your plans just because it appears challenging. Sometimes we exact the biggest gains from difficult changes.

You should continue to notice the similarity between several of the improvement techniques. When you simplify a business process, you also have the opportunity to eliminate bureaucracy. When you eliminate redundancy, you simplify the process. When you look at value-added activities, it leads you to examine bureaucracy. Although the distinctions among the techniques may seem blurry, I encourage you to work through them one at a time because you use slightly different mental filters for each technique. It does not matter what you call something, as long as you reach every nook and cranny in a business process.

Reduce Cycle Time

Kendall Smith wanted to reduce the cycle time required to develop new training by 50 percent. It normally took his training department six months to design and develop a new course, but Kendall wanted to reduce the development time to 90 days because of the upcoming bank merger.

Chapter 5 defined cycle time as the overall time it takes to complete an entire process—from the first step to the last, including waiting or elapsed time. Clients and customers care about cycle time because they feel it; they recognize how long it takes to receive the result. The business cares about reducing cycle time because doing so increases productivity and frees up resources.

In the recognition bonus award process, we said that one bonus award can take 11 days to process (cycle time), even though the activities involved in producing the award take only about one hour (the process time). (Figure 6-3 shows the cycle time summary we generated in Chapter 5 for this process.) Eleven days may or may not seem too long, but if your clients/customers say that they want a quick turnaround, then 11 days will feel too long to them. In this case, you should reduce the cycle time of the business process.

Look at each activity in the business process to identify where to reduce cycle time, so that you can adapt to business changes and respond faster to your clients. Look at activities that have long cycle times and identify how to reduce their times. Look at Figure 6-3. What activities contribute to the high cycle time? In this example:

Activity Number	Description	Hours	Days
1	Complete form/mail	1 hour	0.125 days
2	Approve/reject request	40 hours	5 days
3	Review form	32 hours	4 days
4	OK to proceed?	n/a	n/a
5	Send authorization	2 hours	0.25 days
6	Notify manager	1 hour	0.125 days
7	Communicate award	8 hours	1 day
8	Update system of record	8 hours	1 day
Total		92 hours	11.5 days

Figure 6-3 Recognition Bonus Award Process: Cycle Time Summary

▶ Approving or rejecting an award by manager 2 can take five days (activity 2).

▶ Compensation's review of the information can add another four days (activity 3).

If we can eliminate the second manager's approval, along with compensation's review of the data and the notification, we eliminate nine days!

At Alistar, instead of slowing down the process on each award, we changed the process and eliminated activity 3. Compensation no longer reviews the form. Instead, they delegate authority to the managers to make decisions on their own employees. Because compensation expressed concern about managers following the guidelines, compensation agreed to perform quarterly audits in order to validate that managers followed the company guidelines for bonus awards. This change reduced the bureaucracy and improved the client's perception of the process because the cycle time went down.

Using the cycle time summary, look at how you can reduce the cycle time of any activity with a high number. Understand why a delay exists. Asking why will prove to be one of your best weapons in completing this work.

▶ Why can't manager 1 use the budget as he or she sees fit?

▶ Why won't a spot audit work instead of reviewing every proposed award?

Even when the project team gives you an answer, you can ask why as a follow-up question to further fine-tune the process.

A cycle time analysis, shown in Figure 6-4, provides you with another tool to help with this technique. In this example, I adapted Figure 6-3 to include the potential reasons for a delay and possible ways to reduce the cycle time for the recognition bonus award process. I added two new columns: *cause(s) of delay* and *possible resolutions*. After building the table and entering the data in the first two columns, start by defining a threshold for the *days* column, which assists you in deciding where to focus the project team's attention.

Activity Number	Days	Cause(s) of Delay	Possible Resolutions
1	0.125 day		
2	5 days	■ Cause 1 ■ Cause 2 ■ Cause 3	■ Resolution 1 ■ Resolution 2
3	4 days	■ Cause 1 ■ Cause 2 ■ Cause 3	■ Resolution 1 ■ Resolution 2
4	n/a		
5	0.25 days		
6	1 day		
7	1 day		
8	1 day		

Figure 6-4 Recognition Bonus Award Process: Cycle Time Analysis

In Alistar's case, the project team set the threshold at four days; that is, they decided to examine any activity that took four days or longer. As a result, we focused our analysis on activities 2 and 3, which appear in the white rows in Figure 6-4.

Once you define the threshold, discuss why these activities take so long and list the potential causes for the delay in the table. After listing the possible causes, move through the causes one by one, identify alternatives that may eliminate or reduce the delay, and write the alternatives in the possible resolution column.

As you work to reduce cycle time, focus on topics like:

► Reducing handoffs.

► Optimizing activities that add value to the process.

► Eliminating activities that do not add value.

► Reducing the cycle time of high cycle time activities or, better still, eliminate them.

► Performing activities in parallel instead of one at a time.

► Combining activities.

➤ Benchmarking the industry standard (benchmarking is discussed in Chapter 12).

In addition to making the business process effective for your client/customer, reducing cycle time also leads to an efficient process for the business, thus increasing productivity and freeing up resources to do more valuable work.

Automation

Now that you have squeezed every last bit of efficiency from the process using your analytical and mental skills, you can look at how technology can help the process become even more effective and efficient.

In this discussion of the use of technology to automate the process, I focus on technology that you probably have available to you or that you can purchase inexpensively. I do not talk about major system implementations because one employee trying to improve an everyday business process does not have the authority to spend a few million dollars on a new computer system. Even if you can purchase a new application, you probably have to suffer through a long procurement process. If you have implemented company-wide systems, you should still follow the techniques presented in this chapter to ensure that you have an efficient process that maximizes your technology investment.

You may hear different schools of thought about whether automation belongs at the beginning or the end of business process improvement. You may have heard this basic question:

> Does the technology drive the process?
> Or . . .
> Does the process drive the technology?

If your background includes large system implementations, you have probably seen the technology drive the business process. A company buys a new enterprise resource planning system, and everyone gets busy defining new business processes on the basis of the system's available functionality.

You find technology at the end of the improvement technique wheel because I lean toward the second scenario; I like to see an efficient process drive the technology. We want to focus on automating an efficient, not an inefficient process.

If you think of technology right away during the improvement phase, you can too easily start thinking about building a spreadsheet or a database, when in reality you should probably eliminate the activity altogether because it provides no added value to the client/customer. Therefore, I like to apply the other five techniques first, *then* look at the new business process for points in the process where technology can increase efficiency.

Bill Gates is credited with saying, "The first principle for any technology you contemplate introducing into a business is that automation applied to an efficient operation will magnify the efficiency. The second is that automation applied to an inefficient operation will just entrench the inefficiency." I could not agree more!

Alistar Corporation's recruiting process provides an example of how automation can help improve a business process. The company has a volume-driven hiring process, which requires them to fill an unusually large number of hourly jobs that pay little more than the minimum wage. Recruitment departments, like Alistar's, often measure their success by a series of statistics such as time to fill, number of open requisitions, or number of hires. Alistar had cumbersome reporting techniques, so we redesigned a couple of their reports to take advantage of the data sitting in their recruiting system and combined that data with additional data in a Microsoft Access database to deliver reports that provided the appropriate statistics to senior managers.

Alistar's recognition bonus award process offered many opportunities to apply improvement techniques. Figure 6-5 shows an updated version of the process map after we applied

Improved Recognition Bonus Award Process

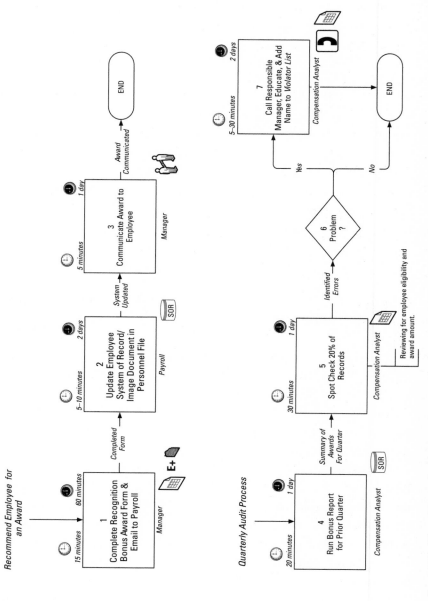

Figure 6-5 Alistar Corporation Improved Process Map

all the techniques. The figure shows that we made the following changes to the recognition bonus award process:

▶ We gained agreement on eliminating the second manager's approval and allowing the original manager to manage his or her own budget.

▶ Although we could not gain agreement to eliminate the form entirely, we simplified it and introduced technology in activity 1 by creating the form in Microsoft Excel so that the manager can email the form to payroll instead of using the slower interoffice mail to send the hardcopy.

▶ We eliminated the requirement for compensation to review every form. Instead, we instituted a new quarterly audit process, depicted at the bottom section of Figure 6-5. Compensation now audits 20 percent of awards submitted for the prior quarter by running a standard report from its system of record.

▶ Compensation agreed to permit the managers to determine the appropriate justification for an award, so the only items left to audit include the award amounts and the employee's eligibility.

▶ Compensation still felt the need to keep track of managers who did not follow the guidelines so that repeat offenders could receive constructive feedback through the performance management process.

As this walkthrough shows, we reduced the cycle time from 11 days to three, a meaningful improvement to the business process. Managers like the authority they now have, and compensation feels that it can still hold managers accountable for following the guidelines.

Spend time learning about the existing technologies in your company so that you are aware of the tools you can use in the automation phase. Get familiar with the existing systems that support your company's business processes. In addition to existing systems, some of the common, inexpensive tools you probably have available are:

➤ Microsoft Office tools like Word, Excel, PowerPoint, and Access

➤ File-sharing and collaboration software like Microsoft SharePoint or Open Text's Hummingbird Connectivity

➤ Network drives where you can store shared documents

➤ Email and the capability to design forms

➤ Text messaging

➤ Workflow

➤ Portals or intranets

All these simple, everyday tools can help automate your business processes.

Chapter Summary: Step 6

Applying the six improvement techniques one at a time assists you in evaluating your business processes in a thoughtful, planned approach. The improvement technique wheel guides you through eliminating bureaucracy, evaluating value-added activities, eliminating duplication and redundancy, simplifying the process/reports/forms, reducing cycle time, and applying automation tools.

Although the differentiation among the techniques may appear blurry at times, you should use the techniques one at a time because the project team will use slightly different mental filters for each. Applying the techniques one at a time ensures that you squeeze every last drop out of each one.

Remember that:

➤ Bureaucracy is "productivity's enemy."

➤ Use SALT as a filter to eliminate bureaucracy.

➤ Keep it simple, silly.

➤ "Simplicity is the key to happiness in the modern world."

➤ "Automation applied to an efficient operation will magnify the efficiency."

➤ "Automation applied to an inefficient operation will magnify the inefficiency."

Either use color coding on your process map to highlight the six improvement techniques, or capture the data in a table like the value-added analysis in Figure 6-2 or the cycle time analysis in Figure 6-4.

Saving the automation technique until last guarantees that you apply technology to an efficient, not an inefficient process.

Time Estimate

Figure 6-6 summarizes the time you should expect to spend applying the improvement techniques (step 6).

Project Team Meeting

During the project team meetings, spend at least one hour to apply each technique as thoroughly as possible. I like to start this meeting by introducing the improvement technique wheel, then define one technique at a time. For example, define bureaucracy and ask the team to share an experience they have had with bureaucracy. This starts the conversation flowing. If you leave a technique too soon, you miss some of the opportunity for improvement, so demonstrate patience and hesitate if

Event	Time	Purpose
Project team meeting: individual improvement techniques	1–2 hours per technique (depending on the size of the process map)	■ Identify points in the process to apply a technique, moving clockwise along the improvement technique wheel.
Postmeeting work	40 hours	■ Update the process map and documentation to incorporate changes made. ■ Gain approval, if required.

Figure 6-6 Time Estimate—Step 6: Apply Improvement Techniques

the project team seems ready to move to the next technique. Let everyone feel somewhat uncomfortable and squirm a bit before moving to the next technique.

Postmeeting Work

This time provides you with the chance to update the process map and the corresponding documentation on the basis of the changes the project team made. You may also have to gain approval for some of the changes that the process team has suggested, with either the sponsor or a stakeholder.

What You Have Achieved

In this chapter, you have achieved the following:

- ► An awareness of six improvement techniques
- ► An understanding of how to create a value-added analysis
- ► A grasp of how to use SALT as a filter for bureaucracy
- ► An awareness of how to eliminate nonvalue-added work
- ► An insight into how to eliminate duplication or redundancy
- ► An understanding of how to simplify, or streamline, a business process
- ► A grasp of how to reduce cycle time
- ► An awareness of how to develop a cycle time analysis
- ► An insight into how to automate a business process
- ► Most important, the *power* to understand how to look systematically for ways to improve a business process

CHAPTER 7

Step 7: Create Internal Controls, Tools, and Metrics

Making It Real

Establishing internal controls, developing tools to increase the effectiveness, efficiency, and adaptability of a business process, and developing metrics bring the process to life beyond just creating a process map:

▶ Internal controls help prevent errors.

▶ Tools help employees perform their job more easily.

▶ Metrics show whether the process works as planned.

Internal Controls

Imagine the level of embarrassment when an employee received congratulations from a colleague on her promotion to an executive-level position *before* her vice president had a chance to share the good news directly with her. This happened at a bank that brought me in after this occurrence to help them put internal controls in place for their key business processes. It seemed that the colleague had viewed the employee's new title when they right-clicked on the colleague's name in their email system even though no update had occurred in the human resource information system.

Senior management had chastised and embarrassed the

department responsible for the error before I came in to work with the firm over the next six weeks. In this case, it was a simple human error that caused all the commotion. Yet the department ended up spending an unanticipated $150,000 in labor and travel costs to create appropriate internal controls for their business processes to prevent future mistakes.

Human errors or employee misunderstandings occur every day in business, costing billions of dollars nationally. Think about the current economic situation and the debacles we face with banking, insurance, and auto companies because proper processes, procedures, or controls simply did not exist. Human error in health care alone claims the lives of close to 100,000 Americans a year, making human error in health care the eighth leading cause of death in the United States. Balbir S. Dhillon, in *Human Reliability and Error in Medical Systems* (World Scientific Publishing Company, 2004) estimates the annual national cost between $17 billion and $37.6 billion.

Internal controls ensure accuracy and reliability at crucial points in a business process and can help reduce the number of errors introduced in the process. When you start looking at a business process to identify internal controls, you may be surprised that none exist. In my experience, this happens frequently. Employees more often than not try to do a good job, but mistakes happen and a systematic approach to preventing the same error from recurring is not always in place. To establish internal controls, identify the points in the business process where something can go wrong. At this point, you might ask how you should begin.

Start by walking through the improved process map you created in step 6 and move through it box by box, asking the project team what can go wrong with each activity. If a mistake can happen, signify this likelihood with an icon to denote that an error might occur. I like to use a warning symbol, as shown in Figure 7-1, to denote that an internal control should exist because everyone recognizes what this cautionary sign means.

Move through the entire process map, and put warning symbols next to each activity that may cause an error. Do not discuss the details about the mistakes or how you can avoid the

Figure 7-1 Warning Symbol

error until you have identified *all* the potential problem spots. If the project team members have trouble identifying potential problems, ask them, "What can go wrong at this point?" If an activity includes the use of spreadsheets or other tools, delve into those items and again ask what problems can occur. Think of what can go wrong with everyday tools, like formulas in spreadsheets, and look for ways to avoid the errors.

Once the project team identifies the potential problems, discuss how to avoid each one. I suggest listing all the problem spots *first* before discussing each one in detail because it takes quite a bit of time to adequately discuss what can go wrong and how to avoid the pitfalls for each activity marked with a warning symbol. If you stop and have a thorough discussion each time you put a warning symbol on the process map, human nature comes into play, and the team may get discouraged with the degree of work involved in error proofing. As a result, participants may fail to identify as many potential problem spots as they should.

Once you have gone through the entire process map and added a warning symbol wherever a mistake can happen, lead the project team through a discussion of exactly which errors can occur, then agree on how to avoid them in the future.

Figure 7-2 shows a table you can use to list the internal controls on an electronic dry-erase board, as discussed in Chapter 3, to keep the conversation visible to the project team.

Activity Number	Activity Description	Possible Issue(s)	Internal Control(s)

Figure 7-2 Internal Controls

➤ **Activity Number:** This is the number you gave the activity on the process map.

➤ **Activity Description:** The text description comes from the activity box on the process map.

➤ **Possible Issue(s):** Identify the various mistakes that might occur with this activity. The project team may find more than one potential mistake because, once they start thinking about errors, they may uncover multiple opportunities for errors. Document each mistake in the possible issue column, using a new row for each potential mistake.

➤ **Internal Control(s):** Identify how to error-proof each of the potential mistakes that the project team identified. This column becomes the list of internal controls for the business process.

Figure 7-3 shows the recognition bonus award process from Chapter 6 (Figure 6-5) with two internal controls identified. Notice the addition of a warning symbol to activity 1, completing the recognition bonus award form and emailing it to payroll, and to activity 5, spot checking 20 percent of the records in the quarterly audit process.

Once the project team identifies potential mistakes, discuss how to solve them. Figure 7-4 on page 172 summarizes the potential errors that can occur with the recognition bonus award process, showing examples of the internal controls for each potential mistake. This figure shows that more than one error may occur for a single activity.

The amount of time you spend on internal controls depends on the purpose of your work. If numerous errors caused you to look at a business process, then you should spend considerable time on internal controls. On the other hand, if your goal is to look for improvement opportunities to increase the effectiveness, efficiency, and adaptability of the process, then spend less time. Think about identifying internal controls for extremely sensitive business processes, whether the business has asked you to do so or not.

When you complete the internal controls document, it should become part of your overall process documentation. In Chapter 4, you saw that we started to define how to package the entire business process for future reference. Figure 7-5 shows

Improved Recognition Bonus Award Process

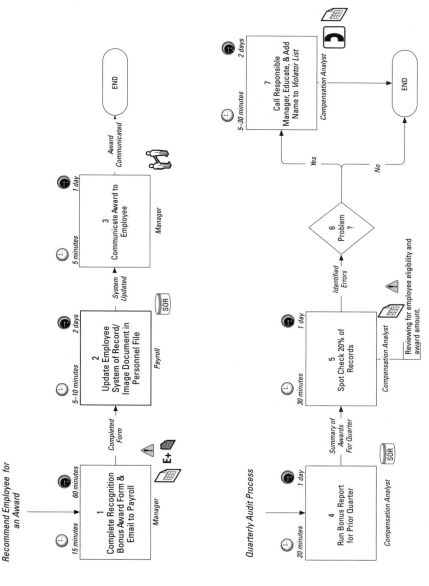

Figure 7-3 Alistar Corporation Improved Process Map: Sample Internal Control

Activity Number	Activity Description	Possible Issue(s)	Internal Control(s)
1	Complete recognition bonus award form and email to payroll	Employee may be bonus or incentive eligible. If so, then the employee is not eligible for a recognition bonus award.	When running the quarterly audit, the compensation analyst will: ■ Check the employee job numbers in the employee system of record to validate that they do not have "bonus" or "other bonus" checked as an attribute of the job. ■ Confirm the employee's eligibility following the criteria outlined in the recognition bonus award checklist.
		Managers across the company may not use the same criteria in determining the amount of money given to an employee.	■ Managers will use the justification criteria and award guidelines outlined in the recognition bonus award job aid created for them by the compensation department. ■ Compensation analyst will validate the award amounts in the quarterly audit. ■ Compensation analyst will provide feedback to managers who do not follow the guidelines and will regularly audit those managers.
5	Spot-check 20% of records	Compensation analyst may forget a step in the audit.	■ Compensation analyst will use the recognition bonus award checklist when conducting the audit.
		Compensation analyst may forget a step in the audit.	■ Compensation analyst will use the recognition bonus award checklist when conducting the audit.

Figure 7-4 Recognition Bonus Award Process: Internal Controls Document

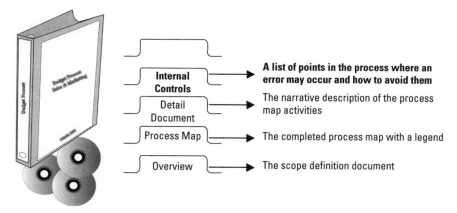

Figure 7-5 Summary Binder Tabs

the internal controls table as an additional piece of the documentation set.

Tools

In Chapter 6, you learned about the existing technologies used by your company, and you took advantage of those tools to improve the business process. Now is the time for you to develop those tools, whether you build a database, create job aids to help employees follow the business process, or make a change to an existing system.

Figure 7-4 made reference to a recognition bonus award checklist and job aid in the internal control column. You can convert the entire internal controls table into a checklist for the process workers to serve as a tool to help minimize errors. From reading the controls identified in Figure 7-4, it appears that managers could cause errors in the business process because the compensation department delegated them the authority to administer their own recognition bonus awards. It also seems that the compensation analysts may make additional errors in running the spot audits. So let us take a look at two job aids I developed to help the managers and compensation analysts.

Job Aids

Simple, quick job aids can provide easy step-by-step directions or guidelines to help drive consistency in a business process. They can help with complex tasks and provide reference information at employees' fingertips that they otherwise have to repeatedly look up. Try to keep job aids to a one-sheet document that is either single or double-sided for ease of use. Figure 7-6 shows an example of a job aid that you can create for managers so that they have the necessary information at their fingertips.

Figure 7-7 on page 176 shows an example of a checklist you can create.

As these two examples demonstrate, you can create countless tools, depending on the complexity of your business process. You can create a tool to simplify a step in the process, to drive consistency across multiple departments, or to explain how to use a particular item like a Microsoft Access database. Job aids can help process workers and stakeholders more easily understand a complex business process.

Custom Email Forms

Figure 7-8 on page 177 and Figure 7-9 on page 178 show that you can create custom forms in Microsoft Outlook by using the forms feature of the software. You can then use the normal capabilities of the email system to send the form to other employees. These two figures resulted from working with a client in the compensation department who expressed concern that his recruiters did not always provide the necessary information for the department to provide a pay quotation on a new employee; the client had to make multiple phone calls to collect the required information. The tool I created improved the workflow and eliminated the missing information because the recruiter could not send the form without filling in all the fields.

Use tools like this when you need to ensure that a requester supplies the required information for either making a

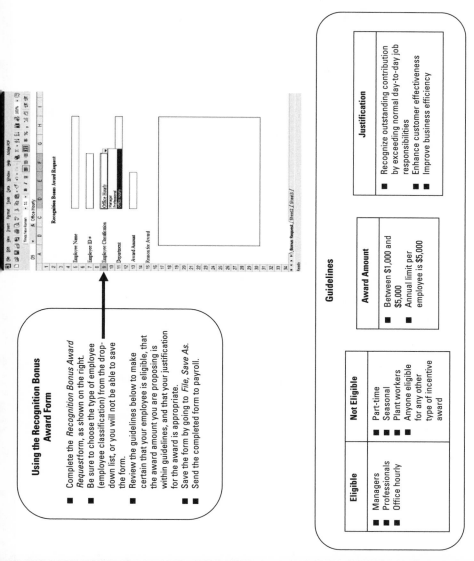

Recognition Bonus Award Reference Card

Using the Recognition Bonus Award Form

- Complete the *Recognition Bonus Award Request* form, as shown on the right.
- Be sure to choose the type of employee (employee classification) from the drop-down list, or you will not be able to save the form.
- Review the guidelines below to make certain that your employee is eligible, that the award amount you are proposing is within guidelines, and that your justification for the award is appropriate.
- Save the form by going to *File, Save As.*
- Send the completed form to payroll.

Guidelines

Eligible	Not Eligible
- Managers - Professionals - Office hourly	- Part-time - Seasonal - Plant workers - Anyone eligible for any other type of incentive award

Award Amount
- Between $1,000 and $5,000 - Annual limit per employee is $5,000

Justification
- Recognize outstanding contribution by exceeding normal day-to-day job responsibilities - Enhance customer effectiveness - Improve business efficiency

Figure 7-6 Sample Manager Job Aid

Done	Action	Tool
❑	■ Look up the employee's record and obtain his or her job number. Check the job number to validate that the job does not have a check mark in the bonus or other bonus field.	System of record (SOR)—job catalog
❑	**Eligibility Criteria** ■ Validate that the employee falls into one of the following categories: ➤ Manager not eligible for any other incentive program ➤ Professional employee not eligible for any other incentive program ➤ Office hourly employee	Employee classification
❑	■ Validate that the employee does *not* fall into one of these categories: ➤ Part-time employee ➤ Seasonal employee ➤ Plant worker	Work status
❑	**Justification Criteria** ■ Use the following criteria to evaluate the reasonableness of the justification: ➤ Accomplishment clearly demonstrates the employee going above and beyond the normal day-to-day responsibilities; or ➤ Action or idea that enhances customer effectiveness; or ➤ Action or idea that improves the efficiency of the business.	Validate with compensation consultant, if in question
❑	**Award Amount** ■ Validate that the proposed award amount falls within the following guidelines: ➤ It is between $1,000 and $5,000. ➤ The employee has not exceeded the annual maximum of $5,000.	SOR (employee history)

Figure 7-7 Recognition Bonus Award Process: Sample Checklist

decision or acting on a transaction and to avoid the need to call the requester and ask for the missing information.

In Figure 7-8, you see the normal email features available with the *to* and *cc* fields displayed and the beginning of the *subject* line. Someone using the form simply had to type the name of the candidate on the subject line and enter the message in the white text section.

In Figure 7-9 on page 178, the second tab, internal candidate, is selected, and the recruiter now enters the current infor-

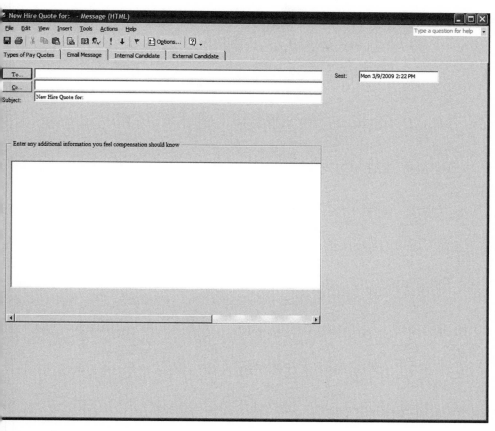

Figure 7-8 Custom Microsoft Outlook Form, Tab 1: Email Message

mation when requesting a new pay quotation. Compensation then fills in the percentage increase, which populates the new salary fields. When creating a custom Microsoft Outlook form, you can designate a data entry field as mandatory, or you can make one field populate another field. In Figure 7-9, once compensation enters a number in the percentage increase field and clicks the calculate button, the new salary automatically appears in the hourly, weekly, and annual fields.

You can also add different tabs across the top of the form to separate the information. Figure 7-9 shows that I created four tabs: types of pay quotes, email message, internal candidate, and external candidate. Creating tabs keeps the form uncluttered

Figure 7-9 Custom Microsoft Outlook Form, Tab 2: Internal Candidate

and makes it simple for users to pick the appropriate tab to complete.

Figure 7-10 shows another job aid I created to complement the custom Microsoft Outlook form.

Creating custom Microsoft Outlook forms is a simple way to standardize information required for a process while benefiting from tools already available in most companies. As Figure 7-11 on page 180 shows, you simply go to: Tools, Forms, Design a Form in Microsoft Outlook to create a custom form. Several books on the market can provide additional detail on designing custom forms, which you might need if you want to develop complex ones.

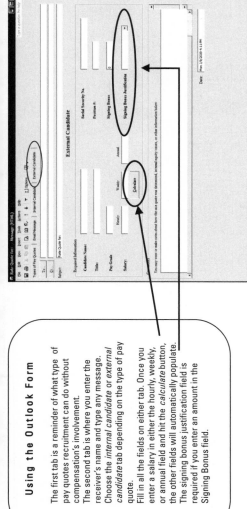

Pay Quote Reference Card

Using the Outlook Form

- The first tab is a reminder of what type of pay quotes recruitment can do without compensation's involvement.
- The second tab is where you enter the receiver's name and type any message.
- Choose the *internal candidate* or *external candidate* tab depending on the type of pay quote.
- Fill in all the fields on either tab. Once you enter a salary in either the hourly, weekly, or annual field and hit the *calculate* button, the other fields will automatically populate.
- The signing bonus justification field is required if you enter an amount in the Signing Bonus field.

Saving the Outlook Form to your Personal Forms Library

- Move the form to your Desktop.
- Open the form.
- Go to TOOLS, FORMS, PUBLISHING FORM AS
- The Look In: drop-down box will show your *Personal Forms Library*, which is probably empty. If this doesn't show, click on the downward arrow and select *Personal Forms Library*.
- Type in whatever name you want to give the form.
- Click PUBLISH.
- Each time you want to use the form in the future, choose Tools, Forms, Choose Form, use the drop-down arrow to select your *Personal Forms Library*, and the form will open without the Enable/Disable Macro message.

Figure 7-10 Sample Job Aid

Figure 7-11 Getting to Design a Form

Excel Tools

Almost everyone knows that Microsoft Excel allows you to create spreadsheets, but I find that not many people have taken the time to delve deeper into what they can accomplish with this application. Many managers (unless they come from finance) tend to shy away from using Excel because they do not have adequate knowledge on how to create formulas or pivot tables. Their reluctance presents you with an opportunity to make spreadsheets seem less intimidating and simple to use. To do so, you can create ones that do not look like spreadsheets at all. Figure 7-12 shows an example of a spreadsheet that looks not so threatening.

This spreadsheet includes functionality behind each of the buttons that automatically calculates the appropriate pay range for a particular job. Although you may need an intermediate skill level with Microsoft Excel to create sophisticated spreadsheets, you can create many tools with a minimum of ability and effort. Think about how to simplify spreadsheets you use every day, and make them more user-friendly. To streamline a business process, instead of waiting for a large system implementation, explore the additional capabilities of software applications already available to you.

Figure 7-13 on page 182 shows that tools now become another part of the overall process documentation.

Figure 7-12 Sample Microsoft Excel Spreadsheet

Metrics

Every day we deal with metrics even though we do not always think of them as such. How quickly did you get out of the house this morning, and how does that time compare to last week's? How has your golf handicap changed over time? How

Tools — Includes a copy of all the tools created to support the process

Internal Controls — A list of points in the process where an error may occur and how to avoid them

Detail Document — The narrative description of the process map activities

Process Map — The completed process map with a legend

Overview — The scope definition document

Figure 7-13 Summary Binder Tabs

many pounds have you lost or gained over the past year? How does your performance rating compare to last year's?

Some people say, "If you can't measure it, you can't manage it." Albert Einstein says the opposite: "Everything that can be counted does not necessarily count; everything that counts cannot necessarily be counted." So this differentiation suggests we should show caution and strike a balance between the value of the metric and its cost. Nevertheless, organizations like metrics, and they should have metrics for their business processes. Just do not go overboard. Think about the metrics you and the project team propose, and balance their usefulness with the expense of capturing the data required for them.

If the project team members spent sufficient time thinking about the client's/customer's needs when they established the foundation in Chapter 3, the scope definition document helps them define the business process metrics. Look at the identified measurements of success, and think about them from three perspectives: effectiveness, efficiency, and adaptability. Remember from Chapter 1 that:

► **Effectiveness** denotes the quality of the process. Does the process produce the desired results and meet the client/ customer needs?

▶ **Efficiency** signifies the productivity of the process. Does the process minimize the use of resources, improve cycle time, and eliminate bureaucracy?

▶ **Adaptability** denotes the flexibility of the process. Does the process remain flexible in the face of changing needs?

You often find that the measurements of success identified in the scope definition document are heavily weighted in favor of effectiveness because the project team wrote them from the client's/customer's perspective and the client/customer is the right place to start. The team may therefore have to think more about metrics that address efficiency and adaptability. Clients or customers also care about the flexibility of the process, and the business cares about efficiency. If the measurements of success do not include any efficiency or adaptability items, consider adding additional measurements of success.

If we use Alistar's compensation budget process as an example, Figure 7-14 shows the measurements of success we defined. Using this information as a starting point, lead the project team through a discussion for each measurement to decide how to measure the item. Make sure to write specific metrics that are

---

Measurements of success:

1. On-demand knowledge for the president's direct reports of their budget balances (the right information at the right time)
2. A process viewed as a reliable tool for use in employee-related activities like planning promotions and developing succession plans
3. Accurate tracking of spending
4. The ability to make better decisions on allocating funds

Figure 7-14 Alistar Corporation Compensation Budget Process: Measurements of Success actionable and that have a time component. Everyone should understand what each metric means.

In the compensation budget process, we defined "on-demand knowledge of the budget balances" as the first measurement of success for Alistar. In other words, the half dozen senior-level executives want assurance that they can identify how much money remains in their salary budget to spend at any time throughout the year. The executives care about the timeliness of the information, which relates to our discussion of cycle time in Chapter 6. In this case, the executives did not want to wait for the normal monthly report; they wanted the information at their fingertips. So how do you meet their need?

Start by defining what *on-demand* means in this case. You may find that a weekly update adequately meets the requirement, or they may want daily updates. When the executives said "on-demand," they may have simply meant something more frequent than the monthly report that they now receive. After defining what *on-demand* means, think about the work involved in delivering against the need and the value of achieving this measurement. In other words, how much labor does it take to provide on-demand knowledge, and how much is it worth?

The project team discussed this measurement of success for some time and considered things like what *on-demand* meant, where the department stored the budget information, whether the executives already had access to the information, and whether the executives knew how to run the reports. We found that the company's human resource system of record held the budget information and that the executives had access to the information any time they wanted it, but they never ran the reports. The project team evaluated several options:

➤ Redesign the report if it did not provide the executives with the information they wanted.

➤ Create a variant (a predefined report format) and teach the executives how to run the report easily using the variant.

➤ Have compensation run the report for the executives and download the information into a spreadsheet.

It turned out that weekly updates would provide senior executives with the information they wanted in the appropriate time frame. Although the budget information resided in the system of record and the executives could retrieve the information at any time, even daily if they preferred, they did not want to take the time to learn how to run the report. Sound familiar? As a result, the compensation department decided to run the report and download the information into a spreadsheet for the executives. Because this needed to be done for only a half dozen executives, meeting this requirement added an additional 15 minutes per week to the overall business process, a labor investment deemed worth the cost.

Pete Hodges, our sales executive from Chapter 3, defined success in multiple ways, but the number of new customers became a key metric that directly led to the lead-generation process. One of his measurements of success read, "Increased number of new customers." Initially, this may seem like an efficiency metric because the statement seems to focus on volume. However, once we discussed how to measure an increase in the volume of new customers, it became obvious that Pete cared about more than the volume; he was also concerned about the *quality* of new customers. So remember not to assume what a word means. Clarify the terminology for each measurement of success before defining a metric. As a result of our discussion, Pete defined the metric as "30 percent increase in the number of qualified new customers over the next six months."

Look at the second Alistar measurement of success in Figure 7-14, and you find the term *reliable* used. Again, what does that term mean?

In the third measurement, it sounds like the compensation department had trouble accurately tracking past spending. The first job is to uncover what occurred in the past so that you understand what this measurement means, and the next step is to establish controls so that the same problem does not happen again.

The fourth identified measurement is an internal metric for the compensation department. When you have internal measurements, spend time discussing how the department knows when it achieves this success. Because it gets easier to create a metric once the project team can share what success looks like, simply ask, "What does success look like?" "How will you know when you achieve success?" For Alistar, this measurement of success really meant how much money remained at the end of the year for each of their compensation funds. Because they forfeit any money remaining at the end of a year, similar to a health flexible spending account, they wanted to make sure that they spent every last dollar. We defined the metric for this last item as "Less than 1 percent of budget will remain at year end."

Once you understand what to measure, establish a baseline measurement to help the business recognize whether the new business process moves the organization in the right direction. In the previous internal metric example, compensation had about 10 percent of the budget left at the end of the prior year. With their new goal of less than 1 percent, they can tell when they are moving in the right direction.

A department that has responsibility for system support provides another example. If reducing the number of reported problems in a specific area like security is important, then they have to start by identifying the number of problems reported today, which becomes the baseline. We could then state the metric as "20 percent reduction in security issues over the next year."

Chapter Summary: Step 7

Identifying points in the business process where a mistake can occur provides the opportunity to introduce internal controls. Using a warning symbol to mark those spots makes the problem areas visible and obvious. Developing an internal control document, which contains the details about how to avoid common errors, provides an effective training tool for new process workers.

Developing tools to support the business process helps train new process workers to avoid errors. Create job aids to simplify or standardize a step in the process, use software applications like Microsoft Excel or Microsoft Outlook to create simple forms, or create checklists and other reminders about important steps in a process. If you have system of record in place or other applications, you can recommend changes to those systems to support the business process.

Creating metrics to support the measurements of success defined in the scope definition document allows you to evaluate whether the process works as planned. Always show caution in developing metrics because you can easily create too many of them. Always balance the usefulness of having a metric against the expense of capturing the data required to supply it.

Time Estimate

Figure 7-15 summarizes the time you should allow to create the internal controls, tools, and metrics (step 7).

Project Team Meeting

This meeting is a continuation of the project team meetings. It generally takes several hours to identify the points in the process where mistakes can happen because most process maps are more complex than our intentionally simple example. After

Event	Time	Purpose
Project team meeting: identify internal controls	3–5 hours	■ Add internal control symbols to the process map and document potential errors. ■ Determine how to make certain that mistakes do not happen.
Postmeeting work: create tools	Varies: ■ 40–80 hours (simple items); ■ 1–2 months (for databases); ■ longer (if system of record changes)	■ Create the job aids and tools identified.
Project team meeting: identify metrics	3–4 hours	■ Identify how to meet the measurements of success.

Figure 7-15 Time Estimate—Step 7: Create Internal Controls, Tools, and Metrics

identifying the potential problem areas, spend the remainder of the meeting identifying how to avoid the potential mistakes. I generally dedicate an entire meeting to this topic because it takes some time to identify solutions to potential errors. Identifying the possible errors is easy; determining how to avoid the problems is the hard part.

Postmeeting Work

During this time, the project team creates the tools identified during the process improvement phase. Depending on the number of internal controls and tools you have to create, this time takes from one to two weeks for simple job aids, a month or more to create databases, and significantly longer if you plan to make changes to your company's system of record.

Project Team Meeting

During this meeting, your entire focus is on reviewing what you identified as the measurements of success on the scope definition document and talking about how you can deliver against those goals.

What You Have Achieved

In this chapter, you have achieved the following:

➤ The ability to identify internal controls to avoid potential problem points in a business process

➤ The knowledge of how to create a variety of tools to simplify the process

➤ The wisdom of when to include a metric and how to use the measurements of success as a starting point

➤ Most important, the *power* to bring the business process to life by including internal controls, tools, and metrics that employees can use

CHAPTER 8

Step 8: Test and Rework

Making Sure It Works

Joanne Wu, training and development manager for a mid-size computer manufacturer, redesigned a half dozen of her department's business processes to increase her department's responsiveness to its clients. She often received complaints that it took too long to design and develop courses to address unexpected training needs that surfaced throughout the year.

Joanne and I worked together for several weeks to change a myriad of steps in her business processes, reduce the approval cycle, and realign resources. Now we had to make certain that the changes worked before introducing the new processes on a wide scale. Joanne identified the area training managers as the test group because she considered them a crucial client group who routinely brought unplanned regional training requirements to her attention. The area training managers had geographically dispersed employees, so using them as the test group would also enable us to assess how the process worked in multiple locations. If the new process worked for the area training managers, it would work for Joanne's remaining clients. We decided to conduct the test during December, a traditionally slow time for the manufacturer to deliver training.

At this point in the roadmap, you have completed the formidable work. You redesigned the business process so that the client/customer sees the process as effective and so that it runs efficiently for the business. You have also documented the process and created new tools and metrics to support the process. Now you want to validate that the process, documentation, and tools work as you expect.

As an example of what you might find out, the custom Microsoft Outlook form I created to support pay quotations (Chapter 7) worked fine when entering information and calculating formulas. However, we found in testing that, once the recruiter received an email from compensation with the new pay quote amounts, the recruiters could not forward the quotation to the hiring manager because we had not enabled the forwarding capability when we designed the form.

Before introducing a new, improved process to the organization, test it and work out any bugs before communicating the change on a wide scale. Testing the business process helps to determine how well the business process will perform in the organization so that you meet your goals, whether they are increased productivity, minimizing errors, or something else. Testing helps in identifying bottlenecks and provides the chance to fix or rework the problems, thus ensuring that the implementation proceeds as smoothly as possible.

In this phase of the work, think about the who, what, where, when, and how of testing:

> **Whom** do you involve in the testing? Consider who will use the process and tools created. If the business process involves only a single department, you may have a small list of people to include in the testing. On the other hand, multiple departments often share responsibility for a business process. In this case, the list of people to include may consist of employees who work with the process daily because they will act as subject matter experts, managers who have a role in the process, and stakeholders who have an interest in the process.

  If you suspect dissimilarity between local and global sites, include both sites in the testing phase. Ideally, you should include local and global site team members early in the overall process work itself, instead of just during the testing phase. This saves rework time in the end.

> **What** do you have to test? Test the business process itself, the associated documentation, and the tools created to sup-

port the process. This includes any job aids created, any new technologies introduced, and any metrics designed.

Even though you may not have any actual data yet for the measurements, create a mock-up of what the measurement will look like and validate that the information meets the requirements of the data recipients. If you plan to create a report, include a mock-up of the report during testing to validate that it works.

► **Where** should the testing occur? Define the different locations where testing must happen.

■ If employees use the process in multiple locations, you may have to test the tools at various business sites because each location may use a different technology or have unusual technical challenges. You may encounter firewall or server challenges at different sites depending on their functions.

■ If you have local sites and global sites, include key locations in the testing to validate that the process and tools work at both types of sites. You may find a step in the process that does not work because of a country's legal requirements. If you work in the United States and have locations in Europe, for example, think about challenges that can arise because of the Safe Harbor framework developed between the United States and the European Union. The following excerpt, taken from the U.S. Department of Commerce Web site, provides an overview of Safe Harbor's concern with protecting a citizen's privacy. You can read additional information at http://www.export.gov/safeharbor/eu/doc_eg_safeharbor_eu.asp:

> While the United States and the European Union share the goal of enhancing privacy protection for their citizens, the United States takes a different approach to privacy from that taken by the European Union.
>
> In order to bridge these different privacy approaches and provide a streamlined means for U.S. organizations to comply with the Directive, the U.S. Department of Commerce in consultation with the European Commission developed a ``Safe Harbor'' framework.

- Another decision revolves around whether to test the tools from the work location and from home. Do managers frequently work from home? Do managers use handheld devices?

  Think about who will use the business process, where the users work, and how they do their work to identify the parameters to include in the testing.

▶ **When** should the testing occur? Identify the time frame for the testing period. Think about the best time to conduct the testing, and avoid any peak periods for the business. For example, if you work with finance, avoid month- and year-end time periods. If you work with a company that has a seasonal business, avoid those busy times.

  In Joanne Wu's case, she wanted to conduct the testing in December, a customarily slow period for the computer manufacturer. However, other businesses may consider December a busy holiday season.

▶ **How** will the testing happen? Define your testing approach, which you can think of as the series of steps involved in testing. If you participated in a system implementation in the past, you will see similarity with the steps involved in the user acceptance testing phase of those implementations because this testing focuses on subject matter experts who test, through trial and error, that the new or modified process and tools work.

  In systems testing, three key types of testing occur: user acceptance testing, integration testing, and regression testing. Of course, an implementation includes other varieties of testing (like unit, performance, or stress testing), but the three I mention generally involve business partners versus the technical staff. User acceptance testing has the most applicability to business process work, because of the similarity of the steps.

The Five Steps in Testing the Business Process

Figure 8-1 shows the five steps to follow in testing the business process.

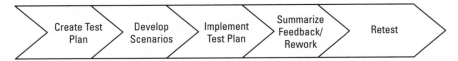

Figure 8-1 The Five Testing Steps

1. Create the test plan.
2. Develop the scenarios (or testing sheets).
3. Implement the test plan.
4. Summarize the feedback received and the challenges encountered, then rework the process and tools.
5. Retest (if appropriate).

Step 1: Create the Test Plan

The test plan provides structure and a systematic approach to testing the business process. Test plans are created when implementing new systems, and you will find them just as beneficial when implementing new or modified business processes. The test plan brings the who, what, where, when, and how together in one location.

Certain of your colleagues may have a negative view of test plans because there is sometimes an inclination to overuse them, but I find that, if you keep them simple, test plans help you avoid mistakes. The discipline alone of developing a test plan forces you to think about things you might otherwise overlook. So think of the test plan as simply a tool used to verify that the business process works as expected. Before signing up and joining a gym for a year, you might want to test it out and accept a free trial month. Think of the test plan as your free trial.

The test plan outlines the overall scope of the testing phase. It states the goal of the testing, describes the approach to use, the resources involved, the items to test, and the schedule or timeline. Figure 8-2 shows a completed six-week test plan for Alistar Corporation's new hire pay process.

Step 1, creating the test plan, incorporates the first three activities from Figure 8-2, defining the testing goal, method, and objectives.

ID Number	Task	Person Responsible	Due Date
1	Define testing goal.	Project manager	May 15
2	Define testing method.	Project manager	May 15
3	Define objectives for test items.	Project manager	May 15
4	Develop scenarios for test items (testing sheets).	Project team	June 1
5	Gain support for resources.	Project manager	June 1
6	Create feedback collection tool.	Project manager	June 1
7	Conduct testing.	Project team	June 2–15
8	Rework, as required.	Project team	June 30

Figure 8-2 New Hire Pay Process Test Plan

Testing Goal

The goal is a statement of the overall purpose for the testing. For Alistar Corporation, our testing goal read:

TESTING GOAL:
   To validate that the new hire pay process is simple to use for the recruiters, compensation, and the hiring managers globally and that the tools created to support the process work as expected with no defects.

Testing Method

The method describes the procedures used to conduct the testing. It answers the who, what, where, when, and how questions. It answers:

➤ Who will perform the tests?

➤ What items constitute the test plan?

➤ Where will the testing occur?

➤ When will the testing occur?

➤ How will you communicate with the testers?

➤ How will you report, track, and resolve problems?

Generally in formal system testing, issue tracking software is used. This level of formality seems too complex for business process testing, but if you have the software available, use

it. A simple spreadsheet, though, generally works fine. For the
Alistar Corporation, our testing method read:

TESTING METHOD:
  The following steps document the testing plan for the new hire pay
process.

Resources: The following employees have a role in testing the process:
- Recruiters located in Chicago, San Francisco, and London.
- Compensation analysts at the main headquarters in Chicago.
- Managers located in Chicago and London.

The following software is required:
- Microsoft Outlook, Version 2007 Professional
- Microsoft Excel, Version 2007 Professional
- Microsoft PowerPoint, Version 2007 or later
- Microsoft Word, Version 2007 or later
- Adobe Acrobat Reader, Version 8 or later

TEST ITEMS
  The test plan includes the following items:
- End-to-end business process (Microsoft PowerPoint process map;
  Microsoft Word detail document)
- New hire pay quotation form (Microsoft Outlook)
- New hire pay calculation tool (Microsoft Excel)
- Job aid aimed at the recruiter's ability to use the form and tool
  (Adobe PDF)
- Sample report that summarizes quarterly new hire pay quota-
  tions (Microsoft Excel)

LOCATIONS
  Recruiters and managers located at our domestic and international
locations will test the tools, including:
- Domestic sites: Chicago, San Francisco
- International site: London, England

TIME FRAME
  The testing will occur from June 2 through June 15.

COMMUNICATION PROCESS
  A daily 30-minute phone meeting will occur to discuss testing progress
and issue resolution at:
- 8:30 A.M. San Francisco time.

- 10:30 A.M. Chicago time.
- 4:30 P.M. London time.

At the first meeting, we will review the test plan and the testing responsibilities.

FEEDBACK PROCESS

An issue resolution log will reside on the shared network drive, and each tester will enter:

- Problems that surface during testing.
- Points of confusion that surface in the process.
- General feedback on the process.

All entries will have a category and severity level attached:

- Category: Usability or Technical Problem
- Severity Level: High, Medium, or Low

Testing Objectives

The objectives for each test item assist the project team in writing appropriate test scenarios. For the team to do a thorough job, they have to understand what you want to accomplish for each test item. For Alistar Corporation, the testing objectives read:

TESTING OBJECTIVES:

The following objectives specify the focus for each test item in the new hire pay process.

Item 1: *End-to-end business process (Microsoft PowerPoint and Microsoft Word)*   To make certain that each step in the business process works for every site and that the documentation supports the work.

Item 2: *New Hire Pay Quotation Form (Microsoft Outlook)*   To validate that the fields work as expected (including data entry fields, mandatory fields, and formula-driven fields), that the form appropriately flows through the email system, and that the calculation button works.

Item 3: *New Hire Pay Calculation Tool (Microsoft Excel)*   To make certain that the formulas work, that the user cannot change the field values, and that the tool includes the appropriate scenarios.

Item 4: *Job Aid (Adobe PDF file)*   To validate that the help content answers recruiter questions that may surface and that the file converted to PDF format correctly.

Item 5: *Report (Microsoft Excel)* To validate that the report includes information required to help senior management understand the cost of hire.

Step 2: Develop the Scenarios

When the resources you identified for testing are ready to start, what do they do? Where do they begin? You do not want them sitting around making up their own scenarios because this wastes time and they might not test the items that you want them to test. The test scenarios, or testing sheets, provide the resources with step-by-step guidelines so that they understand how to test the process and tools.

Figure 8-3 shows the overall workflow for the Microsoft Outlook new hire pay quotation form for Alistar Corporation. The six steps involved in the process are repeated under each process worker with their responsibility for the form highlighted. This figure shows that:

- ▶ The recruiter requests the quotation from compensation.

- ▶ Compensation determines the pay rate and sends the quotation back to the recruiter.

- ▶ The recruiter then opens the quotation and forwards the quotation to the hiring manager.

- ▶ The hiring manager opens the quotation on their desktop, home computer, or handheld device.

Test Scripts and Data Sheets

The information in Figure 8-3 assists in creating appropriate scenarios because each highlighted task under *test scripts* in the figure must be accompanied by a testing sheet. For example, look at the first test script under the recruiter's list, *request quote*. Figure 8-4 on page 199 shows the steps involved in testing that step. The text above Figure 8-4 provides the following general information:

Figure 8-3 Test Scenario for New Hire Pay Quotation Form

- ▶ **Test scenario:** The overall grouping of activities that address an activity or tool in a business process (the new hire pay quotation form)

- ▶ **Test script:** The activity or test item (to request a quotation)

- ▶ **Responsible tester:** The person conducting the test (recruiter)

As Figure 8-4 shows, the test script gives testers (in this case, the recruiter) the details required to test the form. The *data* column provides the information they should enter as they move through the test. By providing information in the data column, you speed up the testing because the tester does not have to spend time thinking of phony information to enter. Providing data also enables you to control the test and to test specific scenarios. If you want to test various versions of a report, you can include the report parameters you want used.

The *expected result* column tells testers exactly what they should see after they complete the step, and the *actual result* column gives them space to document what they observe or encounter during testing.

If you want to test many different scenarios, you should separate the test script from the data by using a separate data sheet instead of using the *data* column in the test script, because

Test scenario: New hire pay quotation form
Test script: Request quote
Responsible tester: Recruiter

Step	Description	Data	Expected Result	Actual Result
1 of 7	Open Microsoft Outlook new hire pay quotation form	None	Normal Microsoft Outlook email opens.	
2 of 7	Click in *to* field and search the global address list for compensation consultant's name. Enter the name.	Abigail Adams	Email is addressed to Abigail Adams.	
3 of 7	Enter candidate's name in the subject line after "New hire quote for."	Dennis Schwartz	Subject line shows "New hire quote for: Dennis Schwartz."	
4 of 7	Type a general message on the main page.	Please note that Dennis has been in his present job for fewer than six months.	General message appears on Email message tab.	
5 of 7	Click on the *internal candidate* tab.	None	Outlook message switches to a new screen.	
6 of 7	Enter information for candidate and hit *calculate* button when done.	■ Candidate name: Dennis Schwartz ■ Employee no.: 7489 ■ Current title: Assistant Manager, Retail ■ New title: Manager, Retail ■ Current salary grade: 29 ■ New salary grade: 31 ■ Current salary: $65,000 annually	The hourly and weekly sums under current salary are automatically filled in after $65,000 is entered in the annual salary field and the *calculate* button is clicked.	
7 of 7	Click *send.*	None	Email arrives in Abigail Adams's inbox. (Confirm receipt of email in Abigail Adams's inbox.)	

Figure 8-4 Example of Test Scenario

using data sheets in this case saves everyone time. Figures 8-5 and 8-6 show what the same example looks like if you separate the test script from the data. Notice that the test script in Figure 8-5 provides only the steps involved in testing, not the data. The test script refers the tester to the data sheet to find the exact field values to enter.

Test scenario: New hire pay quotation form
Test script: Request quote
Responsible tester: Recruiter

Step	Description	Data	Expected Result	Actual Result
1 of 7	Open Microsoft Outlook new hire pay quotation form.	See data sheet 5, request quote	Normal Microsoft Outlook email opens	
2 of 7	Click in *to* field and search the global address list for compensation consultant's name. Enter the name.	See data sheet 5, request quote	Email is addressed to Abigail Adams.	
3 of 7	Enter candidate's name in the subject line after "New hire quote for."	See data sheet 5, request quote	Subject line shows "New hire quote for: Dennis Schwartz."	
4 of 7	Type a general message on the main page.	See data sheet 5, request quote	General message appears on Email message tab.	
5 of 7	Click on the *internal candidate* tab.	See data sheet 5, request quote	Outlook message switches to a new screen.	
6 of 7	Enter information for candidate and hit *calculate* button when done.	See data sheet 5, request quote	The hourly and weekly sums under current salary are automatically filled in after $65,000 is entered in the annual salary field and the *calculate* button is clicked.	
7 of 7	Click *send*.	See data sheet 5, request quote	Email arrives in Abigail Adams's inbox. (Confirm receipt of email in Abigail Adams's inbox.)	

Figure 8-5 Example of Test Script

The data sheet in Figure 8-6 provides the data elements to enter for the various scenarios. In this example, you see two data sets, one in the *data set 1* column and a second one in the *data set 2* column. You can add as many columns as desired, to make certain that you include the different scenarios that you want to test.

When you separate the test script from the data, the testers run through the test script multiple times using a different column of data in the data sheet until they have tested all the scenarios.

Gain Support for Resources

Although you defined the resources required when you wrote the testing method, you now have to secure approval from the appropriate managers to include the testers during the scheduled testing period. Gain the resource commitments while the project team writes the testing scenarios.

Create Feedback Collection Tool

During this step, design the spreadsheet that the testers will use to report issues and feedback throughout the testing period. Figure 8-7 shows a simple example of an issue resolution log I have used to capture problems that surfaced during testing. When entering an issue in the tool, the testers had to choose either *usability* or *technical* in the category column by selecting from the drop-down list, and they chose *high*, *medium*, or *low* from the severity column. Use the issue resolution log during the project team's daily phone meetings to discuss the problems encountered and the status of problem resolution.

Step 3: Implement the Test Plan

During the specified time frame, the identified resources use the supplied test scripts and data to follow the new process and use the new tools. You monitor the progress as the testers enter problems they encounter in the issue resolution tool. As you conduct the daily meetings, the project team discusses

Test scenario: New hire pay quotation form
Data sheet: 5, Request quote
Responsible tester: Recruiter

Step	Data Set 1	Data Set 2	Expected Result	Actual Result
1 of 7	None	None	Normal Microsoft Outlook Email opens.	
2 of 7	Abigail Adams	Yvonne Chan	Email is addressed to correct person.	
3 of 7	Dennis Schwartz	Henrie Bette	Subject line shows "New hire quote for: <name of employee>."	
4 of 7	Please note that Dennis has been in his present job for fewer than six months.	Henrie is transferring from the Chicago branch.	General message appears on email message tab.	
5 of 7	None	None	Outlook message switches to a new screen.	
6 of 7	■ Candidate name: Dennis Schwartz ■ Employee no.: 7489 ■ Current title: Assistant Manager, Retail ■ New title: Manager, Retail ■ Current salary grade: 29 ■ New salary grade: 31 ■ Current salary: $65,000 annually	■ Candidate name: Dennis Schwartz ■ Employee no.: 2009 ■ Current title: Sales Promotions Coordinator ■ New title: Marketing Communications Specialist ■ Current salary grade: L3 ■ New salary grade: L8 ■ Current salary: $47,000 annually	The hourly and weekly sums under current salary are automatically filled in after the current salary is entered in the annual salary field and the *calculate* button is clicked.	
7 of 7	None	None	Email arrives in appropriate person's inbox. (Confirm receipt of email in appropriate person's inbox.)	

Figure 8-6   Example of Data Sheet

ID Number	Test Item	Date	Description	Category	Severity	Detected By	Assigned To
1	Calculation tool	6/4	No scenario for an external hire with greater than 10 years' experience	Usability	High	Sarah Jones	Jesus Carrabba
2	Job aid	6/5	Missing step: what to do after you enter the desired percentage	Usability	Low	May Chang	Sue Sams
3	Quote form	6/5	Cannot forward form to hiring manager	Technical	High	Liz Fleet	Jesus Carrabba
4							
5							

Figure 8-7 New Hire Pay Quotation Process: Issue Resolution Tool

known problems and possible resolutions. If the project team resolves a problem, remove the item from the list by moving the problem to a new worksheet called *closed*. Continue working through the issue resolution log until the team fixes the major problems.

Step 4: Summarize Feedback and Rework

Once the test period ends, summarize the findings and determine the next steps. If you do not obtain the results expected, identify the steps required to attain them. You may have to adjust the business process itself, fix errors in spreadsheets, or rectify other problems that surfaced during the testing phase.

Step 5: Retest

Based on the number and severity of problems that surfaced, you may or may not have to retest a portion of the process. View testing as an iterative process when you test an item.

If the item does not work, you fix it, but then you have to test it again.

Chapter Summary: Step 8

Creating a plan to test the new business process helps to make certain that it works as expected and that you do not experience too many surprises during implementation. Consider it your test drive.

The discipline of creating a test plan forces you to answer questions such as who should be involved in the testing, what items to test, where to conduct the testing, when is the best time to conduct the test, and the steps involved in the testing.

Test scripts provide structure for the resources by giving them step-by-step instructions for conducting the test. Gathering information in an issue resolution log or a similar tool gives you the information to understand what may have to change in the business process or tools. Include as many different scenarios in the testing phase that may occur in real life. If you have multiple scenarios, separate the data from the test script by using data sheets.

Once the testing is done, summarize the feedback and make adjustments. If you make a substantial number of changes, retest either the entire business process or the impacted tools.

If you suspect deviation between local and global locations, include participants from both locations in the overall process work itself because including them early in the process saves rework time in the end.

Time Estimate

To plan the time that it takes to work through this step, Figure 8-8 summarizes the time you should allow to test the process (step 8).

Event	Time	Purpose
Create test plan.	16 hours	■ Identify the who, what, where, when, and how of testing.
Write test scenarios, secure resources, create collection tool.	40 hours	■ Write scenarios for test items. ■ Gain agreement on resources. ■ Create feedback collection tool.
Implement test plan/rework.	40 hours (over two weeks)	■ Validate that the process works as expected. ■ Resolve problems.

Figure 8-8 Time Estimate—Step 8: Test and Rework

Create the Test Plan

During this time, think about how you want to conduct the business process testing. This should not take long, but answer the who, what, where, when, and how questions. You should find yourself spending the majority of your time on the how, or testing approach.

Write Test Scenarios

During this time, the project team writes the detailed testing scenarios. While the team writes the scenarios, you should use this time to gain support from the managers who own the resources you want involved in the testing phase and to create a feedback collection tool, like an issue resolution log.

Implement the Test Plan and Rework

During this time, the testing occurs. You can establish the exact hours that you want testing to occur, or you can let the testers plan their own calendars. In the example, I have estimated 40 hours over two weeks. This period also provides additional time to make any minor revisions as the testing progresses.

What You Have Achieved

In this chapter, you have achieved the following:

➤ Insight into how to make certain that the business process works as you expect

- ▶ The awareness to include both local and global locations in the business process improvement work, or at least in testing the process

- ▶ The importance of identifying whom to include in testing, what to test, where to test, when to test, and the method for testing

- ▶ The steps involved in the entire testing cycle

- ▶ Knowledge of how to create a test script and data sheets

- ▶ Most important, the *power* to make certain that you introduce a workable business process into your company

CHAPTER 9

Step 9: Implement the Change

Preparing the Organization

Now that you know your business process and tools will work, think about how to introduce the change to the organization. Who needs to know? What do they need to know? When should you inform them? How should you communicate the change?

The term *change management* simply means taking people in an organization from the current state to a future state. This chapter focuses on managing change because, as we know from our own experiences, change is a constant and "nothing endures but change," as the Greek philosopher Heraclitus wrote.

When the banking industry went through a cycle of rapid acquisitions and mergers in the 1990s, I was asked by an industry giant to help them merge two separate business processes. At the beginning of the work, I developed an implementation plan that included all the roadmap steps, which kept the work organized while ensuring that we did not miss anyone or anything along the way.

The implementation plan acts as your guide to ensure successful implementation of a new or improved business process. Think of it as a project plan that focuses on either an individual business process or a group of processes. It includes everything from start to finish:

➤ Developing the process inventory
➤ Establishing the foundation and creating the scope definition document

- ➤ Drawing the process map and developing the documentation
- ➤ Estimating the time and cost
- ➤ Verifying the process map
- ➤ Applying the improvement techniques
- ➤ Creating internal controls, tools, and metrics
- ➤ Testing and reworking the business process
- ➤ Implementing the change
- ➤ Developing a continuous improvement plan

In this chapter, I cover three new topics to include in an implementation plan that will help you identify the who, what, where, when, and how. The implementation plan acts as the organizing umbrella that pulls the following three components together in one location:

1. *The impact analysis* outlines the changes that must happen in the organization to ensure a successful implementation of the business process.
2. *The communication plan* provides clarity about who needs to know about the change, what they need to know, when they need to know and the best method of communication for each of the defined audiences.
3. *The training plan* covers who requires training on what, who owns the responsibility to conduct the training, where the training will occur, and when and how to deliver the training.

The sponsor, as the champion for the change, has increased responsibility in the implementation phase, and that responsibility includes advocating the change, aligning the business process changes with the organizational strategy, and helping to resolve any resistance or remove roadblocks.

The Implementation Plan

The best implementation plans include phases that break the work down into reasonable chunks that function as a guide to keep the work on track. Figure 9-1 shows an example of an implementation plan with three phases identified:

▶ **The design phase** identifies the work involved in defining and improving the business process.

▶ **The development phase** includes creating the tools required to make the improved business process work before moving to step 8, where you test the process.

▶ **The implementation phase** includes testing the process, determining how to roll out the new business process, how to communicate and train the affected people, and how to continually improve the business process so that it remains relevant over time.

For a complex business process, it helps to use project management software. For a simple business process, on the other hand, a table or a spreadsheet may work fine. If you use a table or spreadsheet, though, you must manually calculate how long a task takes (the duration), which can be a disadvantage because manual calculations increase the time required to create the original timeline and then to make adjustments to the dates as the work progresses. Figure 9-1 shows an implementation plan created with Microsoft Office Project. That figure shows the following standard Microsoft Office Project columns:

▶ **Task Name**: Create the phases in this column and include specific tasks associated with each major phase. Figure 9-1 shows three phases (design, development, and implementation). The implementation phase then includes four separate tracks (change management, testing, communication, and training). Using tracks within a phase helps to further organize the work. Although this layout works well for general business process implementations, feel free to customize the list of tasks to fit your situation.

▶ **Duration**: This column states how long a task will take to complete. After entering the number of days for each task, Microsoft Office Project automatically rolls up the subtasks and shows the total duration for a phase in bold text. For example, Figure 9-1 shows a duration of:

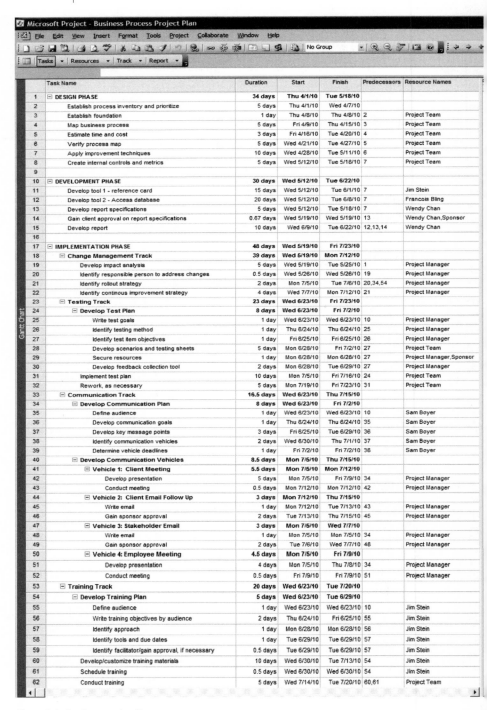

	Task Name	Duration	Start	Finish	Predecessors	Resource Names
1	⊟ DESIGN PHASE	34 days	Thu 4/1/10	Tue 5/18/10		
2	Establish process inventory and prioritize	5 days	Thu 4/1/10	Wed 4/7/10		
3	Establish foundation	1 day	Thu 4/8/10	Thu 4/8/10	2	Project Team
4	Map business process	5 days	Fri 4/9/10	Thu 4/15/10	3	Project Team
5	Estimate time and cost	3 days	Fri 4/16/10	Tue 4/20/10	4	Project Team
6	Verify process map	5 days	Wed 4/21/10	Tue 4/27/10	5	Project Team
7	Apply improvement techniques	10 days	Wed 4/28/10	Tue 5/11/10	6	Project Team
8	Create internal controls and metrics	5 days	Wed 5/12/10	Tue 5/18/10	7	Project Team
9						
10	⊟ DEVELOPMENT PHASE	30 days	Wed 5/12/10	Tue 6/22/10		
11	Develop tool 1 - reference card	15 days	Wed 5/12/10	Tue 6/1/10	7	Jim Stein
12	Develop tool 2 - Access database	20 days	Wed 5/12/10	Tue 6/8/10	7	Francois Bling
13	Develop report specifications	5 days	Wed 5/12/10	Tue 5/18/10	7	Wendy Chan
14	Gain client approval on report specifications	0.67 days	Wed 5/19/10	Wed 5/19/10	13	Wendy Chan,Sponsor
15	Develop report	10 days	Wed 6/9/10	Tue 6/22/10	12,13,14	Wendy Chan
16						
17	⊟ IMPLEMENTATION PHASE	48 days	Wed 5/19/10	Fri 7/23/10		
18	⊟ Change Management Track	39 days	Wed 5/19/10	Mon 7/12/10		
19	Develop impact analysis	5 days	Wed 5/19/10	Tue 5/25/10	1	Project Manager
20	Identify responsible person to address changes	0.5 days	Wed 5/26/10	Wed 5/26/10	19	Project Manager
21	Identify rollout strategy	2 days	Mon 7/5/10	Tue 7/6/10	20,34,54	Project Manager
22	Identify continous improvement strategy	4 days	Wed 7/7/10	Mon 7/12/10	21	Project Manager
23	⊟ Testing Track	23 days	Wed 6/23/10	Fri 7/23/10		
24	⊟ Develop Test Plan	8 days	Wed 6/23/10	Fri 7/2/10		
25	Write test goals	1 day	Wed 6/23/10	Wed 6/23/10	10	Project Manager
26	Identify testing method	1 day	Thu 6/24/10	Thu 6/24/10	25	Project Manager
27	Identify test item objectives	1 day	Fri 6/25/10	Fri 6/25/10	26	Project Manager
28	Develop scenarios and testing sheets	5 days	Mon 6/28/10	Fri 7/2/10	27	Project Team
29	Secure resources	1 day	Mon 6/28/10	Mon 6/28/10	27	Project Manager,Sponsor
30	Develop feedback collection tool	2 days	Mon 6/28/10	Tue 6/29/10	27	Project Manager
31	Implement test plan	10 days	Mon 7/5/10	Fri 7/16/10	24	Project Team
32	Rework, as necessary	5 days	Mon 7/19/10	Fri 7/23/10	31	Project Team
33	⊟ Communication Track	16.5 days	Wed 6/23/10	Thu 7/15/10		
34	⊟ Develop Communication Plan	8 days	Wed 6/23/10	Fri 7/2/10		
35	Define audience	1 day	Wed 6/23/10	Wed 6/23/10	10	Sam Boyer
36	Develop communication goals	1 day	Thu 6/24/10	Thu 6/24/10	35	Sam Boyer
37	Develop key message points	3 days	Fri 6/25/10	Tue 6/29/10	36	Sam Boyer
38	Identify communication vehicles	2 days	Wed 6/30/10	Thu 7/1/10	37	Sam Boyer
39	Determine vehicle deadlines	1 day	Fri 7/2/10	Fri 7/2/10	38	Sam Boyer
40	⊟ Develop Communication Vehicles	8.5 days	Mon 7/5/10	Thu 7/15/10		
41	⊟ Vehicle 1: Client Meeting	5.5 days	Mon 7/5/10	Mon 7/12/10		
42	Develop presentation	5 days	Mon 7/5/10	Fri 7/9/10	34	Project Manager
43	Conduct meeting	0.5 days	Mon 7/12/10	Mon 7/12/10	42	Project Manager
44	⊟ Vehicle 2: Client Email Follow Up	3 days	Mon 7/12/10	Thu 7/15/10		
45	Write email	1 day	Mon 7/12/10	Tue 7/13/10	43	Project Manager
46	Gain sponsor approval	2 days	Tue 7/13/10	Thu 7/15/10	45	Project Manager
47	⊟ Vehicle 3: Stakeholder Email	3 days	Mon 7/5/10	Wed 7/7/10		
48	Write email	1 day	Mon 7/5/10	Mon 7/5/10	34	Project Manager
49	Gain sponsor approval	2 days	Tue 7/6/10	Wed 7/7/10	48	Project Manager
50	⊟ Vehicle 4: Employee Meeting	4.5 days	Mon 7/5/10	Fri 7/9/10		
51	Develop presentation	4 days	Mon 7/5/10	Thu 7/8/10	34	Project Manager
52	Conduct meeting	0.5 days	Fri 7/9/10	Fri 7/9/10	51	Project Manager
53	⊟ Training Track	20 days	Wed 6/23/10	Tue 7/20/10		
54	⊟ Develop Training Plan	5 days	Wed 6/23/10	Tue 6/29/10		
55	Define audience	1 day	Wed 6/23/10	Wed 6/23/10	10	Jim Stein
56	Write training objectives by audience	2 days	Thu 6/24/10	Fri 6/25/10	55	Jim Stein
57	Identify approach	1 day	Mon 6/28/10	Mon 6/28/10	56	Jim Stein
58	Identify tools and due dates	1 day	Tue 6/29/10	Tue 6/29/10	57	Jim Stein
59	Identify facilitator/gain approval, if necessary	0.5 days	Tue 6/29/10	Tue 6/29/10	57	Jim Stein
60	Develop/customize training materials	10 days	Wed 6/30/10	Tue 7/13/10	54	Jim Stein
61	Schedule training	0.5 days	Wed 6/30/10	Wed 6/30/10	54	Jim Stein
62	Conduct training	5 days	Wed 7/14/10	Tue 7/20/10	60,61	Project Team

Figure 9-1 Implementation Plan

- 34 days for the design phase (row 1).
- 30 days for the development phase (row 10).
- 48 days for the implementation phase (row 17).

➤ **Start/Finish:** Microsoft Office Project automatically calculates the start and finish dates once you enter the beginning date of the project and the duration for each task.

➤ **Predecessors:** This column shows the dependency of one task on another and allows you to identify whether one task has to occur before another can start. If you make one task a predecessor to another, Microsoft Office Project appropriately schedules the start and finish dates to ensure that the first task is completed before scheduling the second task. In Figure 9-1, row 4 has the number 3 listed in the *predecessors* column, indicating that you cannot begin mapping the business process (task 4) until you have established the foundation (task 3). In this example, Microsoft Office Project automatically set the task 4 start date *after* the completion of task 3, just as soon as I entered the number 3 in the predecessor's column in row 4.

➤ **Resource Names:** Identify the people responsible for a task.

As an alternative to using project software for the implementation plan, Figure 9-2 shows a portion of Figure 9-1 created using Microsoft Office Word. In this case think through the task dependencies and schedule the tasks using the predecessor concept.

Overview of the Three Phases of the Implementation Plan

The next few sections help you to develop an implementation plan by explaining the three phases in greater detail.

The Design Phase

The design phase tasks in Figure 9-1 or 9-2 should seem familiar because these include the roadmap steps 2–7 covered in previous chapters:

Task ID	Task Name	Duration	Time Frame
1	Design phase	34 days	April 1–May 6
2	Establish process inventory and prioritize.	5	April 1–7
3	Establish foundation.	1	April 8
4	Map business process.	5	April 9–15
5	Estimate time and cost.	3	April 16–20
6	Verify process map.	5	April 21–27
7	Apply improvement techniques.	10	April 28–May 11
8	Create internal controls.	5	May 12–18
9	Development phase	30 days	May through June
10	Develop tool 1: reference card	15	May 12–June 1
11	Develop tool 2: access database	20	May 12–June 1

Figure 9-2 Implementation Plan (Alternative)

► **Step 1:** Develop the process inventory: identifying and prioritizing the process list

► **Step 2:** Establish the foundation: identifying the scope and process boundaries

► **Step 3:** Draw the map process: flowcharting and documenting the business process

► **Step 4:** Estimate time and cost: estimating the process/cycle times and calculating the process costs

► **Step 5:** Verify the process map: validating and gaining buy-in

► **Step 6:** Apply improvement techniques: improving the business process

► **Step 7:** Create internal controls, tools, and metrics: error-proofing the process and creating measurements

The Development Phase

In this phase, identify the tools that the project team needs to create to enable the business process to work (see step 7 in the roadmap). Figure 9-1 shows that the team has to develop a reference card (row 11) and a Microsoft Access database (row 12) to support the process. The team will also determine the data elements required for the report (row 13), gains agreement from clients to verify that the report meets their needs (row 14), and then develops the report (row 15).

The *predecessors* column on row 15 tells us that the report development cannot begin until after the project team creates the database (task 12), develops the report specifications (task 13), and gains client approval (task 14).

The Implementation Phase

This phase, which covers roadmap steps 8–10, includes several different components that require further explanation.

▶ **The change management track** includes developing an impact analysis, identifying who has responsibility for each proposed change, determining the overall rollout strategy, and developing the continuous improvement plan. I discuss continuous improvement as a separate topic in Chapter 10.

▶ **The testing track** focuses on step 8 of the roadmap and includes the tasks that must happen to make sure the process works.

▶ **The communication track** includes developing the communication plan and associated communication vehicles.

▶ **The training track** includes developing the training plan, course materials, scheduling the training, securing facilitators for the training, and conducting the training.

The Four Tracks in the Implementation Phase

Now that you have an overview of the four tracks in the implementation phase, let me explain each of them in more detail.

Change Management Track (Impact Analysis)

As the project team worked to improve the business process, they undoubtedly identified changes that need to occur in the organization to obtain the expected degree of improvement.

The impact analysis provides a tool to capture the changes that must occur to ensure the success of the new business process.

Build the impact analysis by walking through the process map and identifying the required changes. Each time you recognize that a change has to occur to accomplish an activity in the process map, make a note of the necessary change in the impact analysis table, along with the rationale or reason for the change, the department or business area affected by the change, the audience affected by the change, and any expected pushback or problem with the proposed change.

Figure 9-3 provides an example of an impact analysis

Reference Number	Process Change(s) That Affect External Groups	Rationale	Area Impacted	Population/ Group Impacted	Change Management
1	<List the change that has to occur.>	<State why the change is important.>	<List the department (e.g., training) or business area (e.g., retail).>	<List the affected groups.>	<Identify the potential problems with the proposed change.>
2	Eliminate three of the approval levels required on purchases today.	Reduces cycle time by speeding up the approval process. Gets product into retail stores quicker, thus better positioning the business in a competitive environment.	Purchasing; finance	Senior buyer; purchasing manager; finance manager	Only one person in purchasing and finance will now approve buyer purchases. Because multiple levels of managers are accustomed to approving purchase orders over $10,000 today, the managers may not feel comfortable with the change.

Figure 9-3 Impact Analysis

table. In this example, the impact analysis captures only changes that affect external groups, as shown by the title of the second column, because the sponsor's concern revolved around departments outside of his or her control. You can capture all changes in an impact analysis or just those that impact external groups.

As seen in this example, the new process eliminates three approval levels, which improves the cycle time, thus getting product into stores quicker. However, purchasing and finance may not support the change because they may fear that an unwarranted purchase could be made without their approval. The change management column lists any potential pushback that you or the sponsor should address.

Sponsors appreciate the impact analysis because they often own a fair portion of the responsibility for gaining agreement on the required changes to the business process, and the impact analysis provides them with the information they need to make the changes happen.

Testing Track

I do not cover the testing track here because it is discussed in depth in Chapter 8, and you can refer to that chapter for the list of items to include in this track.

Communications Track (Communication Plan)

The third track in the implementation phase involves the communication plan. In developing this plan, think about what communication has to occur to make sure that all parties receive the appropriate information to prepare them for the change. Introducing a new business process is like introducing any other change to an organization. After defining the audience (the *who*), determine the following for each audience:

▶ The key message points (the *what*): What each audience group has to know about the change

▶ The best communication vehicles to use (the *how*): The best way to communicate with each audience

▶ The right timing for the communication (the *when*): The best time to communicate with each audience

If you have an internal communication group in your company, and you have limited experience with communications, ask whether they have a communication template that they use when introducing a new system, initiative, or benefit. Then adapt it for the business process implementation.

Figure 9-4 shows an example of a general communication plan to use when implementing new business processes. Each of the columns in the communication plan has its role to fill.

Audience

List the different category of people who need to know about the process change. Figure 9-4 lists three different audi-

Audience	Communication Goal	Key Message Points	Communication Vehicles (Method)	Due Date
Client/ customer	Feedback and support	■ What's changing linked to the client/customer needs defined in the scope definition document ■ Benefits to the client/customer ■ Timeline	Meeting; email follow-up	July 5 July 7 (email)
Stakeholders	Awareness	■ What's changing and why ■ Benefits ■ Timeline	Email	July 8
Process workers	Education	■ What's changing and why ■ Their role and responsibility ■ Training schedule ■ Contact resources for help	Meeting (live and via video conference); intranet site; network drives; process binders	July 9

Figure 9-4 Communication Plan

ences: the client/customer, the stakeholders, and the process workers.

Communication Goal

State what you hope to accomplish with each audience. Typical examples include providing awareness, gaining approval, obtaining feedback, gaining support, or educating.

In the example, the goal for the clients/customers is to gain their feedback and support for the changes, whereas the stakeholders simply need awareness of the changes, and the process workers require education on the changes so that they can support the new process.

Key Message Points

List the key points to cover for each audience. Think about different cultures that you may have to communicate with because you may need to design different messages to work for those audiences.

Notice in the example that for the clients/customers, a key message point is to connect the process changes back to what the project team defined as important to the clients/customers in the scope definition document created in step 2. Getting the key message points correct is critical to a successful implementation, so do not rush through this step. The key message points make writing the presentation or emails easier because they guide you through the creation of the communications.

Communication Vehicles

Identify the methods to use to communicate with each audience. Consider the different vehicles available, including face-to-face meetings, email, brochures, flyers, newsletters, and video conferencing. The method(s) chosen may differ because of local cultures; for example, some cultures prefer face-to-face communications.

For clients/customers, our example shows that we plan to conduct face-to-face meetings with them, along with a follow-up email to reinforce the key message points. A simple email message suffices for the stakeholders, and a video conference meeting will occur for the process workers in order to engage the geographically dispersed employees. The project team also plans to replace content that resides on the company's intranet, on network drives, and in the current process binders.

Due Date

Identify the timeline for the each communication piece. Think about who needs to know the information first, second, and third.

In our example, we wanted to communicate with the clients/customers first to gain their support before letting the stakeholders and process workers know about the new process. In this way, any changes that have to occur to the business process can happen before introducing the new process on a wide scale.

As part of the communication plan, develop responses to any anticipated concerns, in the form of a frequently asked questions list. This may seem similar to the change management column in the impact analysis, but in this case the list is much broader and has to include questions or concerns that could surface from anywhere, both within and outside the department making the changes. If the new process significantly changes the current work of any of the process workers, you should include this fact in the impact analysis so that the sponsor can assume responsibility for presenting the change to the affected employees.

The keys for successful communication include using simple language and terminology that the audience understands, as well as putting the message in the appropriate context so that the recipients of the message can relate to the key points.

Training Track (Training Plan)

The fourth track in the implementation phase entails the training plan. In developing this plan, think about what training has to occur to make sure that all parties understand and can perform their process responsibilities. Consider:

➤ Who needs training

➤ Who owns the responsibility to conduct the training

➤ What they need training on

➤ Where to conduct the training

➤ When to train

➤ What methods to use to conduct the training

Although some people use the terms *training* and *communication* interchangeably, they are two different streams of work, and anyone in the training field probably has experience with a client trying to make a communication problem a training problem. I differentiate the two terms this way:

➤ **Communication** transmits or exchanges information and messages.

➤ **Training** provides a person with the knowledge and skills to perform a task.

If you have an internal training group in your company, and you have limited experience with training, ask for its help on this part of the implementation. Tools may exist that you can use when analyzing audience needs, deciding how to deliver the training, and developing the training.

Figure 9-5 shows a general example of a training plan that you can use as a starting point for implementing any new business process. Let us look more closely at each of the columns in the training plan.

Audience

Here you list the different categories of people who require training on the process change.

You may notice that we omitted the stakeholders from the training plan in Figure 9-5, although we included them in

Audience	Learning Objectives	Approach	Tools	Facilitator	Due Date
Client/ customer	■ *Run* the newly designed report.	Meeting	Reference card	Sponsor, project manager	July 16
Process workers	■ *Identify* the five steps in the business process. ■ *Explain* how to handle an exception to the business process. ■ *Complete* the <name> template.	Instructor-led training session	■ Process documentation ■ Job aids ■ Personal computers with access to email	Project team member	July 12–15

Figure 9-5 Training Plan

the communication plan because our only priority with this group is awareness. We do not have to train them on anything.

Learning Objectives

State the learning (or training) objectives in this column, or what the audience will learn as a result of the training. In our example, the project team plans to train the client/customer on how to run a new report and train the process workers on multiple items. If we had different groups of employees with different training needs, we could have added additional rows in the training plan to identify the learning objectives and approach for each group of learners.

Although developing learning objectives falls into an entire field of study called "instructional system design," I share the relevant highlights to support what needs to occur in this step.

Notice in Figure 9-5 that each learning objective starts with an action verb: *run, identify, explain, complete.* An action verb denotes the ability to do something. What should a person be able to do after completing training? In business process work, you generally want a person to either:

▶ Know something.

▶ Absorb or grasp something.

▶ Apply something.

Each of these three action verbs denotes a different level of cognition with *know* at the lowest level, *absorb* at a higher level, and *apply* at an even higher level. Figure 9-6 summarizes how these action verbs relate to one other.

The *know–absorb–apply* example demonstrates a hierarchy that exists where the person attending training achieves a

Action Verb	General Description	Learning Objectives	Example
Know	If people can identify or define something, they have proved that they *know* something.	■ *Identify* the five steps in the business process.	If people can state the five steps, then they obviously *know* them.
Absorb	If people can explain or summarize something, they have proved that they *absorbed,* or grasped, something because they can translate the concept into their own words.	■ *Explain* how to handle an exception to the business process.	If an employee can explain how to handle exceptions, then they *absorbed*, grasped, or comprehended the concepts presented in the training. The ability to explain constitutes a higher level of knowledge than simply identifying the five steps because you need to know the five steps before you can identify an exception.
Apply	If people can complete or demonstrate something, they have proved that they can *apply* what they learned.	■ *Complete* the <name> template.	If people can successfully complete the template, then they *applied* what they learned. The ability to apply constitutes an even higher level than either identifying or explaining, because people can perform a task as a result of the training.

Figure 9-6 Levels of Learning Objectives

higher level of competence as they move up in the hierarchy. Figure 9-7 shows another way to depict the hierarchy of learning. In this figure first you *know*, then you *absorb*, and finally you *apply*. When you write objectives, try to reach the *apply* level so that employees demonstrate their knowledge. Confucius said, "What I hear I forget, what I see I remember, but what I do, I understand."

Avoid using verbs that do not support the ability to observe a result, for example, *understand*. How can you tell if people understand something because the process of comprehension is an internal mental process? Unless they can define, identify, explain, or demonstrate their understanding, you do not know if they truly understand.

To continue explaining the columns in Figure 9-5, the remaining columns include:

Approach

Identify how you plan to deliver the training. Will you conduct face-to-face training, Web-based training, self-directed training, or something else?

Tools

List the training tools required to deliver the training. These should include the process documentation, but define

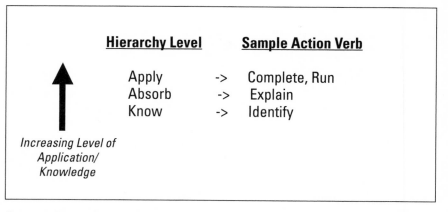

Figure 9-7 Training Objectives Hierarchy

what other tools you require. For example, do you need personal computers so that the people attending the training can access your company's intranet and email system, or do you require a wireless connection?

Facilitator

Identify who will deliver the training to each audience. You, a project team member, or your sponsor may own a portion of this responsibility.

Due Date

Identify the timeline for the training and think about who needs the training first, second, and third, similar to the way we thought about the order in the communication plan. In our example, we trained the employees first so that they could support the clients/customers when they had questions running the report.

The keys for successful training include developing good learning objectives that articulate what the participants should know at the end of training, matching delivery styles with learner preferences, and delivering the training at the right time.

Chapter Summary: Step 9

Planning the entire business process improvement endeavor up front, by creating the implementation plan, will give you confidence that you have the right steps and the right people in place to improve the business process and implement the changes required to bring it to fruition. The implementation plan is the framework that brings the separate components together, and Figure 9-8 shows a summary of the implementation plan components.

The new topics introduced in this chapter include the:

➤ *Impact analysis* that identifies the changes that have to occur, the rationale for the changes, the area and population impacted, and potential pushback.

```
┌─────────────┐
│ 3 phases:   │
└─────────────┘

1. Design
2. Development
3. Implementation
```

```
┌─────────────┐
│ 4 tracks:   │
└─────────────┘

1. Change management: Impact analysis
2. Testing: Testing plan
3. Communication: Communication plan
4. Training: Training plan
```

Figure 9-8 Implementation Plan Components

▶ *Communication plan* that identifies who needs to know what about the new process.

▶ *Training plan* that tells who needs training on what.

If you leave one of these components out of the implementation plan, you risk decreased productivity caused by confusion or anxiety, as well as the inability to deliver client/customer satisfaction. Spend the time at the beginning of the work developing the implementation plan and continually adapt it as the work progresses.

Time Estimate

To plan the time that it takes to work through this step, Figure 9-9 summarizes the time you should allow to complete the implementation plan and its components (step 9).

Develop the Implementation Plan

Develop the details for each of the implementation phases, determine how long each task will take, identify the responsible person, and sequence the tasks. Developing the plan goes faster if you have the project team help develop the separate components of the overall plan. For example, have one per-

Event	Time	Purpose
Develop the implementation plan.	5 days	■ To make sure that you understand the individual tasks that have to occur to address the business process
Develop the impact analysis.	5 days	■ To identify the changes that have to occur to implement the new business process
Develop the communication plan.	1 day	■ To identify who has to know about the process changes, what they need to know, and when and how you will communicate with them
Develop the training plan.	3 days	■ To identify who requires training on the new process, who will deliver the training, where you will deliver the training, when you will deliver the training, and how you will deliver the training
Gain sponsor buy-in.	1 day	■ Ensure that the sponsor agrees with the components of the implementation

Figure 9-9 Time-Estimate—Step 9: Implement the Change

son work on communications, another on training, and another on testing.

Develop the Impact Analysis

This can take quite some time to develop, and it helps to write a draft, take a break, and revisit it again. Do not rush developing the impact analysis because it can have a significant effect on the success of the implementation of the new business process.

Develop the Communication Plan

During this time, develop the audience profile, using the matrix introduced earlier in the chapter that identifies the audience for the communication, what they need to know, and when they need to know the information.

Develop the Training Plan

Develop the detailed training plan and spend sufficient time writing the learning objectives. If you have no experience writing learning objectives, try to find someone, if possible, with a training background to validate them.

Gain Sponsor Buy-in

Once you have completed the implementation plan, review it with the sponsor and make adjustments to either the content or the timeline. In my experience, the timeline generally needs adjustments because the sponsor wants to have the work done sooner than you estimate.

What You Have Achieved

In this chapter you have achieved the following:

➤ An understanding of the tasks required to implement the new business process

➤ Insight into how to use phases and tracks to organize implementation tasks

➤ An analysis of the changes that need to occur

➤ A grasp of how to develop a communication plan that provides details surrounding who needs to know about the changes and what they need to know

➤ A plan to train those affected by the change

➤ A tool to help you stay on track

➤ Most important, the *power* to have a successful implementation

CHAPTER 10

Step 10: Drive Continuous Improvement

Embracing the New Mindset

Joanne Wu, the training and development manager from Chapter 8, led the effort each year to create the annual budget for the training department, which required her to gather the training requirements for the next year from client groups, determine priorities, and allocate the department's resources to address the forecasted training needs. Joanne found the time required to conduct this annual process excessive, just as in every prior year. Only about 40 percent of the projects specified in the plan ever happened. Joanne felt her clients requested unnecessary projects, which did not allow her to plan her department's resources or budget as tightly as she would like.

My first observation was that Joanne viewed the annual plan as an end in itself, not as an ongoing process. Although Joanne's team had streamlined the process of collecting input, she still did not like the result; so she asked me to evaluate the process and help make additional changes to improve the process. An analysis of the situation showed me that Joanne's staff spent most of their time focusing on the process efficiency, streamlining it so that their clients would find it simple. Although they did make the process easier for the clients, they overlooked the effectiveness aspect because the process could not adapt to changing business needs. Because the clients could not always foresee issues that might surface during the year, like new competitive products or a changing economy, the business process had to include flexibility so that it could address new needs as they surfaced throughout the year.

Continuous improvement, a term derived from the total quality movement, means monitoring a business process and making adjustments to it so that it continually improves over time. Developing a continuous improvement mindset ensures that the process continues to deliver the gains achieved. This means continually measuring the business process, regularly re-evaluating client/customer needs and expectations, engaging the process workers on a regular basis, and not allowing the documentation to sit on the shelf.

Although you may consider skipping over this chapter because it sounds like more theory than practicality, I urge you to reconsider because this step enables you to sustain the effectiveness, efficiency, and adaptability introduced into the business process. If you decide to skip this step, you will find that the business process works fine for a while. Then it starts slipping backward a little, then a little more, until eventually it becomes outdated, and you have to start the improvement effort all over again. Think about losing weight. If you successfully lose 20 pounds but never weigh yourself, you will probably start regaining the pounds—perhaps not overnight, but gradually until you find yourself back at your original weight or higher.

The same scenario applies to business processes for a variety of reasons. You have to stay on top of your business processes in order to stay competitive, to continue meeting the changing client/customer needs, or to keep pace with changing technology. Change and external factors demand that you continuously improve business processes.

Even business processes that went through reengineering in the 1990s required a focus on continuous improvement to retain the strategic gains made. During the reengineering rage, though, continuous improvement did not enter many people's minds, probably because it stems from the total quality management field. Proponents of reengineering dismissed total quality management as too slow because total quality techniques delivered incremental, not dramatic change. Some people incorrectly theorized that when you reengineered a business process, it would remain competitive.

Continuous improvement requires the mindset that improvement never ends and that you may never achieve perfection. Practitioners of yoga or followers of Buddhism strive to reach nirvana with the full knowledge that, at best, they may only become more serene and self-disciplined. Just as you set goals to fulfill your personal vision, set goals also to sustain the improvements made to a business process.

As you follow the 10 steps to business process improvement, you acquire a unique level of understanding about the business process, which positions you to act in the role of innovator, influencer, and communicator. You can then:

► Demonstrate innovation by continually identifying new ways to improve the business process.

► Influence others to continuously think about their work from a process perspective.

► Continue to talk and communicate with the clients/customers, stakeholders, and process workers to make sure the process continues to deliver what they require.

So let me share a model that will help you think about continuous improvement and some tools that can help. Because continuous improvement can seem like an obscure concept, the model and tools assist in keeping this step at the forefront and in perspective.

The Continuous Improvement Cycle

The continuous improvement cycle wheel in Figure 10-1 shows four phases that can help you achieve the new mindset. Each phase in the wheel provides a degree of structure to keep you thinking about how to continually improve a business process. You can move through the four phases quickly, but do so often. The four phases are:

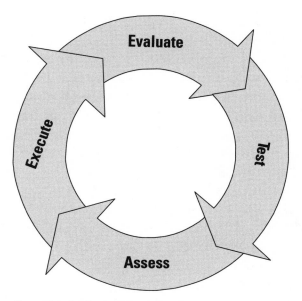

Figure 10-1 Continuous Improvement Cycle

1. *Evaluate:* Determine the opportunities.
2. *Test:* Make the change and try it out on a limited basis.
3. *Assess:* Determine whether the change worked.
4. *Execute:* Deploy the change on a wide scale.

Evaluate

In this phase of continuous improvement, examine all aspects of the business process to identify opportunities for improvement. To accomplish this you have to understand the expectations for the business process. Start by asking a few questions. Does the process continue to deliver the effectiveness, efficiency, and adaptability intended? What bottlenecks exist? Have client/customer needs changed?

To answer these questions, go back and review the client/customer needs defined when the project team created the scope definition document in Chapter 3. Review their needs and expectations to see if the business process still delivers against them. Also look at the measurements of success defined in the scope definition document and the metrics established in Chapter 7 to see how the process has performed over time against the baseline and goals.

You should spend the majority of your time in the evaluate phase of the continuous improvement cycle. How frequently you revisit this phase depends on how often the business uses the process. If it is an ongoing process used daily, go through this phase more frequently, but if it is a cyclical process used annually or semiannually, go through this phase less often. The continuous improvement schedule (discussed later in this chapter) provides a tool to set a timeline for how often to go through this phase for each business process.

This first phase of the continuous improvement cycle requires you to ask yourself several questions:

- ► Does the process deliver what the project team identified as client/customer needs? Clients have a way of raising the bar over time because, as the process meets their expectations, they tend to expect a new level of service. They may not be explicit about their expectations, so stay focused on how the clients/customers feel about the business process. To stay on top of their expectations, revisit the client/customer needs and measurements of success over and over again. Make sure that you do the right things well, and stay fresh and connected to any new expectations. As Joanne Wu learned, client needs do not stay static but change as the business changes. Joanne needed increased flexibility in her budget to accommodate changing business needs.

- ► Do the process workers follow the documented process? Keep the documentation up-to-date, make sure that employees use the documentation and tools created, and see that new employees receive training on the business process. Problems can easily occur simply because no one thoroughly trains new employees.

- ► Do the stakeholders receive what they require from the business process? Although the client/customer is our primary focus, do not ignore the stakeholders. Review the scope definition document, and validate that the process continues to meet their requirements.

> ▶ Do any identified third parties deliver what they said they would deliver? Make sure that any vendors or suppliers follow through on their commitments.

Thinking about the client/customer, process workers, stakeholders, and vendors/suppliers makes it easier to regularly evaluate the effectiveness, efficiency, and adaptability of a business process.

In step 7 the project team developed metrics and established the baseline. Evaluating these metrics becomes one of the most important components of the *evaluate* phase because it immediately highlights a problem. As you collect the quantitative and qualitative data, evaluate the performance of the business process against the metrics and identify any trends. Plot the data and compare it to your baseline data.

As an example of the need for evaluation, recall Pete Hodges, the regional sales manager from Chapter 7, who cared about the number of new customers. The metric we established said that Pete wanted a "30 percent increase in the number of qualified new customers over the next six months." To track the number of new customers, Pete used the table in Figure 10-2, where he captured the:

> ▶ Number of leads generated (supplied by the marketing department)

Evaluation Criteria	1st Quarter	2nd Quarter	3rd Quarter	4th Quarter
Number of leads generated	250	400	450	
Number of customer calls	100	150	250	
Number of qualified leads	50	75	100	
Number of new customers	25	45	50	
Ratio of qualified leads to new customers	2:1	5:3	2:1	
Percentage of qualified leads converted to new customers	50%	60%	50%	
Percentage increase of qualified new customers		80%	11%	

Figure 10-2   Sales Metrics: Percentage Increase in New Qualified Customers

▶ Number of customer calls (the number of leads that sales representatives followed up)

▶ Number of qualified leads (the number of leads that fell within the sales department's definition of "qualified," ones that the sales representatives would call on)

▶ Number of new customers (the number of new accounts closed)

▶ Ratio of qualified leads to new customers

▶ Percentage of qualified leads converted to new customers

▶ Percentage increase of qualified new customers

According to Figure 10-2, something seems to have happened between the second and third quarters because the *percentage of qualified leads converted to new customers* dropped by 10 percent (from 60 percent to 50 percent), although the total increase of qualified new customers increased by 11 percent. Pete was happy with the second quarter results, which exceeded his expectations, but not with the third quarter results because they fell below his 30 percent criteria.

At this point, Pete came to me wanting to dig deeper into the decrease in the ratio between the second and third quarters. I tried to determine the cause for the drop, and we set new goals for the next measurement period. Pete had to reach a number equal to or greater than the second quarter to get at least back up to the 60 percent conversion rate. This would put him back on track to achieve his overall target of a 30 percent increase in the number of qualified new customers over a six-month period. With two months behind him, he was averaging a 45.5 percent increase, which looked good, but he knew that he had to focus on the monthly statistics to ensure meeting his 30 percent target.

After assessing how the sales representatives performed their day-to-day responsibilities, it appeared the problem rested with a dozen new sales representatives who did not follow the guidelines established for qualifying leads. As a result, Pete did not have to introduce any new steps in the process; he simply had to make certain that the new sales representatives received the appropriate training on how to qualify sales leads. Pete added this training to the onboarding process to help new sales representatives in the future.

In Joanne Wu's case, we designed flexibility into her annual budgeting process to accommodate new client expectations, technology improvements, or changing business priorities. We changed the process so that Joanne's staff captured only a handful of initiatives for the next year, ones that clearly supported the company's stated priorities and that would not change. We introduced changes to allow Joanne and her staff to regularly evaluate incoming requests. Having a half dozen identified projects gave Joanne at least some sense of control and yet gave her clients the flexibility they wanted.

During the evaluation phase, look at the process itself and confirm that everyone follows the process, uses the tools as planned, and gathers the metrics as defined. This includes items like:

► Determining the effectiveness of the internal controls put in place: Do they help in eliminating errors?

► Talking to the clients/customers and stakeholders to assess how they feel about the effectiveness of the process: This provides qualitative feedback instead of numbers, and both qualitative and quantitative data aid in determining the effectiveness of the process.

► Evaluating the roles and responsibilities and making changes if appropriate.

► Making sure that the organization trains new employees.

► Evaluating the effectiveness of any communication processes.

► Making sure employees share information and knowledge.

► Making sure that vendors or suppliers deliver what the process expects.

After conducting some analysis and talking to the appropriate people, propose any needed changes, either to the business process itself, to client/customer needs, to the measurements of success, or to the process metrics.

By the end of this phase, you have identified the points in the process that present improvement opportunities and have created a plan of action to focus on them.

Test

Once you have identified a problem or opportunity, made the process changes, and established an improvement goal, implement the change on a small scale to validate that the change(s) work. In this phase of continuous improvement, you want to make certain that any changes work before introducing them on a wide scale.

This task should seem familiar since Chapter 8 covered testing in detail. You can use many of the same techniques from that chapter here, just on a smaller scale. Remember to think about the who, what, where, when, and how of testing the change:

➤ **Whom** to involve in the test

➤ **What** items to test

➤ **Where** the test should occur

➤ **When** the test should occur

➤ **How** to measure the success of the change

During the second phase of the continuous improvement cycle, plan how to test the change. Identify who will participate, what part of the business process to test, what location or area to include in the test, how long the test will run, how to collect and analyze the data, and how to define success. Include the process owner or sponsor to make sure that you have the appropriate support.

Testing in the continuous improvement phase should be on a smaller scale than what we covered in Chapter 8, so involve a smaller number of participants and test items in the testing. A good example of the extent of testing is the follow-up on the bank merger from Chapter 9, where we merged the business processes from two banks into one after an acquisition. In this example, the merger of two highly visible areas, private banking and investment banking, worked fine because the merger team placed significant effort on making their transition seamless. However, after evaluating the new process three months later as part of our continuous improvement plan, problems surfaced at the retail banking sector with their level of customer service and increased operating expenses. This sector had not received as much attention during the merger, and so the retail team made adjustments to their business processes. In deciding where to test the changes, the project team decided to test them with one branch before implementing the changes at all branches.

Depending on what you uncover in the evaluate phase of continuous improvement, you may not always have to test because in some cases employees simply require training, as in the Pete Hodges case, or the project team may simply make adjustments to the measurement data. At other times, though, as in the retail banking example, the project team makes significant changes and you have to test those changes before implementing them on a wide scale. If you find yourself making major changes, revisit Chapter 8 and create a test plan.

It often helps to look first at the process workers if a problem in the measurement data surfaces because you will find it easier to retrain employees on the process or tools than to change the process. Understand why employees perform the way they do, and make sure to differentiate between an employee and a process issue.

At the end of this phase, you have data that tells whether the proposed changes to the business process work.

Assess

In this phase of continuous improvement, keep track of how the changes work as you implement the change on a small scale to understand what has to occur to introduce the change on a wider scale. Did the change deliver the value expected? What other criteria should you consider?

In this phase, review the data collected during the testing phase, make any adjustments deemed appropriate, and decide whether to proceed with the changes. You may also want to bring in benchmark data to help you form an opinion on what changes to introduce.

Benchmarking consists of measuring a business process against a standard of excellence, either an internal group in your company or an external company well-known as being of world-class or best-in-class caliber. For example, Disney is known for delivering outstanding guest service, Toyota for its high-quality cars, and Apple for its innovative designs. Benchmark data can help introduce greater effectiveness, efficiency, and flexibility into your business processes so that they can be adapted to changing needs. Chapter 12 includes a real-life example of a benchmarking study.

Gathering external benchmark data can present a problem because some companies do not like to share information about their business processes. Not all external companies present a problem, though, particularly if they belong to a different industry and do not compete in the same market as your company. Internal benchmarking can be just as effective as external benchmarking, and it may seem easier because you do not have to worry about confidentiality.

If you choose to proceed with benchmarking, work with a colleague who has designed a benchmark study in the past because conducting an effective benchmark study requires experience. Spend enough time planning the benchmark study, and have a solid understanding of your own business process before talking to other people about their processes.

To conduct a benchmark, start with the client/customer needs identified in the scope definition document and prioritize them so that your benchmarking study focuses on the most important client/customer needs. Joanne Wu, the training and development manager introduced earlier in this chapter, identified "quality training experience" as one of her client's top needs.

Start a benchmark study by conducting internal interviews because these assist in defining terminology and in developing a list of external companies and internal groups to benchmark. As you conduct the internal interviews, ask the interviewee to define terms. In Joanne's case, for example, I had to find out what a *quality training experience* meant. By talking to Joanne's clients, I found that they wanted their employees who attended training to apply what they learned on the job upon their return, and they wanted their employees to have reference materials that they could use on the job. The clients also wanted only experienced instructors teaching classes. Once you understand what a term means, ask the interviewee to identify best-in-class companies or internal groups who demonstrate excellence in the type of client/customer need being discussed. For example, I asked Joanne's clients if they knew of any companies or internal groups that delivered a quality training experience.

As this example shows, the internal clients interviewed can help you develop a clear list of client/customer needs and build the list of companies to benchmark because they know their field and they know the best-in-class companies. Once you identify the benchmark list, comprised of both internal and external contacts, develop a set of questions that focus on the business processes' critical success factors. The questions should delve into how the benchmark companies or internal groups achieve the critical success factors.

The project team can also use benchmarking during the evaluate phase of the continuous improvement cycle and during step 6 (when looking at improving the business process) to help determine how the business process compares to best-in-class companies, which in turn can help establish improvement goals.

At the end of this phase, you have all the information necessary to make a decision on how to proceed.

Execute

After assessing the success of the changes to the business process and perhaps comparing the process to other internal groups or external companies, in this phase of continuous improvement you deploy the updated business process across the organization.

This phase should seem similar to the implementation step discussed in Chapter 9, but on a smaller scale. In this phase, communicate the change and train the process workers on the change. Although you do not have to recreate a communication plan or a training plan, you should create a new impact analysis.

The same audience defined in the original communication plan has to know about the process changes if the changes affect them. You can probably use the same goal, key message points, and preferred communication vehicles defined in the plan.

The training plan will have a reduced number of learning objectives and perhaps a different, simpler approach, but the audience probably remains the same.

Create a new impact analysis any time a change occurs because it ensures that nothing falls through the cracks. Always engage the sponsor in introducing the proposed changes.

At the end of this phase, you have introduced the business process change(s) to the organization.

Continuous Improvement Plan

Although continuous improvement introduces many new points to remember, the continuous improvement plan assists you in developing a continuous improvement mindset. The plan summarizes the activities necessary to maintain a focus on the business process and outlines how frequently to perform each activity, any sources of data used, the technique or method used, and who performs the activity.

Before leaving the business process you just worked on and moving to the next one, create a continuous improvement plan for the existing process so that everyone can see the tasks required to keep the process alive and adaptable to the changing business climate. Figure 10-3 shows a sample plan for Joanne Wu's training department. Use this template as a starting point to create a plan for your own business process. The activities listed in Figure 10-3 remain fairly consistent for any business process because they represent the components of the foundation established in Chapter 3 or the process map created in Chapter 4. Make sure to include these activities in your continuous improvement plan:

Activity	Frequency	Data Source	Method	Person Responsible
Review measurement data	Monthly	Weekly activity reports	Observation; conversation	Training manager
Revisit client/ customer needs	Quarterly	Scope definition document	Conversation (phone call)	Director, training and development
Test internal controls	Monthly	Process map and internal control checklist	Observation; conversation	Training manager
Validate process workers follow process	Quarterly	Process map	Observation; conversation	Training manager
Revisit stakeholder needs	Semiannual	Scope definition document	Conversation (phone call)	Director, training and development
Evaluate third-party performance	Annual	Process map	Phone call	Training manager

Figure 10-3 Continuous Improvement Plan

▶ **Review measurement data:** Review what the project team identified as measurements of success in Chapter 3 and how you decided to measure those items in Chapter 7.

▶ **Revisit client/customer needs:** Look at the expectations identified by the clients/customers in Chapter 3.

▶ **Test internal controls:** Review the process map created in Chapter 4, looking for the internal control icon and reviewing how the project team stated the business would overcome the potential problems in the internal control checklist.

▶ **Validate process workers:** Go through the process map and validate that the employees involved in the process follow the steps outlined.

▶ **Revisit stakeholder needs:** Look at the expectations identified in Chapter 3.

▶ **Evaluate third-party vendors/suppliers:** Go through the process map and validate that the vendors or suppliers are delivering what the process specifies.

If you customized the scope definition document and added additional sections, include them in the activity column in the continuous improvement plan.

Over time, as you improve multiple business processes, keeping track of all your business processes becomes more difficult. As the inventory of improved business processes increases, create one continuous improvement *schedule* that covers all the business processes to keep track of the various activity. Translate the frequencies, from Figure 10-3, to actual dates so that the business has an annual schedule to follow.

Figure 10-4 shows an example of a schedule with the activities from Figure 10-3 now listed horizontally as columns. This allows you to list the business processes vertically down the left-hand column, which provides a summary of all business processes in one continuous improvement schedule. Figure 10-4 shows a continuous improvement schedule for part of a recruitment department's hiring processes. Notice how the table lists the requisition, sourcing, and orientation business processes down the left-hand column.

You can see how much easier it gets to manage multiple business processes by having this snapshot because you can quickly see what the business has to focus on at any point in

Business Process	Review Measurement Data	Test Internal Controls	Revisit Customer/ Client Needs	Validate Process Workers	Revisit Stakeholder Needs	Evaluate Third Parties
Requisition	1st of month	1st of month	Q1–3/1 Q2–6/1 Q3–9/1 Q4–12/1	Q1–3/1 Q2–6/1 Q3–9/1 Q4–12/1	5/1 11/1	January
Sourcing	15th of month	15th of month	Q1–3/15 Q2–6/15 Q3–9/15 Q4–12/15	Q1–3/15 Q2–6/15 Q3–9/15 Q4–12/15	5/15 11/15	April
Orientation	30th of month	30th of month	Q1–3/30 Q2–6/30 Q3–9/30 Q4–12/30	Q1–3/30 Q2–6/30 Q3–9/30 Q4–12/30	5/30 11/30	August

Figure 10-4 Continuous Improvement Schedule

time. In this example, the business decided to look at the metrics for the requisition process on the first of each month, sourcing on the fifteenth, and orientation on the thirtieth. Figure 10-4 also demonstrates that the business wants to review the measurement data and test internal controls the most frequently (monthly) and the third-party performance the least frequently (annually).

In developing the continuous improvement plan, the project team identified how often to evaluate each activity, but, after creating the combined schedule, you may decide to reduce some of the frequencies because it may seem overwhelming. Continue to develop the continuous improvement plan for each business process even if you create a continuous improvement schedule because the plan provides additional data that the business requires to conduct the appropriate evaluations.

Chapter Summary: Step 10

The continuous improvement cycle confirms that the business process continually delivers effectiveness, efficiency, and flexibility to the organization. The four phases (evaluate, test, assess, and execute) provide the necessary structure. You can move through the four phases quickly, but do so often. Let the frequency of how often the business uses a business process drive the continuous improvement schedule. During continuous improvement, spend the majority of your time in the evaluate phase because improvement opportunities surface in this phase.

Throughout continuous improvement, you will find yourself using some of the tools created during previous steps, like the scope definition document from step 2 or the communication, training, and impact analysis plans from step 9. Continually evaluate the information defined in the scope definition document because it helps to keep the business process aligned with the changing business needs.

Benchmarking can influence how to approach a business process and assist you in thinking about different goals. Focus any benchmarking effort on the most important client/customer needs, use internal and external parties in the benchmarking, and use data available in research studies as part of the analysis. Identify how best-in-class companies deliver against your client/ customer needs.

The continuous improvement *plan* lays the foundation for verifying that the business process remains relevant and adapts to changing business needs. Combining all your business processes into one continuous improvement *schedule* provides a tool to better manage the work throughout the year.

Time Estimate

To plan the time that it takes to work through this step, Figure 10-5 summarizes the time to allocate to this step.

Develop the Continuous Improvement Plan and Schedule

Outline the details for the steps to follow in the evaluate phase of the continuous improvement cycle. Identify how frequently to conduct each item in the plan, where the data comes from, the persons responsible for the items, and how they will handle them. Implementing the plan goes faster if you include the people identified as the responsible parties in the overall planning. Creating the plan takes only an hour or two, but gain-

Event	Time	Purpose
Develop continuous improvement plan (evaluate phase); create or add to schedule	3 days	■ To put a focus on ongoing improvement and to confirm that everyone involved understands their responsibility ■ To either start a continuous improvement schedule or add the newly completed process to the existing schedule
Gain sponsor buy-in	1 hour	■ Make certain that the sponsor agrees with the components of the plan
Test/assess/execute	Varies	■ To validate that the proposed changes work before introducing them on a wide scale

Figure 10-5 Time Estimate—Step 10: Drive Continuous Improvement

ing other people's support adds to the time it takes to complete this step. Also develop the continuous improvement schedule during this time, or add the newly improved business process to the existing schedule and make any adjustments.

Gain Sponsor Buy-In

Once you complete the continuous improvement plan, review it with the sponsor and adjust the tasks as necessary. If you created a continuous improvement schedule, show the sponsor how the newest business process fits into the overall schedule. You may need the sponsor to gain the agreement from executive-level persons if you list them as responsible for any action items in the plan.

Test, Assess, Execute

During these phases, you or a project team member makes the decision on how to test the changes on a small scale, evaluate the effectiveness of the proposed changes, and then implement them on a full scale.

What You Have Achieved

In this chapter you have achieved the following:

➤ An understanding of what continuous improvement means and why you should care

➤ Details about how to keep adapting the business process to changing business needs

➤ A plan that includes the appropriate steps to regularly review the business process

➤ A schedule that provides a snapshot of when to evaluate multiple business processes so that you can manage a group of business processes

➤ Most important, the *power* to sustain the improvements

CHAPTER 11

Create the Executive Summary

Getting the Recognition

After all the work you have gone through with each step of the roadmap, now is your time to get some well-deserved recognition. Do not relax yet, but rather help management recognize what you have accomplished. Recognition for improving a business process does not come as easy as getting a compliment on a new haircut or a new suit because the new process may not immediately stand out. You have to let management know, in an acceptable way, the work you have done, and that becomes the challenge. This chapter shows how you gain recognition in a professional way by summarizing your business process work in an executive summary, a package that management will find useful.

Executive summaries always seem to differ and I do not recall any two that looked exactly alike. Every executive summary I completed for the scenarios presented throughout this book has a different look because each has its own unique circumstances. My executive summaries have ranged from two to ten pages, but there is no standard, so feel free to create what seems right for your particular situation.

The most important point when writing an executive summary is to make certain that it addresses what the sponsor cares about, so tailor the summary to address those known concerns. For example, let me summarize the chief concerns of the people discussed so far:

➤ Stuart Wang, the compensation director, wanted to understand the labor requirements to support the business processes that his team delivered and how to sustain the improvements that the project team achieved.

▶ Joanne Wu, the training and development manager, cared about adequately planning her resources.

▶ Kendall Smith, the senior vice president of human resources, cared about anything that impacted bringing new employees on board, which meant that his initial interest lay with the training process.

▶ Wendy Chan, manager of workforce analysis, wanted accurate head count reporting for the entire company to use.

The executive summary is usually one part of a larger document, like a business plan, and most busy executives read only that section. In business process work, the executive summary provides a high-level overview of the entire project. Write the summary in a clear and concise manner, but provide sufficient detail of the completed work; then provide additional information in an appendix, as needed. When writing the executive summary, remember that not every reader has the same degree of familiarity with the topic as you and the project team, so write with the novice reader in mind.

The Six Sections of the Executive Summary

Always start the executive summary with an intriguing or compelling statement that grabs the reader's attention, and remember to include the following sections:

▶ Project focus
▶ Goals
▶ Summary
▶ Key findings
▶ Deliverables
▶ Appendix (if applicable)

Let us walk through an explanation of each section of the executive summary and provide some examples.

Section 1: Project Focus

Start the executive summary with a story about the current predicament that illustrates the problems that caused you to take on the work. I use *project focus* instead of problem statement, because the word *focus* is more positive than *problem*, putting the reader in a more positive mindset. Include information in the project focus that shows the business need that drove the analysis; for example, did the work result from a reorganization, the formation of a new business, an increase in errors, or another reason? The following four examples illustrate several different project focus statements, one for each of the three themes just described, plus one for the recognition bonus award process:

EXAMPLE 1: A REORGANIZATION

The fall 2009 reorganization of the home improvement segment caused the human resources organization to realign its support network. Departments no longer have responsibility for employees at a single geographic location, but now have employees who reside in multiple worldwide locations.

The sales and marketing department executives, for example, now have employees that reside in multiple countries and . . .

EXAMPLE 2: A NEW BUSINESS

The project focused on developing the recruitment process that the new Los Angeles division will use to hire their storefront employees. We expect a high volume of candidates to apply for a limited number of jobs. Due to the expected volumes, the project team paid close attention to the timing of each activity in the process.

The team also kept in mind the local . . .

EXAMPLE 3: ERROR REDUCTION

Transactions that cause a change to employee data usually involve multiple departments, and, as a result, handoffs between departments become critical. Over the last 18 months, we have noticed a lack of integration between the departments, causing ineffective handoffs, increased errors, and ultimately inefficient business processes.

Although each department does a thorough job at their individual responsibilities . . .

EXAMPLE 4: RECOGNITION BONUS AWARD PROCESS

Managers have increasingly complained about the turnaround time associated with providing their employees with recognition bonus awards. As the company faces increasing competition in the labor market, the compensation department wanted to streamline the business process and make it easier for managers to give employees a bonus award as part of the company's retention strategy.

The project team focused its work on reducing the overall time required to process a bonus award, which now averages 11 days. The . . .

The intent of these opening paragraphs is to enable the reader to instantly understand why the project team focused on these specific business processes. Provide enough detail so that you paint the picture of the current situation from the reader's perspective rather than from your own. Often when we write emails or memos, it is natural to include everything we know about a subject, believing that everything is important and losing sight that most readers care only about a quarter of the information provided. Make an effort to keep the project focus simple, and give readers only what they want to know. They should grasp the issue and want to read further.

In the previous four examples, the reader cares that:

▶ The human resources organization is proactively supporting the company's reorganization.

▶ The recruitment department is concerned with staffing a new location.

▶ Management is focusing on integration among departments to make sure that the process runs smoothly.

▶ Compensation is concerned with retaining employees in competitive times.

From reading the project focus alone, the reader either continues reading the remainder of the executive summary or loses interest and decides to stop. The more engaging this section, the more likely it is that the reader will continue reading.

Section 2: Goals

The project goals become the second part of the executive summary. Think of a goal as an objective or the purpose of your work. When listing the goals of the project, revisit the scope definition document you created and review what the client/customer and stakeholders told you they wanted from the process. Then look at the measurements of success that you defined. This information assists you in articulating the goals to include in this section. Simply state the goals in bulleted fashion and keep them short. For example:

► Provide executives with up-to-date budget balances.

► Develop a common understanding of the end-to-end business process.

► Balance client/customer needs of the learning environment with prevailing technologies.

If you feel that you have to provide additional detail, write the information as a subset of the main point. For the first example, it might read:

PROVIDE EXECUTIVES WITH UP-TO-DATE BUDGET BALANCES:
Make certain that executives can see the dollar amounts that they have already spent on a compensation program, the amount of money they have planned for the next quarter, and the remaining balance that they have to spend.

If you worked on multiple business processes, you might identify general goals, not specific ones targeted at a business process. In this case, the goal section of the executive summary may start with a statement like:

The goals of the process work are to ensure that the business processes:
■ Provide our clients/customers with an effective process.
■ Deliver efficiency to the operation.
■ Integrate with our key stakeholders.
■ Drive consistency across the business groups.

- Have the appropriate internal controls.
- Reflect the future direction.

Section 3: Summary

The summary should tell the story of your journey. You can think of this third section of the executive summary as an executive summary within the executive summary. I find that executives generally spend their time reading the project focus and the summary sections, skimming over goals and deliverables. As a result, devote sufficient time to this section.

If your work included a cross-functional group of employees, identify the project team members to show the integration between departments, a point that management will appreciate. Link what you write in this section to the goals identified in the prior section, and include various analytical results to give the reader a few concrete statistics to identify with, like a labor summary or information from the impact analysis or implementation. A few examples of different ways to include statistical information in an executive summary might help you better understand what I mean.

Example 1

An executive I worked with at a consumer products company accepted responsibility for a new department and he did not have familiarity with the new group's work. While the new department was located in California, Jim resided in New Jersey, so he rarely had occasion to interact with them face-to-face. He wanted to understand the details of their work, if the department had the right number of employees, and if he should change any reporting relationships.

With Jim's goals defined, I worked with the employees in the personnel administrative services group over six weeks to better understand what they did. I started by identifying the business processes that the department owned, and then identified the process activities and timing involved. I used the simple process map template that I presented in Chapter 4, repeated here in Figure 11-1, as a tool to capture my discussions with employees.

When talking to employees one on one, I do not enlarge the template, as I would when I work with project teams, or draw the process map on a dry-erase board because that seems too formal and perhaps threatening. I simply use the template to jot down the activities as an employee explains them to me. Sometimes, I do not even bring this template with me, but just make notes on a pad of paper. I always have a mental picture of this template, though, and complete it, including the inputs and outputs.

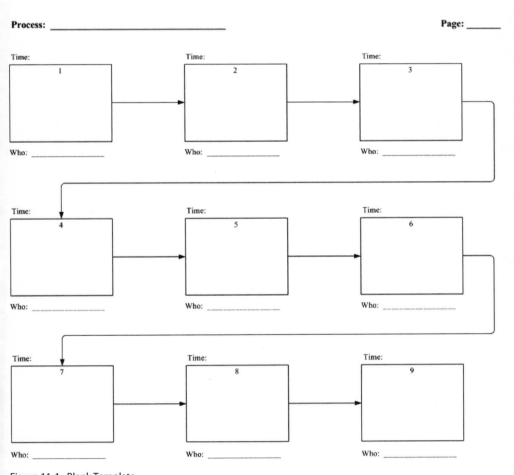

Figure 11-1 Blank Template

After documenting the process, I revisit each activity and ask employees for an estimate of the time they feel each step takes. As discussed in Chapter 5, strive to get the activities right before asking for time estimates. After I draw the process map in Microsoft Visio· I find it helpful to ask the employees to review it and validate the data. Rarely do I need to make significant changes after doing this, only some minor tweaks. Having employees validate the information removes any later concerns about estimating process times.

Over six weeks, I gathered process data and conducted some follow-up analysis for Jim's personnel administrative services group. My analysis revealed several areas for improvement that led me to create the work analysis shown in Figure 11-2. The labor calculation box at the top of the figure should look familiar; we discussed it in Chapter 5. This figure shows:

▶ The personnel administrative services department responsibilities listed in the *process* column.

▶ Current total time employees spend on each process, broken into annual hours and full-time equivalent (FTE, or head count) in the *current* columns. (Recall from Chapter 5 that we use the full-time equivalent to account for percentages of an employee's time spent on a business process.)

▶ Future projections of the total time employees will spend on each process, if Jim follows the recommendations, appear in the *future* columns.

You can skip this paragraph unless you want a reminder of how I arrived at the calculations. I calculated the FTE number in Figure 11-2 just as we did in Chapter 5: Divide the annual hours for each business process by the labor calculation number (1,840) shown at the top of the figure. For example, for the *maintain personnel records* process, divide 2,157 hours (the annual hours spent on this process) by 1,840 (the labor calculation used for employees in this work group) to arrive at 1.2 FTE.

Figure 11-2 shows that if Jim applies the improvement recommendations, he can reduce his full-time equivalents from 16 to 10. These figures do not account for the amount of time

Labor calculation used: 1,840

Annual hours	2,080	
Less 3 weeks vacation	(120)	(due to long-term employees)
Less 1 weeks sick	(40)	
Less 10 paid holidays	(80)	
	1,840	

Current head count: 18
PAS (Personnel Administrative Services) Work Analysis Table

Process	Current		Future	
	Annual Hours	FTE	Annual Hours	FTE
Maintain personnel records	2,157	1.2	1,500	0.8
New employee orientation	500	0.3	450	0.2
Payroll processing and issue resolution	4,129	2.2	2,800	1.5
Benefits administration	1,950	1.1	1,300	0.7
Terminations and exit interviews	481	0.2	240	0.1
Administrative activities (for example, leaves of absence, bereavement pay, minor work permits)	4,095	2.2	2,020	1.1
Employee complaint resolution	7,868	4.3	3,500	1.9
Time card maintenance	894	0.5	650	0.4
Policy and procedures manual maintenance	1,114	0.6	950	0.5
Annual survey participation	160	0.1	150	.08
Workers compensation management	1,780	1.0	1,780	1.0
Audit support	1,445	0.8	1,445	0.8
Reporting (standard and ad-hoc)	2,976	1.6	1,500	0.8
Grand total	**29,549**	**16.1**	**18,285**	**9.9**

Figure 11-2 Executive Summary Work Analysis

employees become involved in other administrative activities, like attending staff meetings or writing weekly reports. Taking these factors into consideration, the future full-time equivalent number probably looks more like 12.

I also included an impact analysis in the executive summary to show the changes that need to occur to achieve the projected savings. In Chapter 9 you learned that an impact analysis shows the changes required to implement an improved business process.

Figure 11-3 shows one portion of the impact analysis for

| Activity | Current | | Recommended Change | Rationale | Change Management | Future | |
	Annual Hours	FTE				Annual Hours	FTE
Administrative activities ■ Leave of absence (LOA) ■ Bereavements ■ Minor work permits	4,095	2.2	LOA tracking: Assess East and West coast group processes (very different) and drive toward process consistency. Bereavements: Move responsibility for checking an employee's right to take a bereavement leave to his or her manager.	West coast group's LOA process takes half the time as the East coast's process. Managers own responsibility for implementing company policies.	East coast has to feel comfortable with automatic letter generation. Managers have to learn employee eligibility rules.	2,020	1.1

Figure 11-3 Executive Summary: Impact Analysis

the *administrative activities* process from Figure 11-2. The analysis includes:

➤ A description of the change, in the recommended change column.

➤ The rationale for the change, in the rationale column.

➤ The department or population affected and the potential controversy or pushback with each proposed change, in the change management column.

Example 2

Sometimes my clients want only a summary of the total time their organization spends on their business processes to understand how their staff spends most of their time. Usually, this analysis leads to new business process improvement work.

Figure 11-4 shows an example of what this might look

Process	Annual Hours	FTE
Needs analysis	12,480	6.6
Program design/storyboard	10,400	5.5
Content development	16,620	8.8
Evaluation plan	3,120	1.7
Course material development	4,160	2.2
Delivery	29,120	15.5
Logistics management	10,816	5.8
Total	**86,716**	**46.1**

Figure 11-4 Executive Summary: Training Example 1

like for a training department. In this figure, I used 1,880 as the labor calculation number (or the standard annual employee hours) to perform the FTE calculations. The figure shows the training processes in the order of how the work is performed, starting with needs analysis and ending with logistics management.

Figure 11-5 shows the same processes organized by the most labor-intensive process first. In this figure, we can tell that delivery is the most labor-intensive process. Using the format in Figure 11-5, you can immediately spot the time-consuming processes and quickly know where to focus your attention.

So far I have shared two different ways to present a statistical component to the summary section of the executive summary. Let me share one more example.

Process	Annual Hours	FTE
Delivery	29,120	15.5
Content development	16,620	8.8
Needs analysis	12,480	6.6
Logistics management	10,816	5.8
Program design/storyboard	10,400	5.5
Course material development	4,160	2.2
Evaluation plan	3,120	1.7
Total	**86,716**	**46.1**

Figure 11-5 Executive Summary: Training Example 2

Example 3

A program management group asked me to help them move responsibility for some business processes from human resources to the operations department. In this case, the goal did not include reducing head count but instead required me to examine the business and make sure that the business processes resided closest to where the work originated, thus reducing handoffs, cycle time, and errors.

Figure 11-6 shows the final summary analysis in this case. You can see that I listed the business processes, current labor requirements, and future labor requirements on the left three-quarters of the figure and summary information on the right quarter of the figure. It took eight weeks to obtain the information necessary to put together this analysis, but having all this information in one table provided the sponsor with a snapshot of the business.

Figure 11-6 shows:

▶ What work the program management group will keep ("PMG Retain . . ." columns).

▶ What work my process evaluation recommends eliminating (processes in the new responsible party column marked n/a to denote they are not applicable).

▶ Work that should move to other departments (also reflected in the new responsible party column).

In addition, this figure shows two summaries on the right-hand side: the total labor moving to each of the new departments in the *labor shifts* section and a total summary of all movements in the *grand summary* section. As it turned out, the program management group retained 5.4 head count, shifted 7.4 head count to the operations, and reduced head count by 0.7 (the not applicable items).

Figures 11-2 through 11-6 show examples of including important analytical information in the executive summary. They also show different ways to provide this type of analytical data. Base this section on whatever drove you to do the work in

Labor calculation used: 1,840	
Annual hours	2,080
Less 3 weeks vacation	(120) (due to long-term employees)
Less 1 week sick	(40)
Less 10 paid holidays	(80)
	1,840

Current head count: 16
Program Management Group Analysis

Process Number	Current		Future				Labor Shifts	
	Annual Hours	FTE	PMG* Retain Annual Hours	PMG* Retain FTE	New Responsible Party	Labor Shifts	Department	FTE
1	2,157	1.2	1,563	0.8	Department A	0.4	Department A	6.3
2	166	.09	0	0	n/a		Department B	0.5
3	4,129	2.2	1,763	1.0	Department A	1.2	Department C	0.6
4	7,868	4.3	459	0.2	Department A	4.1	**Total Labor Shift**	**7.4**
5	4,095	2.2	3,050	1.7	Department A	0.5		
6	1,152	0.6	0	0	n/a			
7	894	0.5	0	0	Department B	0.5		
8	1,114	0.6	0	0	Department C	0.6		
9	572	0.3	572	0.3	Retain			
10	481	0.3	481	0.3	Retain		**Grand Summary**	
11	35	0.02	35	0.02	Retain		PMG retains	5.4
12	607	0.3	607	0.3	Retain		Labor shifts	7.4
13	50	0.03	0	0	n/a		Head count Reduction	0.7
14	92	0.05	0	0	Department A	0.05		
15	1,445	0.8	1,445	0.8	Retain			
Grand total	**24,857**	**13.5**	**9,975**	**5.4**		**7.4**	**Total**	**13.5**

PMG = program management group

Figure 11-6 Executive Summary: Labor Analysis

the first place, and strive to summarize a multitude of data into a single table to show the big picture.

Section 4: Key Findings

The purpose of this section of the executive summary is to make management aware of the key points uncovered during the work. The topics may relate to what the project team learned or to cautions about crucial points in the process. Here are some examples:

▶ The project team developed a shared knowledge of the effect that the actions of one person has on the other. Prior to the business process improvement work, each department completed their actions without understanding the end-to-end process and was thus unaware of the effect on other departments.

▶ We created internal controls to address crucial points in the business process where the highest likelihood of error existed.

▶ Human errors will persist if the department does not follow the processes put in place and bypass the internal controls. Although internal controls add time to the overall process, they offset the increased time by mitigating human error.

▶ The department should review the business process at least annually.

The information included in this section should focus on the few points important for the reader to remember.

Section 5: Deliverables

In this section, identify the materials created as a result of the business process work. List the title and description of each deliverable. The recap helps readers understand what information to ask for if they need additional details. Deliverables can include documents like:

▶ **Process Overview:** A narrative description explaining the purpose of the process, boundaries or scope, clients/customers and their needs, key stakeholders and their needs, measurements of success, and other relevant information.

▶ **Process Maps:** A visual representation of the business process outlining key activities.

▶ **Detail Document:** A narrative description of the process map to assist in understanding and to provide a framework for additional training.

► **Internal Controls Document:** The crucial points in the process where an error can occur, the potential reasons for the errors, and the proposed solution.

► **Checklists:** Tools that document the internal controls or other important information.

► **Impact Analysis:** A summary of the changes that have to occur to ensure the success of the new business process.

► **Implementation Plan:** A project plan that identifies the key phases of the work and their associated timelines.

► **Training Plan:** An outline of who requires training on the new business process, what they require training on, who owns the responsibility for the training, and how to conduct the training.

► **Communication Plan:** An audience profile of who has to receive communication on the new business process, the key message points, the best vehicles to use, and when the communications should happen.

Section 6: Appendix

Include any additional content in the appendix. If you want to include numerous pieces of information, break the appendix down into separate ones and number them. The appendix may include feedback you received from the project team, how the team completed the work, a customized version of the roadmap, the scope definition document, process definitions if you addressed multiple business processes, and perhaps the process map(s). Include whatever material you feel supports your conclusions.

Chapter Summary

Creating an executive summary gives you the opportunity to summarize your work for management and gain recognition, while appearing like a normal part of any project closure.

Keep the readers in mind when writing the executive summary, and include the information you know they care about reading. The project focus sets the tone for the entire executive summary and either draws readers in or bores them. Include the goals of the work, a summary of the work itself, the key findings, and a list of the deliverables. Include process data in the summary section of the executive summary to show the analytical nature of your work because managers always care about the efficient use of head count and the delivery of effective processes to the clients/customers. Keep effectiveness, efficiency, and adaptability in your thoughts as you write the executive summary.

Time Estimate

To plan the time that it takes to work through this step, Figure 11-7 summarizes the time you should expect to spend creating the executive summary.

Create Analytical Tables

During this time, study what information you have gathered and decide what you can summarize in a table format. Build your labor or work analysis using the process times from the process map. Completing this analysis for one business process can easily take a week. If you worked on multiple business processes and have to summarize a group of them, you might need more than 40 hours.

Event	Time	Purpose
Create analytical tables	40 hours (for 1 process)	■ Summarize data into tables that are appropriate to include in the executive summary.
Write executive summary	40 hours	■ Write the project focus, goals, key findings, and deliverables sections of the executive summary.

Figure 11-7 Time Estimate—Create Executive Summary

Write the Executive Summary

At this time, take a step back and reflect on what you have accomplished. Write each of the sections and have a colleague—who is not familiar with the work—review what you wrote. Keep streamlining the executive summary until you feel that it tells the story of your journey in a tight, compressed way.

What You Have Achieved

In this chapter, you have achieved the following:

► The opportunity to summarize your work

► The knowledge of how to write an executive summary

► An understanding of how to create analytical summaries of the work

► What senior managers care about reading

► Most important, the *power* to gain the recognition for your work

CHAPTER | 12

Case Study

Sharing a Real-World Example

Now let us put all the pieces together by stepping through a complete BPI project that I completed for a major bank that I call BB&Z. We all read stories about how someone lost weight, climbed a difficult mountain, or ran a marathon. If you are like me, you find them inspiring because reading what others went through helps me realize that I can do things I might previously have thought were impossible. I chose this particular case because it introduces several new bends in the road and demonstrates how you can adapt the 10 steps to any situation. As we move through the study, you can reference the previous chapters in this book for clarification or for additional details. Hopefully, this case study motivates you and jump-starts you on your own road to improving business processes. I selected a training and development business process.

Background

Pam Borzak, senior vice president of human resources for BB&Z, called me for help with improving the business processes in her organization. As a result of that call, I spent the next year tackling each business process within her departments. Because Pam had responsibility for all the human resource functions, we decided to start her process inventory at the department level to decide which of the human resource departments we should start with first.

In previous chapters we looked at individual business processes. This time we raise the bar a notch and start at the department level. Using this approach, I created a process inventory and process prioritization table by listing the departments in BB&Z's human resource function, and then I applied the prioritization criteria at the department level to determine which department's processes to focus on first.

Step 1: Develop the Process Inventory

In Chapter 2, we built the business process inventory, created prioritization criteria, applied the criteria to each process, and created a process prioritization table that summarized the business processes. We did all that in one table to enable a process-by-process comparison, which then helped us decide where to start our improvement efforts.

I proceeded the same way in Pam's case, only this time I built the process inventory at her department level and applied the prioritization criteria used in Chapter 2 to the list of human resource departments. As you recall, the four main categories of criteria we used in Chapter 2 are:

▶ **Impact:** How much the business process affects Pam's business, including the number of employees impacted by the business process and the client level of the impacted employees.

▶ **Implementation:** How the complexity of the business process, the cost to improve the process, and the timing of the next cycle (or how long before the organization uses the process again) affect Pam's ability to drive any process changes through the organization.

▶ **Current State:** How well the business process works today for Pam's clients and her internal organization.

▶ **Value:** How well the business process delivers worth to the organization, or the quantitative and qualitative benefits that the process delivers.

I used the same 1–3 scale from Chapter 2 to keep the scoring simple and did not apply any weighting to the criteria.

Figure 12-1 shows the completed process prioritization table for Pam's human resource organization. This table shows that we should initially focus on the business processes within training and development (T&D) because that department has the highest total score (20). The high score for T&D resulted from the bank's ongoing acquisition of other financial institutions through mergers, forcing Pam's organization to have to integrate new employees into the company continually. You can see that the merger and acquisition focus is the driving force behind all four categories. Looking at the categories across the T&D row in Figure 12-1 leads to the following observations:

► Many employees are affected by the T&D processes (impact).

► It will not take too long or require too much money to make the necessary changes, and the next cycle appears imminent because of an upcoming merger (implementation).

► The T&D processes have an average client satisfaction and pain level (current state).

► If new employees can quickly get immersed in the existing culture, the process will deliver a benefit to the bank (benefit/return).

Once we decided to start by focusing on training and development, I built the department's process inventory by listing all the T&D business processes. Figure 12-2 on page 266 shows the process prioritization table I created for BB&Z's T&D department. The figure shows the common business processes one might find in a training and development department, which include:

► **Curriculum development**, which includes designing and developing curricula and courses.

► **Forecasting/scheduling**, which involves estimating student demand and developing a class schedule to meet the demand.

	Impact		Implementation			Current State			Value	
	Number Affected 3 = large number 2 = average number 1 = small number	**Client Level** 3 = senior 2 = management 1 = other	**Time to Market** 3 = short 2 = average 1 = long	**Funding** 3 = small 2 = medium 1 = large	**Timing of Next Cycle** 3 = close/ongoing 2 = intermediate 1 = far	**Client Satisfaction** 3 = low 2 = medium 1 = high	**Pain Level** 3 = high 2 = medium 1 = low	**Process Exist?** 1 = no 0 = yes	**Benefit/ Return** 3 = high 2 = average 1 = low	**Total Score**
Compensation and benefits	3	2	1	2	2	2	1	0	2	15
Recruitment	1	2	2	3	2	2	1	0	1	14
Training and development	3	1	3	3	3	2	2	0	3	20
Personnel administration	3	1	1	1	1	2	1	0	1	11
Workforce analysis	1	3	1	2	1	3	2	1	1	15

Figure 12-1 BB&Z Human Resource: Process Prioritization Table: Human Resource Functions

	Impact		Implementation			Current State			Value	
	Number Affected	Client Level	Time to Market	Funding	Timing of Next Cycle	Client Satisfaction	Pain Level	Process Exist?	Benefit/ Return	Total Score
	3 = large number 2 = average number 1 = small number	3 = senior 2 = management 1 = other	3 = short 2 = average 1 = long	3 = small 2 = medium 1 = large	3 = close/ongoing 2 = intermediate 1 = far	3 = low 2 = medium 1 = high	3 = high 2 = medium 1 = low	1 = no 0 = yes	3 = high 2 = average 1 = low	
Curriculum development	1	2	2	3	2	3	1	0	2	16
Forecasting/ scheduling	1	2	3	2	3	3	3	0	2	19
Enrollment	3	1	2	1	3	2	3	0	3	18
Delivery	3	3	3	3	3	3	2	1	3	23
Resource management	1	1	1	2	3	1	3	0	2	14
Evaluation	1	1	2	2	3	3	1	0	2	15
Budgeting	1	3	3	2	2	3	3	1	2	20

Figure 12-2 BB&Z Process Prioritization Table: Training and Development Group

➤ **Enrollment**, which allows students to enroll in a learning event.

➤ **Delivery**, which includes the facilitation of a class, either by an instructor or by alternative methods.

➤ **Resource management**, which involves securing all materials, equipment, and facilitators required to deliver training.

➤ **Evaluation**, which assesses the impact of training.

➤ **Budgeting**, which tracks all spending.

Based on the results of the process prioritization table in Figure 12-2, I normally would start with the delivery process because it has the highest score (23), but before moving to the next step, I reviewed the results of this exercise with Pam. I expressed concern that the score given to delivery may be because it is one of the only business processes, besides enrollment, that her clients experience. All others reflect the internal workings in the department, which are not visible to clients.

At this point, a bend in the road occurred in my work with Pam. I encouraged her to think about the lack of client interaction throughout the process, and she agreed not to rush in and start with the delivery process just yet, but rather to take a fresh look at how her organization functioned and interfaced with the client. Pam agreed that her key goal was making sure that her organization delivered training that supported the company's business objectives. As a result of our discussion, we decided to take a high-level look at the training and development process before getting into the details of any single business process.

The change in direction meant that I had to adjust how we approached step 2, building the foundation. Any change you make along the way subsequently causes other changes down the line as you move through the roadmap, and these changes are perfectly acceptable. In Pam's case, instead of developing a scope definition document on the delivery process, we created one for the entire training and development process.

The roadmap is a flexible and dynamic tool that provides overall direction on how to perform business process improvement work, but remember to adapt it to changing circumstances.

Step 2: Establish the Foundation

In Chapter 3 we learned that in this step we create the scope definition document to establish the boundaries for the business process, so that we can stay on track and avoid scope creep. At this point, you also form the project team, if one is necessary. Because we chose to look at the end-to-end training and development process, Pam elected to include on the team her training and development director, a delivery manager, an instructor, two instructional designers, one of her training specialists who helped with resource scheduling, and her business manager.

During the initial project team meeting, I walked the group through the roadmap in Figure 12-3 so that they could see the steps we would go through and provide them with an opportunity to ask questions. Pam joined us for the first 15 minutes of the initial team meeting.

After reviewing the objectives of business process improvement and answering the project team's questions, we moved on to setting the foundation for our work. All team members had a copy of the blank scope definition document so that they could see the information we would discuss. I kept track of the team's conversation on an electronic dry-erase board so that everyone could see the results of our conversation. Figure 12-4 on page 270 shows the completed scope definition document that the team created for the training and development process.

A look at the scope definition document tells us a great deal. We can see where the project team decided to start and end the process by reading the *scope (boundaries)* section. It starts when Pam's organization works with the finance depart-

Roadmap to Business Process Improvement

Objectives of business process improvement:

- *Effectiveness:* Does the process produce the desired results and meet the customer/client needs?
- *Efficiency:* Does the process minimize the use of resources, improve cycle time, and eliminate bureaucracy?
- *Adaptability:* Is the process flexible in the face of changing needs?

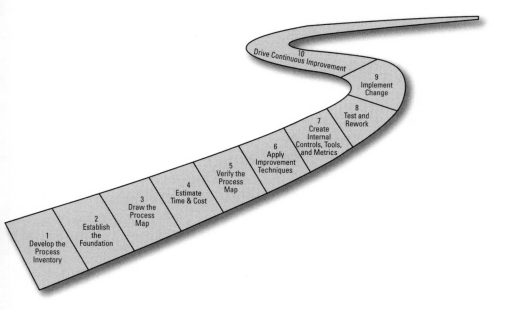

Figure 12-3 Roadmap

ment to establish T&D's annual budget and ends when Pam's management team reviews the annual summary of course evaluation results.

While reviewing the scope definition document with Pam after the first meeting, we made a few changes. Pam wanted to make it explicit that, going forward, business goals will drive where she invests her budget and that she wanted to add another measurement of success related to return on investment. As a result, I added another sentence to the *description* stating that business goals drive training investments and a fifth mea-

Process name: Training and Development

Process owner: Jenny Borzak

Client: Business unit leaders

Description (purpose):

This process covers delivering products and services that enable employee learning to support the business objectives.

All types of products and services are covered, including calendar classes, seminars, conferences, Web-based training, and self-directed learning, whether internally or externally delivered.

Client needs:

- Employees who can perform on the job
- Quick turnaround
- Lower cost

Key stakeholders and interest:

Finance	■ Improved fixed/variable cost ratio
	■ 10% total cost/performance improvement per year

Scope (boundaries):

Start   Establishing annual budget

End   Annual management review to evaluate effectiveness

Process responsibilities:

- Forecasting/scheduling
- Curriculum/course development
- Enrollment
- Resource management
- Delivery
- Evaluation
- Communications
- Business planning/budgeting

Measurements of success:

1. On-the-job performance
2. Reduced development time
3. Cost reduction target
4. Ability to integrate new businesses

surement to show a linkage between the business goals and training. Figure 12-5 shows the updated scope definition document with these two additions.

At the second project team meeting, I reviewed the formatted scope definition document with the team and highlighted the changes that Pam and I made to the description and measurements of success. Because this is the first time that the team sees the document typed, it will seem more formal, and you should feel comfortable making edits. At our meeting, the team expressed concern over how to measure the linkage of training to business goals. I urged them to wait and discuss the *how* when we moved to step 7 on the roadmap, which addresses establishing metrics. This kept the team from veering off course. As side questions emerge in the meetings, refer to the roadmap to show how you will address a question at a later time. This assures participants that you heard them and that you will not overlook their concerns.

Once the project team felt comfortable with the scope definition document, we moved to step 3 and began drawing the process map.

Step 3: Draw the Process Map

As pointed out in Chapter 4, drawing the process map in step 3 gives the project team a tool to help them understand the end-to-end business process, shows them where handoffs occur between departments, and provides a background to apply the improvement techniques in step 6.

You may recall that, in this step, you decide whether to draw a standard or cross-functional process map, depending on how you plan to use it, and select the level of detail for the map. You can draw a high-level map, like the morning routine process in Chapter 4, Figure 4-6, or a detailed process map.

In Pam's case, I decided to draw a high-level process map for three reasons:

▶ Her organization had limited shared understanding of the end-to-end business process.

Process name: Training and Development

Process owner: Jenny Borzak

Client: Business unit leaders

Description (purpose):

This process covers delivering products and services that enable employee learning to support the business objectives. In all cases, the business goals drive the learning investment.

All types of products and services are covered, including calendar classes, seminars, conferences, Web-based training, and self-directed learning, whether internally or externally delivered.

Client needs:

- Employees who can perform on the job
- Quick turnaround
- Lower cost

Key stakeholders and interest:

Finance	■ Improved fixed/variable cost ratio ■ 10% total cost/performance improvement per year

Scope (boundaries):

Start   Establishing annual budget

End   Annual management review to evaluate effectiveness

Measurements of success:

1. On-the-job performance
2. Reduced development time
3. Cost reduction target
4. Ability to integrate new businesses
5. Clear linkage of training to business goal

Process responsibilities:

- Forecasting/scheduling
- Curriculum/course development
- Enrollment
- Resource management
- Delivery
- Evaluation
- Communications
- Business planning/budgeting

► The process had numerous subprocesses, making it complex.

► This level of detail would provide Pam with an overall view of the entire process.

We agreed to delve into a single business process as required, to answer questions or to address problems.

Deciding to start at a high level of detail leads to both positive and negative repercussions for the facilitator. On the one hand, this decision makes it easier to draw the process map because you do not need a detailed level of understanding and you can do so quickly. On the other hand, managing the project team becomes more difficult because part of the team almost always likes to delve into detail. Although you will hear various, reasonable-sounding explanations for the need to go deeper, recognize that the root of team members' anxiety usually revolves around not seeing their own job reflected in the process map. Your challenge, as the facilitator, becomes keeping everyone grounded and feeling secure.

To draw Pam's high-level process map, the team met for three hours every week for four weeks to create the two-page, high-level process map shown in Figures 12-6 and 12-7. Between each meeting, I created and updated the process map using Microsoft Visio.

Notice that in these two figures that the process map spans two pages because it did not fit onto a single page; notice how I used the two types of connectors discussed in Chapter 4 (Figures 12-8 and 12-9 on page 276). The connector symbols help readers understand how to follow the process map by telling them where to move next. I used the off-page connector in Figure 12-6 to tell the reader to move to page two, activity 8, after estimating the annual budget in activity 7. Also notice the off-page connector in Figure 12-7 entering activity 8, which lets the reader know that this activity comes from a prior page in the process map. After moving to activity 8 on the second page of the process map, the on-page connector in Figure 12-7 tells readers that, after activities 10 and 11, they move to delivery of

(*text continues on page 276*)

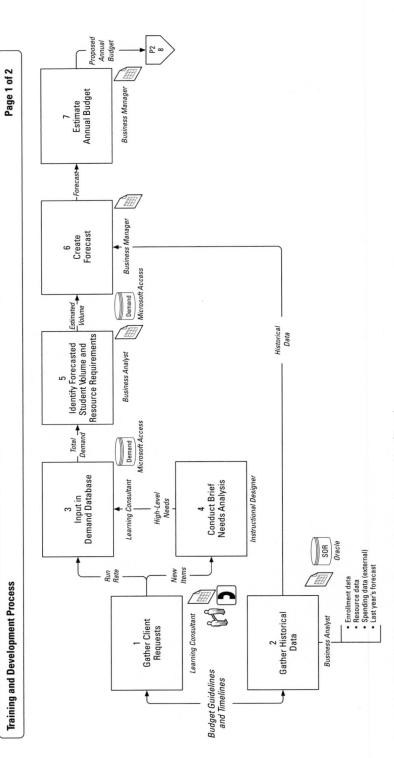

Figure 12-6 BB&Z Training and Development Process: Process Map (Part 1)

Figure 12-7 BB&Z Training and Development Process: Process Map (Part 2) the products and services in activity 18 on the *same* page of the map.

Figure 12-8 Off-Page Connector Symbol

Figure 12-9 On-Page Connector Symbol

In reviewing Figures 12-6 and 12-7, we see that Pam's process starts after she receives the budget guidelines and timeline from the finance department. Figure 12-6 shows one way to draw a business process that starts with two activities occurring at the same time after an event enters the process. In Pam's case, as soon as her team receives the budget guidelines and timeline from finance, the learning consultants collect input from their clients to cover their needs for the next year. Simultaneously, the business analyst gathers historical data from the prior year. In looking at the process map, it becomes apparent, by the addition of the Microsoft Excel icon, that Pam's team uses a spreadsheet for many of the activities identified as well as two databases: the demand database (a Microsoft Access database) and their system of record (an Oracle database).

Once finance approves the annual budget in activity 8, the instructional designers begin design work on courses, curriculum, and evaluation strategies. As the instructional designers design and develop the training products throughout the year, the evaluation specialists get involved and create the evaluation tools and the delivery team identifies the resources required to facilitate the planned training.

Once the delivery team identifies the resources, the resource management team starts evaluating the available resources and secures any additional resources required. Once the resource management team secures the resources, communications can begin to tell employees of the upcoming training schedule. As students enroll and attend training, the evaluation specialists gather the performance data in preparation for the annual review meeting that occurs at the end of every year. Meanwhile, the enrollment specialist updates the system of record to reflect the employee's completion of training.

Figures 12-6 and 12-7 include many symbols to denote the various tools used to accomplish each activity, and Figure 12-10 shows the legend page of the process map that explains the meanings of the symbols used. The legend page can go at the beginning or end of the map.

In addition to updating the process map between meetings, I spent time documenting the conversation in the detail document, shown in Figure 12-11. Remember to document the conversation as you proceed so that you do not lose track of the rich dialogue, and include examples when possible. The project team usually accepts a higher level process map as long as you capture sufficient information in the detail document that accompanies the map.

After drawing the high-level process map and capturing the narrative to accompany the map, the team moved to step 4. We added the process timing to the process map and identified the cost of the business process.

(*text continues on page 283*)

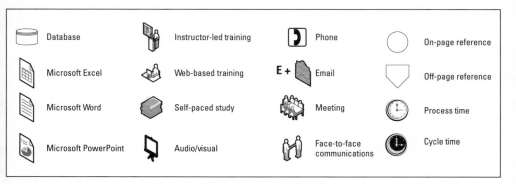

Figure 12-10 Legend

Number	Activity Description	Responsible Party	Tools	Output
1	**Gather client requests:** At this step in the process, the learning consultant, who works with a client group throughout the year, discusses the client's training needs for the upcoming year. They discuss existing and new courses that the client requires to meet their business objectives.	Learning consultant	Excel spreadsheet Phone Face-to-face meetings	**Run rate:** The products and services already delivered by the training and development organization that the client wants to continue using **New items:** New needs that the client identifies
2	**Gather historical data:** At the same time that the learning consultants gather client input, the business analyst gathers data for the prior year using existing sources to collect attendance numbers, identify resource usage, spending on external resources, and to compare last year's forecast to this year's actual.	Business analyst	Excel spreadsheet System of record	**Historical data:** All historical data is available to assist in creating the forecast for next year.
3	**Input in demand database:** Once the learning consultant determines the client's estimate on what existing training it plans to take advantage of during the next year, the learning consultant enters this information in the demand database to assist in forecasting the next year's demand. After the instructional designer conducts a high-level needs analysis with the client (4), the learning consultant enters the new items in the demand database.	Learning consultant	Demand database	**Total demand:** The run rate and new demand are available to help with forecasting student volume for next year.

Figure 12-11 BB&Z Training and Development Process: Detail Document

Number	Activity Description	Responsible Party	Tools	Output
4	**Conduct brief need analysis:** If a client identifies a new need for which it does not seem that a training solution exists, the learning consultant works with an instructional designer to create a high-level needs analysis to understand the client's goals. This helps to gain insight into the potential demand and resource requirements that this new request may drive.	Instructional designer		**High-level needs:** This business has a brief summary of new demand items at this point.
5	**Identify forecasted student volume and resource requirements:** The run rate demand from existing courses and the high-level needs from newly identified products or services enter the process in this step. These two pieces of information assist the business analyst in forecasting the next year's student volume.	Business analyst	Excel spreadsheet Demand database	**Estimated volume:** The business has identified the estimated volume for run rate items and new items.
6	**Create forecast:** The business manager combines the forecast from step 5 and the historical data gathered from step 2 to create a forecast for the upcoming year. The forecast includes student volumes, resources requirements, and the number of new products.	Business manager	Excel spreadsheet	**Forecast:** A total forecast is available.

(continues)

Number	Activity Description	Responsible Party	Tools	Output
7	**Estimate annual budget:** The business manager adds the costing elements to the forecast completed in step 6 to determine the cost of delivering the planned products and services.	Business manager	Excel spreadsheet	**Proposed annual budget:** The training and development organization has identified their annual budget requirement.
8	**Approval?** The finance department either approves the training and development organization's budget for next year or asks the request to be refined.	Finance		**Yes:** Finance approved the budget. **No:** Finance has not approved the budget, and the training and development organization must rework their budget request.
9	**Design course/curriculum/ evaluation strategy:** Once the training and development organization has an approved budget, the instructional designers can begin designing products and services, which may include courses, new curricula, or researching external solutions, and deciding how to evaluate a new product or service. The instructional designers use Microsoft PowerPoint to present a high-level visual of the design, accompanied by a detailed design document.	Instructional designer	PowerPoint Word	**Completed design:** The design exists for new courses, or new curricula, and an evaluation strategy outlining how to evaluate the products and services exists.
10	**Develop courses/curriculum:** The instructional designer creates the products and services.	Instructional designer		**Product/service availability:** The business has developed courses and curricula.

Figure 12-11 (continued)

Number	Activity Description	Responsible Party	Tools	Output
11	**Develop evaluation tools:** Once the instructional designer completes the evaluation strategy in step 9, the evaluation specialist can begin developing the evaluation tools.	Evaluation specialist		**Evaluation tools:** Individual course evaluation tools exist.
12	**Identify resource needs:** The delivery team begins assessing what resources they require to deliver against the design. This may include instructors, space, course materials, or equipment, depending on the volume and training type.	Delivery team	Excel spreadsheet	**Resource needs:** The business has identified any resources required to deliver the products and services.
13	**Match supply and demand:** Once the resource manager identifies the resources required, they compare the demand to what the organization already has in place.	Resource manager	Excel spreadsheet	**Shortage:** The business does not have the resources required to meet the need. **Excess:** Too many resources exist.
14	**Acquire resources:** If the resource manager determines that sufficient resources do not exist, they start securing the appropriate resources. For example: ■ If they require additional instructors, they secure them. ■ If they require more space, the resource manager negotiates for additional space. ■ If they require external facilitators, they negotiate vendor contracts. ■ If they have to buy new books or other self-directed resources, the resource manager purchases them.	Resource manager	Phone	**Resource availability:** The business has the resources required to meet the business needs.

(continues)

Number	Activity Description	Responsible Party	Tools	Output
15	**Retire resources:** If the business no longer requires the existing resources, the resource manager retires the resources.	Resource manager	Phone	**Retired resources:** The business retired resources that they no longer require.
16	**Communicate product/service availability:** Once the learning consultant knows that the instructional designer started course development and the resource manager has secured the resources, they can start the communication process with the clients.	Learning consultant	Company intranet Verbal Email	**Awareness:** Notification to potential consumers of product and service availability has occurred.
17	**Schedule enrollments:** As employees enroll in a course or use a resource, the enrollment specialist schedules the employee in a class or checks out a resource for the employee.	Enrollment specialist	Excel spreadsheet	**Students enrolled:** Employees have enrolled in training or have the appropriate self-paced resources
18	**Deliver product or service:** During this step in the process, the instructor delivers the product or service to the employee. This activity has three inputs: ■ The instructional designer has developed the product/service (10). ■ The evaluation specialist has created the evaluation tools (11). ■ The students have enrolled (17). This step can take many forms including instructor-led classes, Web-based training, self-directed study, seminars, or conferences.	Delivery team	Instructor Computer Book Seminar A/V	**Product delivery:** The employee has consumed the product or service.

Figure 12-11 (continued)

Number	Activity Description	Responsible Party	Tools	Output
19	**Collect test and performance data:** Throughout the training and development process, the evaluation team collects feedback regarding an employee's satisfaction with the training and their capacity to apply what they learned on the job.	Evaluation specialist	Excel spreadsheet	**Evaluation data:** Results from the training evaluations exist.
20	**Update attendance in system of record:** If an employee attended a class or completed Web-based training, the enrollment specialist enters this information in the system of record.	Enrollment specialist	System of record	**SOR updated:** The system of record is updated with the employee's attendance.
21	**Conduct annual management review:** Once each year, the training and development management team reviews the results of the evaluations collected throughout the year to identify how to improve their products and services.	Training and development director	Meeting	**Recommended changes:** The business has a list of courses that may require changes to help with the next year's planning process.

Step 4: Estimate Time and Cost

In Chapter 5, we discussed process and cycle times and how to use this information to estimate what a process costs. Recall that:

➤ **Process time** is the time required to complete a single activity in a process.

➤ **Cycle time** is the time required to complete an entire process, from the first to the last step in a process. Sometimes you hear this called "elapsed time."

In Chapter 5, I discussed how well estimating works for this step instead of using a formal data-gathering technique. However, when you work with such a high-level process map, as we did in Pam's case, you will not find the estimate as accurate because you do not have enough detail on all the subprocesses. You should still perform this task, though, because it provides directional information. When you draw a high-level process map, go back and revisit the timing estimates when you move to individual business processes.

During this step, I added process and cycle times to the process map for Pam's high-level T&D process. Figures 12-12 and 12-13 show the process and cycle times added to the training and development process map. As in Chapter 4, the white clock denotes process time, and the dark clock denotes cycle time.

After adding the process time to Pam's training and development process map and asking the project team to identify annual volumes, I had the data necessary to complete a high-level estimate of the labor cost for the T&D process. In Chapter 5, you learned that calculating the labor cost of a business process entails these four steps:

1. List the process activities and process times in a spreadsheet.
2. Identify the annual volume.
3. Determine the full-time equivalent (FTE) formula to use.
4. Determine the salary and employee benefit rate to use for the employees or process workers.

Process Activities and Process Time

After the project team completed the estimates for process and cycle time, I transferred the times shown on the process map to the next two tables. I completed this task after the project meeting, during which we identified process time, cycle time, and annual volume. Figure 12-14 on page 287 shows the process time estimates for the training and development process, and Figure 12-15 on page 288 shows the cycle time esti-

Training and Development Process

Figure 12-12   BB&Z Training and Development Process: Process Map with Time Estimates (Part 1)

Figure 12-13 BB&Z Training and Development Process: Process Map with Time Estimates (Part 2)

Activity Number	Low End	High End	Frequency
1	1 hour	2 hours	Annual
2	8 hours	24 hours	Annual
3	2 hours	40 hours	Annual
4	1 hour	3 hours	Annual
5	4 hours	4 hours	Annual
6	8 hours	20 hours	Annual
7	3 hours	3 hours	Annual
8	n/a	n/a	Annual
9	40 hours	80 hours	By course
10	80 hours	160 hours	By course
11	20 hours	40 hours	By course
12	4 hours	4 hours	Annual (estimate) By course (refine)
13	40 hours	40 hours	Annual
14	80 hours	80 hours	Annual
15	40 hours	40 hours	Annual
16	8 hours	12 hours	By course
17	0.08 hours	0.08 hours	By transaction
18	1 hour	16 hours	By course
19	4 hours	4 hours	By course
20	0.2 hour	0.2 hour	By transaction
21	4 hours	4 hours	Annual

Figure 12-14 BB&Z Training and Development Process: Process Time Estimates

mates. Both tables include a range in some cases, depicted as the *low end* and *high end* columns, because the team could not settle on a single number.

In these tables, I added a fourth column, *frequency*, something I did not include in Chapter 5. I did this in Pam's case because we cannot count every step in the high-level process map the same way. The training and development organization performs the steps in the annual budgeting portion of the process map only once a year, so we cannot count the time consumed by activities 1–8, 13–15, and 21 more than once. However, volume does drive the other activities on the process map. Notice that activity 12, identifying resource needs, has two frequencies because training and development estimates the re-

Activity Number	Low End	High End	Frequency
1	80 hours	80 hours	Annual
2	80 hours	80 hours	Annual
3	80 hours	80 hours	Annual
4	80 hours	80 hours	Annual
5	40 hours	40 hours	Annual
6	40 hours	40 hours	Annual
7	40 hours	40 hours	Annual
8	120 hours	240 hours	Annual
9	320 hours	320 hours	By course
10	160 hours	960 hours	By course
11	80 hours	80 hours	Annual
12	40 hours	40 hours	Annual (estimate) By course (refine)
13	160 hours	160 hours	Annual
14	160 hours	480 hours	Annual
15	80 hours	160 hours	Annual
16	40 hours	40 hours	By course
17	.08 hours	.08 hours	By transaction
18	1 hour	16 hours	By course
19	40 hours	40 hours	By course
20	0.5 hour	0.5 hour	By transaction
21	4 hours	4 hours	Annual

Figure 12-15 BB&Z Training and Development Process: Cycle Time Estimates

source requirements during the annual process and refines them as the instructional designers create the products and services throughout the year.

Since the activities in the process map have different frequencies, we need to reorganize the information from the process and cycle tables by frequency so that we can calculate the labor costs. Figure 12-16 shows a combined view of process and cycle time information organized by the frequency of each activity. The three frequencies we used are:

➤ **Annual activities:** Those performed once a year.

➤ **Per-course activities:** Those performed each time a course is developed.

Activity Number	Description	Process Time	Cycle Time
Annual Activities			
1	Client requests	1.5 hours	80.0 hours
2	Historical data	16.0 hours	80.0 hours
3	Demand database	21.0 hours	80.0 hours
4	Needs analysis	2.0 hours	80.0 hours
5	Student volume	4.0 hours	40.0 hours
6	Forecast	14.0 hours	40.0 hours
7	Annual budget	3.0 hours	40.0 hours
8	Approval	n/a	180.0 hours
12	Resource needs	4.0 hours	40.0 hours
13	Supply/demand	40.0 hours	160.0 hours
14	Acquire resources	80.0 hours	320.0 hours
15	Retire resources	40.0 hours	120.0 hours
21	Mgmt. review	4.0 hours	4.0 hours
Total annual activities		**229.5** hours	**1,264.0** hours
Per-course Activities			
9	Design/develop	60.0 hours	320.0 hours
10	Develop	120.0 hours	560.0 hours
11	Evaluation tools	30.0 hours	80.0 hours
12	Resource needs	1.0 hours	n/a
16	Communications	10.0 hours	40.0 hours
18	Delivery	8.5 hours	8.5 hours
19	Collect performance data	4.0 hours	40.0 hours
Total per-course activities		**385.5** hours	**808.5** hours
Per-transaction Activities			
17	Enrollments	0.08 hours	0.08 hours
20	Update SOR	0.2 hours	0.5 hours
Total per-transaction activities		**0.28** hours	**0.58** hours

Figure 12-16 BB&Z Training and Development Process: Process and Cycle Time Estimates

▶ **Per-transaction activities:** Those performed each time a student consumes a product or service.

Pam wanted to know how long the annual components of the business process took in days or months, so I had to translate the hours consumed by the total annual activities in Figure 12-16 (229.5 and 1,264.0 hours) into days and months using the formula shown in Figure 12-17.

Formula:

$$\frac{\text{Total process or cycle time hours}}{\text{8 hours/workday}} = \text{Process or cycle time total in days}$$

Example 1—Process time:

$$\frac{229\frac{1}{2} \text{ hours}}{\text{8 hours/workday}} = 28\frac{1}{2} \text{ days of process time}$$

Example 2—Cycle time:

$$\frac{1{,}264.0 \text{ hours}}{\text{8 hours/workday}} = \frac{158 \text{ days}}{30 \text{ days/month}} = 5.3 \text{ months of cycle time}$$

Figure 12-17 *Calculating Total Process and Cycle Times in Days or Months*

After performing these calculations, we knew that the annual portion of Pam's business process consumed 28½ days of process time, but it could take as long as five months of cycle time to complete.

Our next step was bringing in volume-related data.

Annual Volume

Before we can calculate the volume and associated labor cost for the activities affected by volume, we must first separate the two volume categories (*by course* and *by transaction*) by the type of employees who do the work because these employees have different rates of pay. In Chapter 5, I used an intentionally simple process, the recognition bonus award process and included only one compensation employee type, but in Pam's case, five types of employees affect the volume calculation:

▶ Instructional designers

▶ Evaluation specialists

▶ Learning consultants

▶ Instructors

▶ Enrollment specialists

To incorporate these employee types into the calculation, Figure 12-18 shows the employee type that delivers the training and development activities added to the table. Notice that this new table only shows the process time for volume-related activities since moving forward, we only care about this information. The new concept you should notice in this table is that one employee type can perform different activities. For example, the evaluation specialist develops evaluation tools (11) and collects performance data (19).

Next, I had to merge activities performed by one employee type into a single row to get us ready to incorporate the volume component. In Figure 12-19 I added the 60 hours that the instructional designers spend designing each course (9) to the 120 hours they spend developing the course (10), giving the instructional designer a 180-hour total in Figure 12-19. From a labor perspective, Figure 12-19 tells us that:

➤ Instructional designers require 180 hours, on average, for every course they develop.

➤ Evaluation specialists require 34 hours per course.

➤ Instructors require 9.5 hours.

Activity Number	Description	Employee Type	Process Time
Per-course Activities			
9	Design	Instructional designer	60.0 hours
10	Develop	Instructional designer	120.0 hours
11	Evaluation tools	Evaluation specialist	30.0 hours
12	Resource needs	Instructor	1.0 hours
16	Communications	Learning consultant	10.0 hours
18	Delivery	Instructors	8.5 hours
19	Collect performance data	Evaluation specialist	4.0 hours
Per-transaction Activities			
17	Enrollments	Enrollment specialist	0.08 hours
20	Update SOR	Enrollment specialist	0.2 hours

Figure 12-18 BB&Z Training and Development Process: Employee Type and Process Time Estimates for Volume-Related Activities

Activity #	Employee Type	Process Time
Per-course Activities		
9, 10	Instructional designer	180.0 hours
11, 19	Evaluation specialist	34.0 hours
12, 18	Instructor	9.5 hours
16	Learning consultant	10.0 hours
Per-transaction Activities		
17, 20	Enrollment specialist	0.28 hours

Figure 12-19 BB&Z Training and Development Process: Process Time Estimates by Employee Type

▶ Learning consultants require 10 hours for this part of the process.

▶ Enrollment specialist requires 0.28 of an hour for every transaction.

Now that I knew how much time each instance of an activity took and who performed the work, I had to determine the annual labor required for each employee type. To perform this calculation, I had to identify the yearly volume. Figure 12-20 shows the volume listed in the *annual volume* column, which shows that, every year, the training and development organization:

▶ Designed and developed about 30 new courses.

▶ Delivered 1,000 classes.

▶ Had a total of 25,000 students attend classes.

Employee Type	Process Time/Activity	Annual Volume	Annual Labor
Instructional designer	180.0 hours	30	5,400 hours
Evaluation specialist	34.0 hours	30	1,020 hours
Instructor	9.5 hours	1,000	9,500 hours
Learning consultant	10.0 hours	130	1,300 hours
Enrollment specialist	0.28 hours	25,000	7,000 hours

Figure 12-20 BB&Z Training and Development Process: Labor and Labor Estimates

Notice that the annual volume for the learning consultant shows 130, instead of just 30, because this employee not only communicates the 30 new products and services developed, but also markets the ongoing calendar of almost 100 products and services.

The last column in Figure 12-20 shows the annual labor calculation, which I derived by multiplying the process time by the annual volume that Pam's team gave me, to get the annual labor hours. So now we know that the instructional designers, for example, require 5,400 hours a year to perform their job.

Now we had to determine how many employees the 5,400 hours equate to, using the full-time equivalent formula (FTE) discussed in Chapter 5.

FTE Formula

The FTE number denotes the total number of hours that an employee can be paid for in a work year. So, if an employee works 40 hours in a week and we multiply that number by 52 weeks, we get 2,080 hours, a starting point for the FTE formula. However, I could not simply use 2,080 hours in the labor calculation because I had to deduct vacation, sick, and holiday hours available to an employee. Figure 12-21 shows the calculation I used for Pam's organization. This figure shows that I used 1,880 as the standard number of hours an employee works in Pam's organization.

Next, I applied the 1,880 labor calculation number to the annual labor hours from Figure 12-20. You can see the formula

Labor Calculation Used:	1,880	
Annual hours	2,080*	----▶ *Starting point*
Less 2 weeks vacation	80	
Less 1 week sick	40	
Less 10 days paid holidays	80	
	1,880	

*40 hours per week × 52 weeks in a year

Figure 12-21 Basis for FTE Calculation

I used to perform this calculation in Figure 12-22, using the instructional designer's 5,400 hours as the example.

Formula:

$$\frac{\text{Annual labor hours}}{\text{FTE hours}} = \text{Total FTE required to support the business process}$$

Example:

$$\frac{5,400 \text{ hours}}{1,880 \text{ FTE hours}} = 2.9 \text{ FTE required}$$

Figure 12-22 FTE Calculation

So now we know that Pam requires three instructional designers to handle the level of work in the training and development organization. I then went on and performed the same calculation on Pam's other employee types, and the table in Figure 12-23 shows the result of this calculation on the five employee types.

Employee Type	Process Time	Annual Volume	Annual Labor	FTE
Instructional designer	180.0 hours	30	5,400 hours	2.9
Evaluation specialist	34.0 hours	30	1,020 hours	0.5
Instructor	9.5 hours	1,000	9,500 hours	5.1
Learning consultant	10.0 hours	130	1,300 hours	0.7
Enrollment specialist	0.28 hours	25,000	7,000 hours	3.7
Total FTE required				**12.9**

Figure 12-23 BB&Z Training and Development Process: Labor Process Time Estimates

At this point, we know that the training and development process requires about 13 employees to support the development and delivery of training. However, remember that we created this process map at a high level and that I did not include the annual component of the process in the labor estimate. I also did not include other day-to-day tasks that Pam's organization must perform to keep the business running. Because Pam wanted only a high-level estimate, we agreed to revisit the labor estimates after we completed the improvement phase.

The next step is normally to introduce the employee salaries into the mix.

Employee Costs

In Pam's case, we did not calculate the employee costs, even though we had the necessary information. I recommended we wait to perform the employee cost calculations until after we finished our work because creating the process map at such a high level would guarantee changes in the estimates.

To calculate the employee costs, follow the process outlined in Chapter 5. Start by identifying the pay rate for each employee type, and add an employee benefit rate (EB rate) to each salary. For example, we could say that the instructional designers earn $80,000 a year, that Pam's company uses a 30 percent EB rate, and that the designers dedicate 100 percent of their time to design and development activities. Using these numbers, Figure 12-24 shows the employee cost calculation that we could perform for the instructional designer.

Formula:
Employee labor cost × (100% + EB rate) = Total employee cost dedicated to business process

Example:
$80,000 × 130% = $104,000 per instructional designer

Figure 12-24 Employee Cost Calculation

This figure shows that each instructional designer costs Pam about $104,000 a year. Even though Pam wanted to move to the improvement phase, we had one additional step to complete.

Step 5: Verify the Process Map

Before moving to the improvement phase, we did a quick check-in with Pam's managers to test whether we had captured the big pieces of work and used the right volume numbers. We completed this task at her weekly staff meeting and made minor changes to the volume numbers.

Step 6: Apply Improvement Techniques

Chapter 6 covered how to use six techniques to improve a business process, including eliminating bureaucracy, evaluating value-added activities, eliminating duplication and redundancy, simplifying the process/reports/forms used, reducing cycle time, and applying automation tools.

I began this step by discussing what happens in activity 1 with the project team, to find places where we could reduce bureaucracy. As the conversation progressed to the value-added technique, we found few value-added activities. I asked why gathering client requests occurred only once a year. The more the team talked, the more they came to realize that activity 1 appeared to be the only activity in the *entire* business process where the client interacted with the process. The team became more and more concerned about the limited interaction their clients had with the business process.

As we talked about their clients and what their clients wanted from the process, the project team began doubting whether they truly understood their client needs. Going back to the scope definition document the team completed earlier, they thought their clients cared about their employee's ability to perform on the job, quick turnaround on training requests, and lower cost. But now the team questioned the validity of those needs and did not even agree on what a particular need meant. Failing to reach any satisfactory conclusions, we chose to stop and conduct a benchmark study to determine how best-in-class companies meet certain client/customer needs.

Benchmarking

In Chapters 6 and 10 we touched on benchmarking, which consists of measuring a business process against a standard of excellence (either of an internal group in your company or of an external company well-known as best in class). Before you can benchmark a process against best-in-class companies, you first have to understand the crucial points in your own business process. Figure 12-25 shows a visual depiction of how to approach a benchmarking exercise, with three distinct phases.

Now let us look at how I led Pam's training and development organization in conducting a benchmark study and how to apply each of the three phases.

Phase 1: Client/Customer Interviews

In the first phase, the project team had to understand:

▶ What Pam's internal clients deemed important, to see whether they matched what the project team identified as client needs

▶ How the clients recognize when their need is met

▶ Who the clients would identify as best in class for each of their needs

So I directed the project team to begin the benchmarking exercise by conducting 55 client interviews over a four-week period. We then validated the interview results by using a survey that we sent to 700 end users of training and their managers. We received 519 surveys back. As a result of gathering and analyzing the data, we determined that Pam's clients wanted the following from their training investment:

▶ Quality instructors

▶ Training alternatives

▶ The ability to customize courses

▶ Employees applying the training on the job

During the interviews, we asked interviewees how they would know when a need was met. For example, how would they know if they had a quality instructor? What does *quality* mean? In asking how clients would measure a quality instructor,

Phase 1:
Client/customer interviews
to understand the following:

- What clients/customers care about (identify client/customer needs)
- How they measure if a need is met (potential metrics)
- Who is best-in-class in meeting this need (develop potential benchmarking list)

leads to

Phase 2:
Benchmarking
to understand the following:

- How best-in-class companies deliver against the defined client/customer needs
- How they measure success (potential metrics)
- Other trends and general conclusions

leads to

Phase 3:
Performance goals for the process
to define the following:

- Future direction
- Baseline process requirements

Figure 12-25 Benchmarking Phases

I found out that quality, in their eyes, meant they wanted instructors with real-life experience. In other words, they wanted instructors who had industry experience teaching classes. I now had a new gauge by which Pam could evaluate her instructor pool: How many of Pam's instructors taught courses in which they possessed real-world experience? As it turned out, not many.

The final question in the interview asked clients to identify any companies they felt did an outstanding job at meeting a particular need. Could they identify a company that did a good job at having quality instructors, instructors who bring their real-life experience to their teaching? Their answers to this question helped me build a list of companies that we could benchmark against.

At the end of the first phase, we had a validated list of client needs for the training and development business process, we knew how Pam's clients measured success, and we had a list of companies and internal groups that we could benchmark against to find out how they delivered against client needs.

Phase 2: Benchmarking

Now that we understood what Pam's clients cared about, how they would measure success, and who they thought were best-in-class companies, it was time to move the project team to phase two. Next, I asked the team members to focus on:

- ➤ Writing the interview questions and creating a tool to collect the data
- ➤ Working with Pam's internal productivity group to identify contacts at the companies that we wanted to benchmark and then scheduling appointments
- ➤ Reviewing benchmarking studies available in the market on education and training

We created two sets of questions. One set focused on general information to ask every benchmark company, and the second addressed the list of client needs. We did not ask every benchmark company about all four client needs, but rather focused each interview on the single client need for which the company was identified as best in class. We asked certain companies about quality instructors, another group about training alternatives, others about course customization, and finally a fourth group about how they evaluated an employee's performance on the job.

The first list of general questions, which we asked all companies, included items like:

- ▶ How many employees do you have in your company?
- ▶ How many employees do you have in your training and development organization?
- ▶ How do you organize your training and development group (centralized, decentralized, or other)?
- ▶ How do you organize your resources to support your client base (by business, geography, or other)?
- ▶ How do you fund the training and development group (tuition, fully budgeted, other)?
- ▶ What do you consider the top-priority goals for the training and development organization?
- ▶ What do you consider the training and development group's critical success factors (the key goals your organization must attain to compete in your market)?
- ▶ What do you feel differentiates you from other companies in the training and development business (your primary strengths)?

For the second set of questions, we started the interview by providing each best-in-class company with a definition of the client need we wanted to discuss with them. For example, we started an interview on *quality instructors* by defining what we thought quality instructors should possess: industry expertise, technical competence, exceptional platform skills, and credibility.

We then asked five main questions to understand how the particular benchmark company met the client need, for example:

1. How are you organized to support _____?
2. What approach or process do you use to gain _____? How do you determine the best approach?
3. What process do you use to measure the effectiveness of _____?
4. What problems do you encounter?
5. What, if anything, would you change? Why?

To continue with the quality instructor theme, the interview included specific questions like these:

1. How are you organized to support quality instructors?
2. What approach or process do you use to gain quality instructors? How do you determine the best approach?
3. What process do you use to measure the effectiveness of your instructors?
4. What problems do you encounter?
5. What, if anything, would you change? Why?

Phase 3: Performance Goals

After the project team completed the benchmark interviews, I summarized the findings and translated them into performance goals, that is, what Pam's organization cared about:

▶ **Instructor Expertise:** Pam wants her organization to become known for having instructors with real-world experience, which suggests that she will:
  - Focus on acquiring instructors with industry and/or product expertise.
  - Build a core of instructors/developers and outsource delivery, if appropriate, to acquire the content expertise required.
  - Use the same resource, if possible, for the development and delivery of training.
  - Use team teaching/consulting to provide required content expertise.

▶ **Training Delivery Alternatives**: A significant percentage of Pam's training is instructor-led training, and she wants to move toward offering a wider range of formats and increase the use of technology.

▶ **Ability to Customize Courses:** Pam wants to increase the modularity in her course design to enable quicker customization, to offer training for intact groups that uses examples and scenarios from her client's business, and to deliver training at her client's site.

▶ **On-the-Job Performance:** Pam wants her organization to focus on measuring an employee's ability to perform on the job, to offer refresher training in self-paced formats, and to give managers reinforcement tools to support their employees' learning.

Conducting a benchmark study can take some time, so remember these keys to a successful benchmarking study:

▶ Identify the right contacts in the right companies.

▶ Discuss one critical success factor, or client needs, per interview.

▶ Recognize that internal benchmarking can be as effective as external benchmarking.

▶ Include research study findings in your summary.

A New Approach

After reviewing the results of the benchmark study, we took another bend in the road. Pam and the project team did not see how their present process, even after it was improved, would get them to their desired end state. As we discussed the activities involved in the current process map, the team identified instances of bureaucracy, and they created a value-added analysis, but the importance of increasing the client interaction throughout the overall process became obvious. The process map showed that Pam's team interacted with the client most often during the two weeks when they collected annual needs. I helped the project team to recognize that the organization asks the wrong questions during the annual data collection process by focusing on volume instead of on business objectives and that they had not provided a means of addressing changing needs throughout the year. In reviewing the scope definition document created in step 2, I reminded the team of the process definition they wrote:

> This process covers delivering products and services that enable employee learning to support the business objectives. In all cases, the business goals drive the learning investment.

I helped the project team think about how they would redesign the front end of the process to see whether they could simplify the process, how they might reduce the five-month cycle time, and how they could make the planning process more of an ongoing one instead of just an annual process. With the client identified as the central point of the process, we designed a totally new approach to planning for client needs that influenced a redesign of the activities that followed.

Pam's case demonstrates the flexibility required when working on business process improvement. You saw one bend in the road in step 1 when we built the process inventory at the department level, which influenced a change in step 2 and the writing of the scope definition document. Now we had taken another twist because we are about to redesign BB&Z's training and development business process from scratch to place the emphasis on the client.

As you perform process work, try not to put labels on the work other than business process improvement. Perhaps you have noticed by this point that I generally avoid the use of terms like *quality improvement* or *reengineering* because it does not matter what you call it or whether you switch between the two, as long as you focus on improving the process.

Over the next week, we developed a new process map that placed the client at the center of the process. Figure 12-26 shows the beginning of the new process map, and you can easily see how often the new process interacts with the client, denoted by the number of arrows going to and from the client oval.

This process map looks different from our earlier map. Although it has yet to include all the tools used by each activity, it currently shows where data goes in and out of each activity. The project team devoted significant time to identifying the data

Figure 12-26 BB&Z New Learning Process

flow throughout the process (i.e., having the right data at the right time) because of its importance in supporting a more integrated process in the future. Figure 12-26 shows three new databases that support the process:

- **Client Profile:** Holds information about training and development clients, their needs and preferences, and how training and development handled their needs, rejections, and acceptance
- **Offering Profile:** Holds solutions, performance goals, designs, learning objectives, and delivery requirements
- **Process Performance Profile:** Holds evaluation data and other general data on how the learning process performs

Figures 12-27 and 12-28 illustrate the symbols used to denote the flow of data.

Figure 12-27   Data Flowing to an Activity

Figure 12-28   Data Flowing from an Activity

At this point in the work, two major business processes began to surface:

- **Need/Solution Identification:** This business process becomes the focal point for the client partnership and includes the identification of needs and solutions, proposal creation, return on investment, and client acceptance.
- **Business Direction and Measurement:** This business process sets the foundation for the business of the training and development organization and includes the rules for running the business, measuring the overall performance of

the learning process, and the development/coaching/reward of employees who work throughout the learning process.

Most of the activities depicted in the process map so far fall into the needs/solution identification process, except for activity 14 (develop business plans), which falls into the business direction/measurement process. Both business processes jointly own activity 13.

To help you to understand the steps in the new training and development business process, Figure 12-29 shows the beginning of the design document for the new learning process map from Figure 12-26.

The remainder of the learning process map (not depicted) focused on two additional business processes:

▶ **Resource Development and Delivery:** This process secures and develops resources (internal and external) to enable development and delivery of solutions. The process includes managing vendor relationships, assembling the multiple components, and overall applied research and technology.

▶ **Promotion and Communication:** This process creates the promotional and/or communication strategy, and it reviews the results of the strategy. It includes managing the creation of the materials and the distribution of those materials.

In summary, the new learning process demonstrates the following improvements to the business process:

▶ The new business process has ongoing client interaction, increasing the value-added activities of the process.

▶ Performing data collection throughout the year minimizes the time required during the annual planning process, thus reducing cycle time.

▶ The learning process expresses client needs as performance goals, which the training and development employees translate into measurable, observable learning objectives, increasing the value-added activities of the process.

Number	Activity Description	Inputs	Outputs
1	**Client** [Need/solution identification process] Although the client is not an activity, client focus becomes a central theme to the entire training and development process, now known as the learning process. The learning process is the process by which the training and development organization delivers education, training, learning opportunities, and experiences. A set of business plans, created in concert with a corporate charter, establishes the scope of the process. Within the established scope, the process focuses on precisely defining and validating client needs before generating solutions.	**1. Proactive request for plans/needs/clarification** The learning process operates in both a reactive and proactive mode. When operating proactively, the process initiates contact with the client as a request. This input represents that proactive request started by the learning process. **2. Rejection and referral** When the learning process determines that it cannot meet the client need within the charter of the learning process, the process sends a rejection to the client, accompanied by a referral to an external resource or agency that may meet the client's needs. **3. Recommendation** The learning process seeks to generate suitable solutions in response to client needs. The process presents possible solutions to the client as a recommendation. This input represents the recommendation generated by the learning process.	**1. Problems, goals, plans** This output is the primary input that the learning process handles. The entire learning process exists to process this input and produce learning solutions for those client business problems, needs, and plans that fall within the defined scope of the learning process. **2. Rework** In response to processing client needs, the learning process creates a recommendation that proposes a solution to meet the client's need. If the client determines that the need definition requires rework, the client requests rework of the recommendation. **3. Modification request** In response to processing client needs, the learning process creates a recommendation that proposes a solution to meet the client's need. On receipt of the recommendation, the client may request a slight change. **4. Acceptance** In response to processing client needs, the learning process creates a recommendation that proposes a solution to meet the client's need. On receipt of the recommendation, the client may accept the proposal.

Figure 12-29   BB&Z's New Learning Process: Detail Document   *(continues)*

N u m b e r	Activity Description	Inputs	Outputs
2	**Analyze plans and define needs** [Need/solution identification process] The work represented by this activity occurs in two ways: proactively and reactively. When operating proactively, the learning process: ■ Initiates contact with the clients. ■ Gathers plans, problem statements, and goals. ■ Analyzes and clearly articulates the needs. When operating reactively, the learning process: ■ Responds to client-initiated requests for help with resolving problems, achieving goals, and/or developing plans. ■ Analyzes and clearly articulates the needs.	**1. Problems, goals, plans** This input represents the input provided by the clients, either in response to the learning process's request or because they elected to start the process on their own. **2. Consolidated needs** The learning process strives to eliminate waste and redundancy by consolidating needs and responding to them across the organization. When employees analyze plans, they contrast their identified needs to those identified by other training and development employees, so that the learning process can address similar needs in a manner that optimizes resources. **3. Questions** Work within the *validate, evaluate, and balance* activity may raise questions requiring further clarification of the client needs. This input represents such questions.	**1. Client needs** This output represents confirmation by the learning process of a clearly articulated and duly recorded need. These needs are in a form suitable for processing by the *validate, evaluate, and balance* step in the learning process. **2. Proactive request for plans/ needs/clarification** The learning process operates in both a reactive and proactive mode. This output represents that proactive request started by the learning process.

Figure 12-29   (continued)

N u m b e r	Activity Description	Inputs	Outputs
3	**Validate, evaluate, and balance** [Need/solution identification process] The work represented by this activity involves the learning process determining whether the client's stated needs fall within the charter of the learning process. ■ Evaluation represents work completed before the validity check, to determine the scope and nature of the need. ■ Validation addresses whether the needs fall within the business of the learning process. If the needs fall within the domain of the learning process, then the responsible employee attempts to balance them against other needs of the client to establish priorities within the client's business. ■ Balancing also represents the work of relating the needs to other functions, business units, or teams to see if these groups have similar needs. The primary output of the work consists of a list of validated needs, needs that the learning process can address.	**1. Client needs** The primary input to this activity represents the need as expressed by the client. **2. Rework** When the learning process generates a recommendation to a client need, the client may reject the proposal for a variety of reasons. The client rejection provides the learning process with additional clarification of their need. The rejection, containing this new clarity regarding the client need, represents rework that the learning process must accommodate. This activity accepts the rejection and the associated redefinition of the client need and starts the process again.	**1. Rejection/referral** If the learning process determines that meeting the client need would require a solution outside the domain of the learning process, then the training and development employee offers a referral to assist the client in obtaining a suitable solution. **2. Validated need** When the learning process determines that it can meet the client need, the process passes the need to the next step in the process, *characterize need with client,* where the need is translated into objectives.

▶ The offering profile database provides a searchable tool that assists in eliminating duplication. Once the training and development employee translates a client's performance needs into learning objectives, the objectives become the basis for reconciling common needs.

▶ The creation of three databases helps to streamline the information and organize the data around clients, offerings, and performance results.

▶ Streamlining the business process delivers a more adaptable process that can react more quickly to changing business needs.

Pam and the project team liked the new process and reviewed it with a few clients to gain their support. Once the team felt comfortable with the design, we moved to the next step on the roadmap, identifying internal controls, creating tools, and developing metrics.

Step 7: Create Internal Controls, Tools, and Metrics

In Chapter 7, we discussed how internal controls help to identify points in the business process where a mistake can occur and to explain how to prevent those errors; how tools can support and streamline the process, avoid errors, and assist with training new employees to perform their job easier; and how metrics show whether the process works as planned.

Internal Controls

I started this step by asking the project team to identify where something could go wrong in the new process. We then created internal controls to address each of those areas. Figure 12-30 shows the new learning process map with two internal controls added, as depicted by the warning symbol on activities 3 and 13.

The internal control document in Figure 12-31 on page 312 identifies what the project team determined could go wrong with these two activities and describes how they plan to reduce

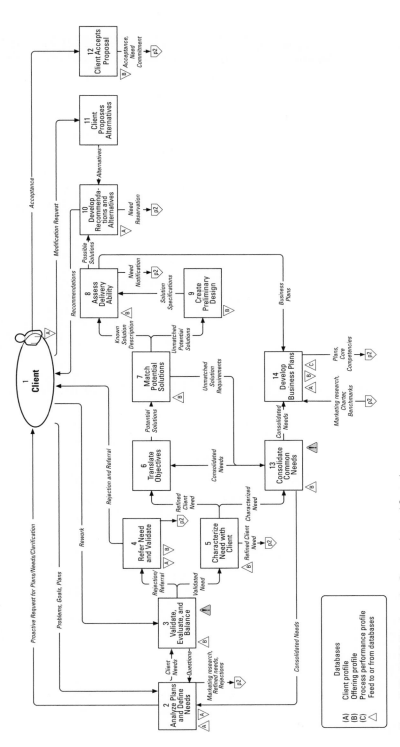

Figure 12-30 BB&Z New Learning Process: Internal Controls

Activity Number	Activity Description	Possible Issue(s)	Internal Control(s)
3	Validate, evaluate, and balance	Employee may misdiagnose whether a client need falls within the learning process scope and could cause an unhappy client if they send a rejection to the client.	■ Before rejecting a client request and referring the client to another vendor, the consultant will obtain a second opinion by asking another employee to validate his or her findings. Once both parties agree that the request appears out of scope, communication with the client can occur. ■ The communication plan, as part of the new process implementation, will reinforce training and development's charter with the client.
13	Consolidate common needs	Employee may not characterize a client need correctly in activity 5, thus providing incorrect data into this activity, and, since this activity affects many other points in the process, preventive controls must be in place.	■ A set of templates, rules, and procedures exist to ensure consistent data entry. ■ Entry into the offering profile in activity 5 is restricted to instructional designers and customer performance consultants (previously known as learning consultants). ■ The business manager acts as the gatekeeper to this data and notifies an instructional designer if he or she enters data not consistent with the guidelines.

Figure 12-31 BB&Z New Learning Process: Internal Controls Document

the number of errors. Having a discussion about what can go wrong in a business process helps the organization to circumvent the potential problems.

Tools

The next part of step 7 involves developing the tools to support the process. Pam's team had to develop several new items to support the learning process, including:

➤ Creating three new Microsoft Access databases to store the client, offering, and performance data.

➤ Creating standards for the documents used throughout the learning process, such as the design document (9) and the business plan (14).

➤ Establishing a process for obtaining and storing external research, competitive analysis information, and the company's corporate charter.

➤ Evaluating solutions to enable class registration and manage resources.

➤ Creating job aids to help employees perform their jobs.

Figure 12-32 shows one example of a job aid we created to help validate that only correct data entered the offering profile database. Because the learning process views the offering database as a crucial tool to enable the matching of common needs, thus reducing duplication, this job aid provides examples of how to translate client needs into performance goals and performance goals into learning objectives. This table shows three examples of translating a client need into a performance goal that a manager can measure or observe.

The highlighted words in Figure 12-32 depict searchable words in the offering database. For example, if you search for the term *sales*, two performance goals appear (examples 1 and 3), with their associated learning objectives. The database accommodates the addition of other searchable words, such as *constructive feedback* for example 2.

I asked the project team members to think about the vari-

	Example 1	Example 2	Example 3
Client need	Sales force needs to bring in more customers.	Managers need to get better at giving employees negative feedback.	Sales reps need to understand how to work through the government bureaucracy.
	⬇	⬇	⬇
Performance goal	Sales reps invest their time and the company's resources only on qualified prospects.	Managers give employees constructive feedback in a timely manner.	Sales force can successfully close sales through the government's acquisition process.
	⬇	⬇	⬇
Learning objective	■ *Identify* criteria that qualify a prospect. ■ *Evaluate* how the criteria can lead a prospect to become a valued customer.	■ *Identify* the root cause of performance problems. ■ *Demonstrate* active listening.	■ *Identify* the phases in the government's acquisition process. ■ *Explain* your role in each of the acquisition phases.

Figure 12-32   Job Aid Example: Link Between Client Needs, Performance Goals, and Learning Objectives

ous tools they had to create and how they would explain the new process to their clients and stakeholders. I suggested that a model would help people outside the department understand the new process because it included so many changes. The model I developed in Figure 12-33, working with the project team, illustrates the interaction throughout the learning process:

➤ The business direction/measurement process acts as the foundation for the entire learning process, supporting Pam's concept that business goals drive learning investments.

➤ Client needs flow through the needs/solution identification business process, while the business direction/measure-

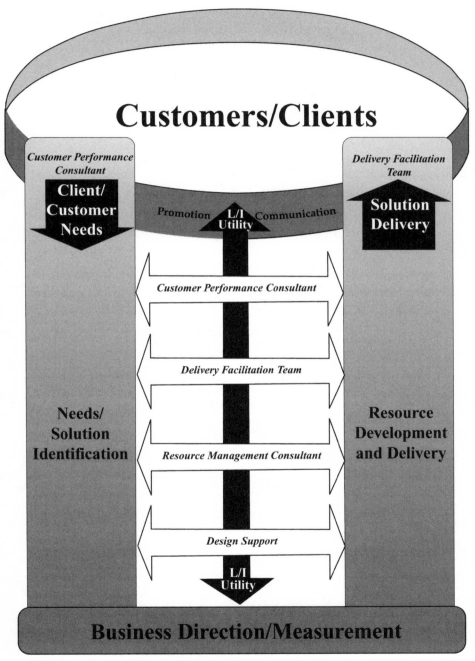

L/T Utility = Learning/Information Utility

Figure 12-33   BB&Z Learning Process Model

ment process and the resource development and delivery processes support those client needs.

➤ Ultimately, the promotion/communication process interacts with the customers/clients to share details about the available products and services.

➤ The horizontal arrows depict the employees in the learning process and show the interaction between client needs and the delivery of products and services.

➤ The learning/information utility reflects the databases that hold information to make the entire process functional, and the model shows that all employees use the utility.

Notice that the learning consultant's job name changed in the new model to *customer performance consultant* to stress the importance of focusing on the clients' businesses and helping them to achieve their goals.

I highly recommend that you spend time creating a visual representation of how your business process works because using a model helps explain a complex business process to people outside the day-to-day business better than a process map, which can seem overwhelming.

Metrics

In the scope definition document we created in step 2, Pam's clients seemed to care about performance on the job and two efficiency-oriented metrics (quick turnaround and lower cost). With this information, we listed five measurements of success in the document:

➤ On-the-job performance
➤ Reduced development time
➤ Cost reduction target
➤ The ability to integrate new businesses
➤ The linkage between training and business goals

After completing the benchmarking study, we learned that training and development's clients also cared about quality instructors, alternative delivery methods, and course customization. Although Pam and the project team cared about every measurement of success, I encouraged them to recognize that the learning process had too many potential measurements to start. I suggested that they limit their metrics for the first year to one metric for each of the following: effectiveness, efficiency, and adaptability. The project team agreed, and after discussing the measurements of success, we developed metrics for the following items:

- ▶ **Effectiveness:** On-the-job performance (We felt that having quality instructors could help us to meet this measurement of success.)
- ▶ **Efficiency:** Reduced development time (We thought that course customization and a new approach to modularity could help reduce the time required to develop courses.)
- ▶ **Adaptability:** The ability to integrate new businesses

We then took each of Pam's measurements of success and translated them into the metrics shown in Figure 12-34.

Using the effectiveness measurement of on-the-job performance as an example, let me share how we approached this item. I suggested they start with instructor-led training, the

Measurement of Success		Metric
On-the-job performance	➡	20% improvement of on-the-job performance after attending training
Reduced development time	➡	100% of new products and services developed will incorporate a modular design.
Ability to integrate new businesses	➡	New employees are trained within two weeks of an acquisition.

Figure 12-34 BB&Z Learning Process: Year 1 Metrics

most expensive type, to measure employees' ability to perform on their jobs after they attended training.

In the training and development field, you typically hear about four levels of training evaluation, depending on what you want to measure:

- ▶ Level 1: Satisfaction
- ▶ Level 2: Learning
- ▶ Level 3: Application
- ▶ Level 4: Return on investment

We decided to create a level-3 evaluation, where we planned to measure an employee's application of what they learned on the job. Pam committed to focus on five high-volume courses throughout the first year. She chose to start with an evaluation of Beating the Competition, a course delivered to the company's financial sales representatives that targets BB&Z's biggest competitor. She felt that she could use the results of this evaluation to demonstrate a linkage between training and business goals.

The evaluation specialist developed a pre- and postassessment for the course; then we established a process where the instructors would capture a student's baseline at the beginning of the course by administering a brief survey. Three months later, the evaluation specialist followed up with the students using the telephone survey in Figure 12-35 to measure increases in their on-the-job performance. In addition to the assessment and survey, I suggested that the evaluation specialist track the sales figures of employees who attended the training.

Pam now had a newly designed business process that included increased client interaction, necessary internal controls, tools to support the process, and metrics to evaluate the effectiveness, efficiency, and adaptability of the process.

With all this behind us, we can move to the next step and confirm that the process and tools will work as expected.

Step 8: Test and Rework

In Chapter 8, you learned to create a test plan to test the process and the tools before introducing the process changes

Beating the Competition
Post Assessment Telephone Survey

The survey started with general demographic questions and then these specific questions:

1. Since completing the course, how many times have you encountered xyz as a competitor?
   (1) 0–5 (2) 6–10 (3) 11–15
   (4) 16–20 (5) 21–25 (6) more than 25

2. Since completing the course, in what percentage of discussions have you been able to present yourself with confidence regarding xyz as a competitor?
   (1) less than 10% (2) 10–25% (3) 26–50%
   (4) 51–75% (5) 76–90% (6) more than 90%

3. Since completing the course, in what percentage of time have you been able to use a broader vocabulary related to the competitive environment?
   (1) less than 10% (2) 10–25% (3) 26–50%
   (4) 51–75% (5) 76–90% (6) more than 90%

4. How well do you feel the course prepared you to use xyz terminology?
   (1) very well (2) well (3) somewhat well (4) not well at all

5. How well do you feel the course prepared you to compare and contrast the company's products against the xyz product family?
   (1) very well (2) well (3) somewhat well (4) not well at all

6. How well do you feel the course prepared you to position the company's messages to circumvent xyz's strategies?
   (1) very well (2) well (3) somewhat well (4) not well at all

7. What percentage of the time have you been able to overcome a competitive objection?
   (1) less than 10% (2) 10–25% (3) 26–50%
   (4) 51–75% (5) 76–90% (6) more than 90%

8. Since taking the course, how many competitive activity reports have you completed to request support from the competitive marketing group?
   (1) 0–5 (2) 6–10 (3) 11–15
   (4) 16–20 (5) 21–25 (6) more than 25

Figure 12-35 Telephone Survey Example

across the entire organization. In this phase of the work, you think about the who, what, where, when, and how of testing:

- ► **Whom** to involve in the testing
- ► **What** items to test
- ► **Where** to conduct the testing
- ► **When** to perform the testing
- ► **How** to conduct the testing

You can see that I use the same general test plan from Chapter 8 for Pam's process, as shown in Figure 12-36. These steps remain consistent for most process improvement work, and so we use this as a boilerplate test plan. The only items that change all the time are the test items. For Pam's learning process, examples of our test items included:

➤ End-to-end business process (Microsoft PowerPoint process map; Microsoft Word detail document)

➤ Customer profile database (Microsoft Access)

➤ Offering profile database (Microsoft Access)

➤ Process performance profile database (Microsoft Access)

➤ Job aid covering the guidelines for entering data into the offering profile database (Adobe PDF file)

➤ Sample report that summarizes annual performance results of the learning process (Microsoft Excel)

➤ Class registration tool

➤ Resource management tool

By testing the learning process, I discovered the need to make the following changes:

➤ We had to do additional work on what constituted a match in activity 7 because it seemed too easy to credit a solution with addressing a performance goal.

ID Number	Task	Person Responsible	Due Date
1	Define testing goal.	Project manager	May 15
2	Define testing method.	Project manager	May 15
3	Define objectives for test items.	Project manager	May 15
4	Develop scenarios for test items (testing sheets).	Project team	June 1
5	Gain support for resources.	Project manager	June 1
6	Create feedback collection tool.	Project manager	June 1
7	Conduct testing.	Project team	June 15–30
8	Rework, as required.	Project team	July 15

Figure 12-36 Learning Process: Test Plan

► We had to train the customer performance consultants on how to use the offering database.

► We redefined the activity called "synthesize/evaluate refinements" because the process workers did not understand what this activity entailed.

► How we set up the resource management application had to be modified.

► We adapted the fields in the customer profile database to accommodate the customer performance consultants.

► We modified the process performance database to meet what Pam hoped to gain from this data.

► We changed the sample report that summarized the learning process's performance.

At the end of the testing phase, the project team made all the necessary changes. The training and development employees that were involved in the testing noticed that we had made substantial changes to the process. They understood the reasons why and expressed excitement about the upcoming implementation.

Step 9: Implement Change

When I first started working with Pam, I created a project plan for the training and development business process improvement effort and continually adjusted the plan throughout the work, especially after deciding to redesign the process.

In Chapter 9, you learned that the implementation plan included phases and that a phase could include tracks. Three key tracks in the implementation phase include the:

1. *Communication track:* Developing a communication plan stating who has to know what when
2. *Training track:* Developing a training plan that tells who requires training on what
3. *Change management track:* The impact analysis that identifies whom to engage in the changes you want to introduce

Communication Track

The project team had to think about what communication needed to occur to verify that everyone received the appropriate information to prepare them for the change. Figure 12-37 shows part of the learning process communication plan, in which I defined the audience, communication goals, key message points, the best communication vehicles to use, and the best timing to deliver the messages.

Figure 12-37 shows training and development employees and clients as the two main audiences that require communication about the process changes. A key challenge for training and development was to refocus the organization's mindset so that everything employees do revolves around the client.

Audience	Communication Goal	Key Message Points	Communication Vehicles (Method)	Due Date
All training and development employees	Engage the organization. Move toward client as number one.	■ What's changing and why ■ Importance of the client ■ More integrated process ■ Training plan and timeline	Department meeting Model Email follow-up	May 1
Client	Gain feedback and support.	■ Learning process redesigned to focus on their business objectives ■ Link new process to the results of the client interviews ■ Review the benefits of the new process including increased client interaction ■ Clarify training and development's charter (what is in and out of scope) ■ Contact resources for additional information	Email Model	May 10

Figure 12-37 BB&Z Learning Process: Communication Plan

Training Track

For the training plan, the project team had to think about what training needed to occur to ensure that all parties could perform their process responsibilities. They had to list the employees requiring training, identify what kind of training the employees required, and identify who owned the responsibility to conduct the training. They also had to decide where the project team would hold the training, along with when and what methods they would use to conduct the training.

Figure 12-38 shows part of the learning process training plan. The figure shows that I designed the training approach to have employees attend training on the basis of how they relate to the four new business processes. This segregation was intentional to reinforce the importance of the new design. It also shows that the customer performance consultant will receive additional training on the client and on the offering profile databases (discussed earlier).

Change Management Track

The impact analysis for the new learning process captured the changes that had to occur to ensure the success of the new business process. In Chapter 9, we built the impact analysis by walking through the process map and identifying the required changes. Figure 12-39 on page 325 shows a portion of the impact analysis plan I created for the new learning process.

Once Pam addressed the items in the impact analysis and after I developed the training and communication plans, Pam felt ready to introduce the new learning process. She now had confidence that the project team had considered the important items and felt ready to move ahead with implementation. Pam felt strongly about the next step, continuous improvement, because she now recognized how quickly a process may have to change. So the team had one last task to complete before disbanding.

Step 10: Drive Continuous Improvement

During this step, Pam had another challenge she had to deal with: how to help the organization adopt a new mindset

Audience	Training Objectives	Approach	Tools	Facilitator	Due Date
All training and development employees	■ *Define* how the learning process meets client needs. ■ *Describe* each step in the learning process. ■ *Explain* your role in the learning process. ■ *Illustrate* how the learning process model supports the business process.	Separate group meetings by the four new business processes: ■ Need/solution identification ■ Business direction/measurement ■ Resource development and delivery ■ Promotion/communication	■ Process documentation ■ Model ■ Job aids	Managers	May 30
Customer performance consultants	■ *Summarize* how to move to a proactive client relationship. ■ *Explain* the charter of the learning process and *demonstrate* the validation of a client need. ■ *Create* performance goals from a client need and *categorize* those needs.	Instructor-led training	■ Process documentation ■ Model ■ Job aids ■ Databases: client profile and offering profile ■ External data sources	Instructional designer	June 15

Figure 12-38 BB&Z Learning Process: Training Plan

where they would always look for ways to improve the learning process. The continuous improvement cycle wheel in Chapter 10 introduced some structure to this phase, and I led the project team in creating a plan to regularly evaluate, test, assess, and execute against improvements. As you recall, the four steps are:

1. *Evaluate:* Determine the opportunities that exist.
2. *Test:* Institute the change and try it out on a small scale.

Reference Number	Process Change(s) that Affect External Groups	Rationale	Area Affected	Population/ Group Affected	Change Management
1	Formalizing the client interaction	To make certain that T&D only works on projects that support a client's business need	Entire company	Clients	Clients will receive formal communication and will be asked to accept or reject various items (e.g., performance goals, designs).
2	The process sends rejections to a client	T&D must stay focused on what the organization is in business to deliver.	Entire company	Clients	Clients are not accustomed to T&D saying "no."
3	Annual budgeting process will change	To ensure success, the budgeting process must occur ongoing throughout the year versus annually.	Entire company	Clients	Clients are not accustomed to asking for help other than during the annual process. Finance prefers an annual cycle.
4	The learning process may end a vendor contract at any time	To adapt to changing business needs, T&D requires flexibility in working with vendors.	Legal Purchasing	Vendors	Must balance shorter contract terms with competitive pricing, which may be a challenge.

Figure 12-39 BB&Z Learning Process: Impact Analysis

3. *Assess:* Determine whether the change worked.
4. *Execute:* Deploy the change on a wide scale.

We developed a continuous improvement plan for each of the four business processes, then developed the continuous improvement *schedule* shown in Figure 12-40, to provide an overview of the timing for each of the business processes.

As each of the timelines in Figure 12-40 became due, the responsible party would use the four steps in the continuous

Process	Review Measurement Data	Test Internal Controls	Revisit Customer/ Client Needs	Validate Process Workers	Revisit Stakeholder Needs	Evaluate Third Parties
	Monthly	*Monthly*	*Semiannual*	*Semiannual*	*Annual*	*Annual*
Need/ solution identification	1st of month	1st of month	Q1–3/1 Q3–9/1	Q2–6/1 Q4–12/1	May	January
Business direction/ measurement	30th of month	15th of month	Q1–3/1 Q3–9/1	Q1–3/15 Q3–9/15	May	August
Resource development and delivery	30th of month	30th of month	Q1–3/1 Q3–9/1	Q2–6/1 Q4–12/1	May	Q1–3/15 Q2–6/15 Q3–9/15 Q4–12/15
Promotion/ communication	Not applicable (n/a)	n/a	March (not semiannual)	n/a	n/a	n/a

Figure 12-40 BB&Z Learning Process: Continuous Improvement Schedule

improvement wheel to address it. For example, in examining the measurement data on the first of every month, the customer performance consultant would evaluate what the data was saying and decide whether something had to change. If something did change, the consultant would test the change and determine whether it worked, then introduce the change to the entire organization. During the *evaluate* step, the customer performance consultant could elect to change the metric itself, alter the product or service, or simply reinforce how an employee should perform a task.

After the project team finished all the work, I included in the executive summary (1) the learning process model from Figure 12-33, (2) the process description summary shown in Figure 12-41, and (3) a process summary that included general assumptions, dependencies, job descriptions, and sizing algorithms.

At the end of our work, Pam Borzak had an organization that focused on the right areas. Her entire organization was client focused and regularly evaluated the effectiveness, efficiency, and adaptability of the learning process. I helped her develop recognition guidelines to reward employees for outstanding performance in support of the new business process.

Need/Solution Identification	Business Direction/Measurement
Overall description: This process is the focal point for the client *partnership*. It includes identification of needs and solutions, proposal creation, impact, and client acceptance.	**Overall description:** This process sets the *foundation* for the business of training and development, the rules for running the business, measuring the overall performance of the learning process, and the development/coaching/reward of employees who work throughout the learning process.
Responsibilities: ■ Defining the client needs entering the learning process ■ Validating and evaluating needs ■ Characterizing needs ■ Translating needs into performance goals and matching needs to potential solutions ■ Assessing the organization's capability to deliver solutions ■ Proposing recommendations ■ Signaling potential resources ■ Measuring solution results ■ Obtaining client acceptance ■ Consolidating common needs ■ Synthesizing end evaluating refinements ■ Ensuring the refinements of the solution and/or resources are integrated and made available throughout the process.	**Responsibilities:** ■ Creating and changing business rules ■ Creating decision support information ■ Developing business plans ■ Developing and conducting benchmarking and competitive analysis activity ■ Capturing, sharing, and applying learning ■ Analyzing process performance ■ Developing accountability and reward systems ■ Using the results of consolidated common needs on a strategic basis

Resource Development/Delivery	Promotion/Communication
Overall description: This process secures and develops resources (internal and external) to enable development and delivery of solutions. It includes managing vendor relationships, assembling the multiple components, and overall applied research and technology.	**Overall description:** This process creates the promotional and/or communication strategy and evaluates the results of the strategy. It also manages the creation of the promotional materials and distributes that material.
Responsibilities: ■ Developing and acquiring resources ■ Assessing the organization's capability to deliver solutions ■ Assessing the delivery of products and services ■ Assembling resources ■ Initiating delivery of the planned solution ■ Refining delivery ■ Synthesizing and evaluating refinements ■ Ensuring the refinements of the solution and/or resources are integrated and made available throughout the process	**Responsibilities:** ■ Developing a promotional/ communication strategy ■ Developing promotional tools and materials ■ Collecting and analyzing promotional results ■ Implementing a distribution plan

Figure 12-41   BB&Z Learning Process: Process Descriptions and Responsibilities

Chapter Summary

Pam Borzak's story at BB&Z demonstrates how to apply the 10 steps to business process improvement and how to adjust the steps as you encounter obstacles or bends in the road. The 10 steps are:

1. *Develop the process inventory:* How to build a process inventory and process prioritization table for either an entire department or the business processes within a department
2. *Establish the foundation:* How to develop the scope definition document for a business process
3. *Draw the process map:* How to decide the level of detail for building the process map and how to create a map that spans multiple pages
4. *Estimate time and cost:* How to calculate process and cycle time, how to incorporate frequency into the calculations, and how to include different types of employees
5. *Verify the process map:* Ways to validate the accuracy of the process map
6. *Apply improvement techniques:* How to incorporate benchmarking into the improvement phase and how to know when to design an entirely new process
7. *Create internal controls, tools, and metrics:* How to develop internal controls, sample tools, and metrics. A reminder of the importance of building a model to explain a complicated process
8. *Test and rework:* How to test all the components of a business process
9. *Implement change:* How to develop the communication, training, and impact analysis plans
10. *Drive continuous improvement:* How to create a schedule to keep track of all the different business processes

What You Have Achieved

In this chapter, you have achieved the following:

➤ A grasp of how to adjust to bends in the road and adapt the 10 steps

➤ An understanding of how to build a model to further explain a complex business process

➤ The ability to calculate employee costs when different types of employees are involved in the process work

➤ The knowledge that you can build the process inventory and prioritization table at either the department or the process level

➤ An understanding of how to incorporate multiple frequencies in the cost analysis

➤ Insight into how to conduct a benchmark study

➤ Most important, the *power* to know that you can do it

Index